WAGE INDEXATION
IN THE UNITED STATES
Cola or Uncola®?

International Standard Book Number: 0-88410-988-7

Library of Congress Catalog Card Number: 84-28430

Printed in the United States of America

Library of Congress Cataloging in Publication Data

Hendricks, Wallace E.
    Wage indexation in the United States.

    Bibliography: p.
    Includes index.
    1. Wages—Cost-of-living adjustments—United States.
I. Kahn, Lawrence, M. II. Title.
HD4928.C72U64   1985   331.2′15   84-28430
ISBN 0-88410-988-7

WAGE INDEXATION IN THE UNITED STATES
Cola or Uncola®?

WALLACE E. HENDRICKS
and
LAWRENCE M. KAHN

BALLINGER PUBLISHING COMPANY
Cambridge, Massachusetts
A Subsidiary of Harper & Row, Publishers, Inc.

To our parents

Contents

List of Figures and Tables

FIGURES

Preface

Our goal in writing this book was to provide a single volume that covered a description of wage indexation in the United States, a review of economic theories of indexation, and empirical work linking theory with evidence. Our primary focus was on the unionized sector of the economy.

Chapters 2 and 3 provide a detailed description of wage indexation in the United States and should be accessible to all interested readers. Chapters 4 and 5 review economic theories, and Chapters 6 through 8 provide our empirical results. These latter five chapters assume more mathematical and statistical expertise on the part of the reader.

This book is one of several outputs of a research program at the Institute of Labor and Industrial Relations, University of Illinois over a five-year period. As such, this research has benefited from financial support from several organizations including the Bureau of Economic and Business Research, University of Illinois; the U.S. Department of Labor; and the Research Board at the University of Illinois. We have also benefited from extensive support from our students and colleagues. Our research assistants provided substantial help in the gathering and analyzing of the data we use extensively in the book. These assistants included Debashish Bhattacherjee, Andrew Bruns, Daniel Burgard, Cynthia Gramm, Steven Merkin, Christopher Pawlowicz, Ronald Seeber, and Roger Wolters. Two of them stand out for special recognition: Steven Merkin did much of the background work necessary for Chapter 2 as part of his tutorial project for his master's degree. Cynthia Gramm gathered the strike data used in Chapter 8 as part of her Ph.D. thesis work. We would also like to acknowledge helpful advice given by our colleagues Francine Blau, Peter Cappelli, Louis Christofides, Ronald Ehrenberg, Henry Farber, Peter Feuille, Robert Flanagan, Daniel Hamermesh, Roger Koenker, and members of seminars at Guelph, Purdue, Iowa, Illinois, Cornell, and Columbia universities. Finally, we thank Carol Halliday and her staff for excellent typing.

*   *Chapter 1*

Introduction

This book concerns wage indexation in the United States and specifically the tying of future wage increases to changes in the level of prices. A sustained rise in the overall level of prices (inflation) can erode the purchasing power of workers unless wages keep pace. Likewise, inflation can reduce profit margins for firms the prices of which do not keep up with increases in the costs of doing business. In many instances, wage increases for workers and price increases for firms come about as a direct result of inflationary pressure. However, individuals tend to credit themselves rather than inflation for any rise in the prices of wages they receive (Solow 1982). The feeling of lack of control that is prevalent in this environment leads the public to demand that the government control inflation or, in the absence of some government control of price changes, to demand private contracts that insure them against future declines in purchasing power or profit margins. Wage indexation is one such contract.

Although inflation has become a pervasive fact of life for Americans in the 1970s and 1980s, it is a relatively recent phenomenon in U.S. history. For example, from 1800 to 1945, there were many periods of falling prices and many periods of rising prices. However, astonishing as it may appear, the overall level of consumer prices by the end of World War II was about the same as it was in 1800.[1] Consumer price increases during this period were associated with wars or new gold discoveries but were always short-lived (Friedman 1974: 26–27). After each bout of inflation, prices fell sharply to their

1

"customary" levels (U.S. Bureau of the Census 1975). Since 1945, in contrast, the price level in the United States has, almost without exception, steadily risen with a marked acceleration in the 1970s and early 1980s. In contrast to the overall price stability of the 1800–1945 period, prices rose by about 460 percent from 1945 to 1983. Further, about three-quarters of this post–World War II inflation has occurred since 1970.[2]

INFLATION AND THE ECONOMY

To understand the effects of inflation on the economy as well as the responses by the public to protect itself against these effects, it is worthwhile to focus on two dimensions that distinguish different types of inflation. The first involves changes in the structure of prices in the inflation. Within this dimension, changes can be categorized as "pure" or "uneven." The second dimension involves the ability of the actors to predict future price level changes. Within this dimension, price level changes can be categorized as anticipated or unanticipated (Solow 1982).

In a pure inflation, all prices rise at the same rate, implying that everyone keeps up equally with inflation. Under such conditions, the only real costs are the efforts people make to manage their cash balances—a seemingly small cost (Solow 1982). However, we do not observe pure inflation; instead, inflation has always been associated with uneven price increases for different goods. For example, rents typically are more sluggish than agricultural prices. In an uneven inflation, relative prices (as well as the absolute price level) change. Thus, there may be changes in resource allocation and income distribution, some of which might be undesirable from a social point of view. A classic example of redistribution would be the fall in real income of retirees living on fixed nominal pensions. With a very rapid, impure inflation, redistribution might be substantial, producing tensions and pitting one group in society against another.

Whatever inflation is experienced, it may or may not have been foreseen. If inflation were quite predictable—for example, if we knew with 99 percent confidence that prices would rise at an annual rate each year of 4 to 4.5 percent—then it would be relatively easy for everyone to engage in planning to avoid any undesirable effects of inflation. Workers could ask for and firms could grant wage increases to cover the anticipated price increase. Interest rates could include an inflation premium equal to the expected inflation rate. Firms could enter into long-term pricing agreements with scheduled increases equal to the expected inflation rate. If people's expectations about prices were always realized, there would need be no unintended redistribution of income or reallocation of resources associated with inflation.[3]

In reality, of course, future price levels cannot be perfectly predicted. The consequence of unanticipated inflation, in the absence of any corrective mechanisms, is the redistribution of purchasing power from buyers to sellers. The opposite happens during an unanticipated deflation. In addition, the less predictable the price level is, the riskier the economic environment becomes. Lenders demand a risk premium, causing a rise in interest rates relative to the inflation rate; risk-averse enterprises might curtail some investment activities; families live in increased fear that their assets will be wiped out. Further, in an unanticipated inflation, the price system conveys less information that aids in resource allocation than if we could forecast inflation accurately. The allocative function of the price system is to convey information about relative prices. The more unpredictable the inflation rate is, the less sure we can be that a rise in one good's price is a relative price increase. We might therefore expect a less efficient market system than if inflation were completely anticipated (Friedman 1982).

Even though the economic environment might be uncertain, people are not powerless to do something about it. One response would be to shorten the period for which a contract is in force. According to Okun (1982), much of the U.S. economy consists of long-term labor agreements or pricing arrangements between firms. The long duration of such contracts saves on negotiation costs and helps maintain customer loyalty. However, the more volatile inflation is, the more quickly a long-term agreement becomes out of date. Incentives for shorter contracts increase, with a net loss to society due to increased transaction costs and reduced customer (or worker) loyalty. Shorter contracts have the further disadvantage of causing a more rapid transmission of inflation throughout the economy (Okun 1982).

An additional response to uncertain inflation, in which the long-term agreement can be maintained, is to index payments to some measure of inflation. The most prevalent example in the United States of such an arrangement is the cost-of-living allowance (Cola) clause in union contracts. Such clauses automatically adjust wages in response to consumer price index (CPI) changes and thus do not require renegotiation every time wages are changed. Other examples of indexation in the United States include the automatic escalation of Social Security payments with respect to consumer prices (Munnell 1977), the occasional indexation of private pensions (Defina 1975), flexible interest rate home mortgages, and the proposed indexation of federal income tax brackets to begin in 1985. It is interesting to note that the widespread emergence of flexible rate mortgages has very close parallels to our experience with Cola clauses. The indexation of these interest payments very often includes "caps," "triggers," and "corridors" similar to those found in Cola agreements.

It is possible under such indexation schemes to fix the real value of payments from one party to another, whether those payments are wages, pensions, interest payments, or taxes. A benefit of such an outcome might well be smaller fluctuations in output and employment — less severe recessions and less vigorous booms. If firms set employment along the demand curve for labor, wage indexation can keep employment stable by reducing real wage movements. A deflationary monetary policy might result in less unemployment under indexation because wages will automatically decelerate as price inflation slows down. Thus, indexation can eliminate the effects of unanticipated inflation or deflation by insulating the "real" sector of the economy from overall inflation (Friedman 1974). However, under widespread indexation, inflation becomes transmitted more rapidly throughout the economy. In addition, a firm the prices of which bear little relationship to overall consumer prices might not wish to tie its wages to the CPI. Further, indexation might prevent a change in real wages from taking place that would help clear the labor market. For example, if productivity falls (rises), the real wage consistent with full employment might also fall (rise); however, wage indexation could prevent such an adjustment from taking place. Finally, by making inflation easier to live with, a system of widespread indexation might tempt the government to make only minimal efforts at fighting inflation (Giersch 1974).

Despite these potential drawbacks to indexation, its benefits have led several countries with high and volatile inflation rates to institute widespread systems of indexation. For example, in Brazil, wages, savings deposits, loans, rents, social insurance, and taxes have all been indexed to the inflation rate (Ahnefeld and Frank 1974). Israel has also maintained a system of indexation in response to its high and volatile inflation rate (Cukierman 1977).[4] With average annual 1976–81 inflation rates of 59 percent in Brazil and 78 percent in Israel, indexation is evidently seen as necessary to prevent dramatic shifts in income distribution and resource allocation (ILO 1982). The volatility of these rates can be illustrated by noting that during this period, Brazil's inflation ranged from a low of 38 percent to a high of 96 percent while Israel's range was from 35 percent to 131 percent (ILO 1982). Presumably, inflation in these countries is very hard to predict. Substantial underprediction of Israel's 124 percent annual inflation rate from 1979 to 1981 could, for instance, have cut real wages in half were it not for indexation (ILO 1982). If workers and firms had anticipated "only" a 58 percent inflation rate during these two years, and set wages accordingly, then this would have occurred. The annual inflation rate in Israel over the 1974–79 period was in fact "only" 46 percent, so such an outcome might not have been unlikely (ILO 1982).[5]

COST-OF-LIVING ALLOWANCE (COLA) CLAUSES IN U.S. COLLECTIVE BARGAINING

Indexation of wages and salaries in the United States is confined almost exclusively to union workers (Sheifer 1979). Among union workers, about 55 to 60 percent have some kind of Cola in their collective bargaining agreements (see Table 2–7). Since at most 25 percent of U.S. workers are in unions (Kochan 1980), only a small minority of U.S. workers have wage indexation. Outside the areas mentioned earlier (Social Security, interest payments, and income taxes), formal indexation is very rare in the United States (Blinder 1977). Although inflation is a major concern in the United States, it is not nearly as high or as volatile as in countries like Israel and Brazil. Table 2–7 shows, for example, that over the same 1976–81 period discussed for these two countries, inflation in the United States averaged a mere 10 percent (compounded) with a range of 6.8 percent to 13.3 percent. With these figures, the possible losses in real wages due to unanticipated inflation must be a good deal smaller than those implied by Israel's and Brazil's inflation. The relative stability of U.S. consumer prices probably accounts for our limited incidence of indexation.

Even though the practice of indexation in the United States is limited, it has become firmly entrenched in certain segments of unionized employment. As Table 2-7 indicates, the fraction of workers under major collective bargaining agreements (i.e., covering at least 1,000 workers) reached about 60 percent in 1976 and has been nearly that ever since. Those workers who are covered by wage indexation are extremely reluctant to give it up and will do so only under dire economic circumstances. For example, in the late 1970s and early 1980s industries hit by severe recession—autos, trucking, and steel, among others—asked workers to give up or modify their Colas. Indexation in these industries was seen as an uncontrollable source of labor cost increases and thus as a contributor to industrial decline. However, the workers were willing to take pay cuts and make many other concessions in order to retain the Cola principle (see Chapter 2).

Colas have become an institutionalized component of collective bargaining in several basic industries including autos, steel, trucking, and rubber. Several features of Colas stand out as distinguishing characteristics of wage indexation in the United States. First, Colas tend to be associated with our stronger unions such as the United Auto Workers (UAW), the United Steelworkers (USW), and the Teamsters. Second, since the 1948 agreement between General Motors (GM) and the UAW, Colas have been associated with long-term (e.g., three-year duration) contracts. Third, among those contracts with indexation, the typical Cola formula leads to only partial indexation. That is, the average Cola raises wages by a smaller percentage than prices rise. Fourth, most Colas provide equal, across-the-board, cents-per-hour wage increases to each worker in the bargaining unit. Thus, Colas usually cause a narrowing of wage differentials by raising low-paid workers' wages by a higher percentage than that of high-paid workers.

Colas have a variety of restrictions and idiosyncrasies in their definitions that affect their yield. For example, the particular formula relating the CPI to wage increases varies: Many UAW contracts now call for a one-cent-per-hour raise for each 0.26-point increase in the CPI; other Colas call for one cent per hour for each 0.6-point CPI increase. Some Colas stipulate maximum ("caps") or minimum payments; others don't allow a payment until a certain CPI level is reached ("triggers") or become inoperative during certain CPI ranges ("corridors"). Some Colas call for quarterly payments; others allow annual adjustments. Because of these kinds of restrictions, two Colas with the same formula (e.g., one cent per hour for each 0.3-point CPI increase) do not necessarily lead to the same yield.

Many of these features of Colas suggest that union bargaining power is an important factor leading to wage indexation in the United States. Both the lack of Colas in the nonunion sector and the rarity of indexing provisions for private sector nonlabor transactions suggest that in the United States some form of seller monopoly power is necessary to induce buyers to grant Colas. This view is reinforced both by the association between long-term contracts and Colas and by the concentration of Colas in contracts negotiated by the strongest unions. As we discuss in Chapter 2, Colas were often granted by firms in return for an agreement by unions for a long-term, no-strike contract. The unions posing the greatest strike threat were best able to extract such an offer. Colas have been viewed by some (for example, Laidler 1974) as a way of guaranteeing labor peace. The absence of Colas from the nonunion sector suggests that a typical firm unconstrained by the presence of a union would prefer not to have its wages tied to the CPI. However, the degree to which a firm resists a Cola and the desire among workers for a Cola might vary along several dimensions. We discuss these dimensions in detail in Chapters 5 and 6. They include such factors as worker and firm risk aversion, the divergence between movements in the CPI and in the firm's value added, and uncertainty about inflation. Thus, bargaining power is not the only factor affecting the presence or generosity of a Cola.

PLAN OF THE BOOK

In this book we perform a detailed study of the determinants and effects of wage indexation in U.S. collective bargaining. Extensive use is made of secondary materials, both historical and contemporary. However, the bulk of our empirical analysis is based on a unique source of data on Colas compiled over a three-year period. The data consist of a time series for the 1967–82 years for about 4,000 collective bargaining relationships. As described in more detail in the following chapters, this data file includes extensive information on wage levels, types of Cola provisions (if any), bargaining unit information (e.g., worker coverage, unit size, the union), and industrial characteristics. These data were collected by hand from the contracts on file with the U.S. Department of Labor in Washington, D.C. The data are not easily reproducible, since the Labor Department destroyed much of the information after we collected it. The richness of our data base permits extensive econometric hypothesis testing that will be of interest to researchers and policymakers alike. In addition, the detailed information on the characteristics of Colas will be useful for practitioners who need to know about collective bargaining trends as well as the cost of various Cola provisions under alternative assumptions about inflation.

Chapter 2 consists of a comprehensive examination of the historical evolution of Colas in the United States in the twentieth century, with some mention of earlier forms of indexation. It provides a link to our later empirical work by focusing on economic variables. The following themes in the evolution of Colas in the twentieth century are stressed in this treatment:

1. change in labor's attitudes toward Colas — from early opposition to advocacy;
2. management views on wage indexation — Colas as a deterrent to union organizing, as the price to pay to gain long-term contracts, as a source of uncontrollable increases in labor costs;
3. changes in the method of measuring consumer prices — the basis for indexation of wages;
4. the relationship of government wage controls to Colas — World War I, World War II, the Korean War, the Kennedy–Johnson guideposts, the Nixon controls, and the Carter guidelines;
5. the role of "key" negotiations in setting patterns — for example, the GM–UAW agreements of 1948 and 1950 or the auto concessions of the 1970s and 1980s;
6. the impact of economic conditions — especially inflation uncertainty — on the incidence and characteristics of Colas, with special emphasis placed on the post–World War II period; and
7. the connection between Colas and long-term agreements beginning with the 1948 GM–UAW contract.

Chapter 3 uses our own data base to provide a detailed discussion of the characteristics that define Colas: types of formulas, timing of reviews, maximum and minimum adjustments, triggers, and corridors. The changing nature of these characteristics over the 1970s is documented. The characteristics are also cross-tabulated with industry- and union-related variables. These tabulations provide a very clear picture of the variations in Cola characteristics in the United States.

Chapter 4 reviews formal economic models and empirical evidence obtained by others on the effects of indexation. We focus on the impact of Colas in the following areas: output and employment fluctuations, inflation, strikes, and wage differentials. Particular attention is paid to the distinction between the effects of indexation under "real" and "monetary" shocks to the economy. For example, it has been hypothesized that Colas can stabilize real GNP under monetary shocks (e.g., unexpected changes in the money supply) but destabilize GNP under real shocks (e.g., an OPEC oil embargo). In addition, some suggest that Colas reduce the incidence of strikes by keeping wages in line with overall economic conditions and by reducing opportunities for striking through long-term agreements. Finally, as noted earlier, Colas are expected to reduce wage differentials within bargaining units.

Chapter 5 surveys theories about the economic explanation for the existence and strength of Colas. Presentation of rigorous economic models as well as some intuitive discussion of employer and employee desires is provided. The following forces are emphasized in these models: inflation uncertainty and risk aversion, industry-specific versus economywide shocks, negotiation costs and contract length, and union bargaining power. For example, risk aversion is hypothesized to raise workers' demand for indexation, and higher union bargaining power raises the likelihood that a Cola will return wage increases equal in percentage terms to price increases.

Chapters 6 through 8 present our empirical work on the determinants of the incidence and strength of Colas (Chapter 6), the effect of Colas on wage inflation (Chapter 7), and the effect of Colas on the incidence and severity of strike activity (Chapter 8). The economic models presented in Chapters 4 and 5 provide the basis for the empirical specifications. Although measuring the incidence of Colas (e.g., whether a contract has a Cola) is straightforward, the measurement of strength is not. Chapter 6 begins with a discussion of this issue. The primary issues center around *ex post* versus *ex ante* measurement of Cola strength and the separation of the response of wages to anticipated inflation from the response to unanticipated inflation. This separation leads to a distinction between the intentions of labor and management with respect to a Cola and the realized payments under a Cola. To measure these intentions, the hypothetical response of each Cola to various inflation rates is computed. Hypotheses derived in Chapter 5 about the demand for indexation are also tested using multivariate techniques.

The actual effects of capped and uncapped Colas on wage inflation are estimated in Chapter 7. Several issues assume particular importance in this analysis. For example, we distinguish the wage response to anticipated and unanticipated inflation. The possibility that current wage setting corrects past mistakes in forecasting inflation as well as allowing for future expected inflation is analyzed.

The final area of empirical testing is the investigation of the impact of Colas on strike activity provided in Chapter 8. The analysis uses a sample of individual contract negotiations containing strike data (i.e., incidence and length of strike if any) matched to our Cola and other contract information. We are primarily interested in estimating the total effects of Colas on strike activity. These effects are broken down into direct and indirect impacts. The direct effect is the impact of having indexation on the expected incidence and duration of a strike associated with a particular negotiation. The indirect effect occurs because having a Cola facilitates negotiation of a long-term contract, thereby reducing the union's opportunities to strike.

The final chapter considers policy and research implications of our empirical and theoretical work.

NOTES

1. According to the U.S. Bureau of the Census (1975: 210–11), the consumer price index (an indicator of average living costs) stood at 51 in 1800 (1967 = 100) and 53.9 in 1945! Of course, such long-range comparisons are tentative because of changes in the mix of consumer goods.

2. See U.S. Bureau of the Census (1975) and the *Monthly Labor Review,* March 1984.

3. To be literally true, such a claim requires that we be able to predict individual prices as well as the overall price level.

4. Other countries that have relied on some form of indexation include West Germany (rents and leases only), Denmark, Italy, Belgium, Finland, Switzerland, the Netherlands, Norway, Iceland, France, Austria, Great Britain, and Sweden (Ahnefeld and Frank 1974).

5. Of course, the overall inflation rate might well have been different without indexation. However, on the micro level, the comparison is valid: An individual worker who had salaries in 1979–81 set according to expected inflation might have had a 50 percent cut in real wages.

REFERENCES

Ahnefeld, Adolf, and K. H. Frank. 1974. "Appendix: Scope and Forms of Escalator Clauses in Various Countries." In *Essays on Inflation and Indexation,* edited by Herbert Giersch, pp. 16-23. Washington, D.C.: American Enterprise Institute.

Blinder, Alan S. 1977. "Indexing the Economy through Financial Intermediation." In *Stabilization of the Domestic and International Economy* (Carnegie-Rochester Series on Public Policy, Vol. 5), edited by K. Brunner and A. Meltzer, pp. 69-105. Amsterdam: North-Holland.

Cukierman, Alex. 1977. "General Wage Escalator Clauses and the Inflation Unemployment Tradeoff." *Economic Inquiry* 15, no. 1 (January): 67-84.

Defina, Catherine C. 1975. "Labor and the Economy in 1974." *Monthly Labor Review* 98, no. 1 (January): 3-16.

Friedman, Milton. 1974. "Monetary Correction." In *Essays on Inflation and Indexation,* edited by Herbert Giersch, pp. 25-61. Washington, D.C.: American Enterprise Institute.

———. 1982. "Inflation and Unemployment." In *The Battle Against Unemployment and Inflation,* edited by Martin N. Baily and Arthur M. Okun, pp. 45-57. New York: Norton.

Giersch, Herbert. 1974. "Index Clauses and the Fight Against Inflation." In *Essays on Inflation and Indexation,* edited by Herbert Giersch, pp. 1-16. Washington, D.C.: American Enterprise Institute.

International Labor Office (ILO). 1982. *Year Book of Labor Statistics 1982.* Geneva: ILO.

Kochan, Thomas. 1980. *Collective Bargaining and Industrial Relations.* Homewood, Ill.: Irwin.

Munnell, Alicia. 1977. *The Future of Social Security.* Washington, D.C.: The Brookings Institution.

Okun, Arthur M. 1982. "Customer Markets and the Costs of Inflation." In *The Battle Against Unemployment and Inflation,* edited by Martin N. Baily and Arthur M. Okun, pp. 35-39. New York: Norton.

Sheifer, Victor. 1979. "Cost-of-Living Adjustment: Keeping Up With Inflation?" *Monthly Labor Review* 102, no. 6 (June): 14-17.

Solow, Robert M. 1982. "The Intelligent Citizen's Guide to Inflation." In *The Battle Against Unemployment and Inflation,* edited by Martin N. Baily and Arthur M. Okun, pp. 20-34. New York: Norton.

U.S. Bureau of Labor Statistics. 1984. *Monthly Labor Review* 107, no. 3 (March): 65-103.

U.S. Bureau of the Census. 1975. *Historical Statistics of the United States, Part 1.* Washington, D.C.: U.S. Government Printing Office.

The History of Wage Indexation in the United States

Automatic wage escalation adjustments triggered by the consumer price index (CPI) have become an entrenched part of U.S. collective bargaining. These Cola clauses represent not only a concern for the effects of inflation on workers' purchasing power, but also result from a desire on the part of workers for reduced uncertainty about purchasing power (i.e., their real wages). This uncertainty is reduced through the *automatic* adjustments that workers with Colas can anticipate during an inflationary period. At the same time, Colas might raise the employer's uncertainty about future labor costs to the extent that inflation is unexpected.

These two themes of real wage protection and the potentially damaging impact of uncertainty pervade the U.S. experience with wage escalation in the twentieth century. Inflation and uncertainty help explain why Colas become widespread in some periods. They also help explain the particular features of Colas that labor and management fashion together. These links will become evident as we trace the evolution of Colas. During this evolution, several issues concerning Colas have persistently troubled labor, management, and government.

First, unions and firms that have chosen to link wages to prices must decide whether that link should be automatic or discretionary. The Cola plans that we are accustomed to seeing today provide automatic protection against inflation. However, many early attempts to compensate workers for inflation involved wage "reopeners" —

contract provisions allowing for renegotiation of wages after a certain time period had elapsed or after a certain level of consumer prices had been reached (Carr 1925). Time- or CPI-triggered wage reopeners remain a common contract provision. Wage reopeners give management more flexibility than automatic adjustments but do not give workers the same kind of guaranteed protection. Second, among those bargaining units that negotiate automatic Colas, the exact formula that ties wage changes to changes in the CPI and the question of possible maximum or minimum adjustments must be decided. Our empirical analysis described below will shed light on the enormous difference in labor costs than can result from placing maximum or minimum values on Cola adjustments. Third, the appropriate index of consumer prices to use in Colas has been an issue of concern to all involved parties. The U.S. Bureau of Labor Statistics (BLS) continually updates the CPI, and each change can cost or save a company millions of dollars in Cola payments. For example, the BLS has recently changed the housing component of the CPI by using a measure of renting costs as opposed to mortgage rates. In a period of rising rents and falling mortgage interest rates, this change could cost companies a great deal (*Business Week,* February 14, 1983). The resolution of each of these first three issues has had a substantial impact on the inflation protection afforded by Cola clauses.

Fourth, since the 1948 agreement between the General Motors Corporation (GM) and the United Auto Workers (UAW), there has been a strong link between long-term contracts and the presence of a Cola.[1] Multiyear contracts with no-strike clauses give companies a reasonable assurance against strikes during the life of the agreement. These companies have often had to grant Colas to gain this labor peace, and our data analysis shows a strong statistical link between long contracts and Colas. However, long-term contracts introduce rigidities into the wage structure by not allowing a rapid union wage response to unemployment (Lewis 1963; Flanagan 1976; Hendricks 1981). For this reason, multiyear union contracts have been blamed by some macroeconomists for reducing the ability of fiscal and monetary policies to restrain wage inflation (Sachs 1980). On the opposite side of the coin, however, is the fact that long-term agreements reduce the inflationary effects of expansionary policies.

Fifth, the federal govenment has had to deal with the Cola phenomenon in designing wage and price controls. Workers with Colas have often received different treatment under government controls from those without indexation. Finally, "key" bargaining units seem to play an important role in setting patterns for Cola terms. These units tend to have strong unions such as the UAW, USW, or Teamsters. For example, the particular formula once used by the UAW (one-cent-per-hour raise for each 0.3-point increase in the CPI) has become a model for many other bargaining units. Such imitation can introduce rigidities into the wage structure similar to rigidities induced by long-term contracts.

EARLY EXPERIENCE WITH INDEXATION: THE PRE–WORLD WAR II PERIOD

Reference to the cost of living in setting industrial workers' wages in the United States began in the early twentieth century and became widespread during the World War I period.[2] For example, the U.S. Anthracite Coal Strike Commission of 1902 used cost-of-living figures in setting wages, and in 1910 several arbitration cases involving railway wages were based on the cost of living. However, such cases were rare until World War I (Carr 1925: 1, 7).

Table 2–1 gives some clues as to why World War I is the period marking the beginning of U.S. wage indexation. In particular, from 1880 to World War I, consumer prices showed a remarkable stability; the CPI (1967 = 100) stood at 29 in 1880 and was 30.1 in 1914. Fluctuations between 1880 and 1914 were very minor, the largest annual change in consumer prices being only 4 percent. This rise was sustained for more than one year in only one case, 1901 to 1903. (Not surprisingly, this was the period that wages in the coal industry were first changed with reference to the cost of living.) In the thirty-five-year period before World War I, most years saw no change in consumer prices. With this long background of price stability, it is easy to see why the cost of living played such a small role in wage setting prior to World War I.[3]

However, beginning with 1915, prices began to accelerate rapidly. From 1915 to 1920 the CPI virtually doubled, as opposed to a net rise of only about 5 percent over the previous thirty-five years. This sudden and large increase in consumer prices forced companies, workers, unions, and government to take account of living costs in setting wages.

For workers and unions, the motivation for this concern was the

Table 2-1.   Consumer Price Index and Inflation Rates, 1880-1950.

Year[a]	CPI	Percentage Change	Year	CPI	Percentage Change
1880	29	3.6%	1913	29.7	2.4%
1881	29	0.0	1914	30.1	1.3
1882	29	0.0	1915	30.4	1.0
1883	28	−3.4	1916	32.7	7.6
1884	27	−3.6	1917	38.4	17.4
1885	27	0.0	1918	45.1	17.4
1886	27	0.0	1919	51.8	14.9
1887	27	0.0	1920	60.0	15.8
1888	27	0.0	1921	53.6	−10.7
1889	27	0.0	1922	50.2	−6.3
1890	27	0.0	1923	51.1	1.8
1891	27	0.0	1924	51.2	0.2
1892	27	0.0	1925	52.5	2.5
1893	27	0.0	1926	53.0	1.0
1894	26	−3.7	1927	52.0	−1.9
1895	25	−3.8	1928	51.3	−1.3
1896	25	0.0	1929	51.3	0.0
1897	25	0.0	1930	50.0	−2.5
1898	25	0.0	1931	45.6	−8.8
1899	25	0.0	1932	40.9	−10.3
1900	25	0.0	1933	38.8	−5.1
1901	25	0.0	1934	40.1	3.4
1902	26	4.0	1935	41.1	2.5
1903	27	3.8	1936	41.5	1.0
1904	27	0.0	1937	43.0	3.6
1905	27	0.0	1938	42.2	−1.9
1906	27	0.0	1939	41.6	−1.4
1907	28	3.7	1940	42.0	1.0
1908	27	−3.6	1941	44.1	5.0
1909	27	0.0	1942	48.8	10.7
1910	28	3.7	1943	51.8	6.1
1911	28	0.0	1944	52.7	1.7
1912	29	3.6	1945	53.9	2.3
			1946	58.5	8.5
			1947	66.9	14.4
			1948	72.1	7.8
			1949	71.4	−1.0
			1950	72.1	1.0

Note: 1967 = 100; rates are increases from previous year.

[a] Pre-1912 data are estimates.

Source: U.S. Bureau of the Census 1975: 210-11.

protection of purchasing power, although workers were reluctant to accept wage cuts during times of falling prices. For companies, the motives were the increase in employee morale and the reduction of turnover. For example, the scientific management movement supported the principle of cost-of-living adjustments as a deterrent of unionization. In 1919 the Holt Manufacturing Company in Peoria, Illinois implemented a plan to review wages quarterly or semiannually to the extent that living costs warranted such a review. Believing that living costs were a source of dissatisfaction, the company decided that it should take account of living costs in order to improve employee relations (Williams and Holt 1919: 32). In addition, the company reported a sharp reduction in turnover in the years immediately following implementation in 1919 of the plan to coordinate wages and living costs. Specifically, in 1918 voluntary turnover equaled 228 percent of employment but fell to only 45 percent by 1920 (Carr 1925: 373). Although high unemployment in the early 1920s could also explain the reduction of turnover, the Holt Company perceived the turnover figures as evidence of the effect of its wage plan (Carr 1925).[4]

Finally, the motive of government in using the Cola principle was to maintain labor peace and thus wartime production. For example, both the National War Labor Board and the Shipbuilding Labor Adjustment Board relied primarily on the cost of living as a criterion for wage changes during World War I. These agencies referred to the need for labor peace for the war efforts (Carr 1925: 32–53). In Chapter 8, our own data for the 1970–81 period will be used to perform a detailed test of the idea that Colas contribute to labor peace.

During this early period (1915–23) in which wages were first linked to prices, most plans were discretionary in the sense that the size of wage adjustments in relation to price adjustments was generally not set in advance (Carr 1925).[5] In addition, a variety of sources for cost-of-living information were used, although in most cases the BLS data on prices were used. In 1919 the BLS published its first cost-of-living index.[6] It was published semiannually for thirty-two cities consisting primarily of shipbuilding and industrial centers. In 1921 the BLS began regular publication of a national index for the United States. These indexes were noteworthy because they were constructed from budget studies of wage earners and clerical workers and introduced the "market basket" concept (Carr 1925). Price data were used in three types of wage-setting contexts: government wage-setting boards, union-management collective bargaining agreements or arbitration decisions, and plans instituted by individual nonunion companies.

Government Wage-Setting Boards, 1915–23

In the 1915–23 period, many government agencies became involved in setting wages: the U.S. Bituminous and Anthracite Coal Commissions; the President's Mediation Commission, the National War Labor Board, the Shipbuilding Labor Adjustment Board, the National Adjustment Commission, the U.S. Railroad Commission and U.S. Railroad Board, many state and municipal agencies. According to a BLS study, during this period:

> The cost of living has entered as a factor into practically every award made by Government arbitration boards. It has also been considered by State and municipal agencies, and by State arbitration boards, and has been the controlling factor in the fixing of wages by minimum wage boards in 13 states and the District of Columbia. (Carr 1925: 431)

Federal arbitration awards directly affected many workers. Table 2–2 shows that about 4 million workers were covered by these awards — a substantial percentage (roughly 15 percent) of the average total U.S. nonfarm employment of about 26 million (U.S. Bureau of the Census 1975: 137). Further, since there were only about 1 million mining workers (all types of mines) and 4 million transportation and public utilities workers at this time, federal awards covered the majority of these industries' workers (U.S. Bureau of the Census 1975: 137).

Federal arbitration boards during the 1915–23 era relied mostly on BLS data for prices. Before 1919 no cost-of-living figures based on retail prices were computed regularly by the BLS; for these earlier

Table 2–2. Number of Employees Covered by Federal Arbitration Awards, 1915–23.

Industry	Number of Employees
Coal	747,000
Meat packing	100,000
Shipping	500,000
Railroad	2,000,000
Other	711,500
Total	4,058,500

Source: Carr 1925: 431.

years, a combination of wholesale and food price data was used (Carr 1925: 433). Although reference was made to living costs in almost all government wage awards, this system could not be called one of indexation. Wage awards were entirely discretionary. In some cases, the award made general reference to the rising cost of living; in others, the arbitrator noted a specific figure for the increase in living costs. Even in the latter, the government did not want to tie itself to a specific formula relating wages to living costs. For example, in 1918 the Shipbuilding Labor Adjustment Board announced that since West Coast living costs had risen 20.1 percent, workers under its jurisdiction were entitled to a 20 percent raise. However, in announcing its general principles, the board stated that it would only consider raising wages again if living costs rose at least 10 percent. Further, the board argued that full wage adjustments should be given only to the lowest paid workers (Carr 1925: 55–56). Such a policy gave the board considerably more flexibility than would have been available with an automatic cost-of-living escalator clause.

Other federal agencies such as the National War Labor Board and the U.S. Railroad Labor Board were even less specific about living costs. In 1920 the U.S. Anthracite Coal Commission made a general reference to a doubling of living costs from 1913 to the U.S. entry into World War I, but its award did not reflect this 100 percent rise. Interestingly, the commission, in making its decision, did not wish "to connect itself to an award which could justly be considered as an encouragement to the so-called 'vicious spiral' in prices" (Carr 1925: 22). Finally, state minimum wage boards often collected their own cost-of-living data but did not tie themselves to any specific wage-setting formulas (Carr 1925: 97–199).

Although government arbitration boards in the 1915–23 period were not engaging in actual indexation, they provided legitimacy to the idea of cost-of-living adjustments and spurred agencies such as the BLS continually to refine cost-of-living data. The government's lead in these areas may well have paved the way for automatic escalator plans for sectors not under the jurisdiction of federal or state arbitration boards.

Union–Management Contracts, 1915–23

Table 2–3 indicates that from 1915 to 1923, union members constituted between 10 and 20 percent of nonfarm employment, the figure

Table 2-3.   Union Membership as a Percentage of Nonfarm
Employment, Selected Years.

1915	11.2%	1926	11.4%	1936	13.7%	1950	31.5%
1916	10.9%	1927	11.6%	1937	22.6%	1960	31.4%
1917	11.9%	1928	11.4%	1938	27.5%	1970	27.4%
1918	13.1%	1929	11.0%	1939	28.6%	1978	24.0%
1919	15.1%	1930	11.6%	1940	26.9%		
1920	18.4%	1931	12.4%	1941	27.9%		
1921	19.5%	1932	12.9%	1942	25.9%		
1922	15.1%	1933	11.3%	1943	31.1%		
1923	12.4%	1934	11.9%	1944	33.8%		
1924	12.4%	1935	13.2%	1945	35.5%		
1925	11.8%						

Sources: Davey, Bognanno, and Estenson 1982: 74; U.S. Bureau of the Census
1975: 137, 178.

falling during the 1920s. Thus, any wage indexation under collective
bargaining covered at most a small minority of the work force. However, several developments in collective bargaining have importance
for current Cola issues and are thus worth noting.

Union–management contracts that explicitly considered the cost of
living generally referred to BLS data, although some adjustments were
made on the basis of data such as those published by Bradstreet on
retail food prices. Most of these agreements were reached after the
dissolution of the government wage-setting boards of World War I.
Some contracts stipulated that cost of living should be the sole factor
used in revising wages; others permitted consideration of the economic condition of the industry as well as the cost of living. There
were several different types of agreements that placed all the weight
on cost of living. Some were discretionary and others called for automatic indexation. The printing industry took the lead in this early
period of Cola formation (Carr 1925).

One type of contract where consumer prices were the sole criterion
for wage charges stipulated that wages should be revised on certain
dates in accordance with the cost of living. An example was the 1919
agreement between the Cleveland Garment Manufacturers' Association and the Ladies' Garment Workers (ILGWU). The contract called
for periodic wage adjustments made by a board of referees in line
with changes in living costs (Carr 1925: 204). This plan seems similar

to modern-day wage reopeners, except that the referees were directed to consider the cost of living; this wage adjustment criterion was therefore also similar to that of the federal arbitration boards in World War I. In practice, under the agreement, the referees also considered the continuity of employment in setting wages, limiting the degree to which wages automatically changed as living costs changed (Carr 1925: 205).

In contrast to the Cleveland garment industry example, a second type of contract stipulated that if the cost of living had changed on a given date by a given amount, the wage scale would also be changed by this amount. Such contracts occurred in the printing industry in Seattle in 1921 and Chicago in 1920. These agreements constitute the first automatic escalator clauses. The Seattle agreement stipulated that if by December 1921 the CPI fell at least 19.1 points from its December 1920 level of 94.1, wages would be cut 10 percent; if prices rose to at least 113, wages would rise 10 percent. This Cola was noteworthy because it allowed for wage cuts — a sensitive subject for union workers — and it permitted only partial indexation. The latter can be seen by comparing the 10 percent wage change with the minimum price change of 20 percent needed to trigger the Cola. Partial indexation can be viewed as a compromise between labor's desire for real wage protection and management's desire for stable labor costs. The Chicago contract had similar provisions (Carr 1925: 205-6).

A related kind of Cola stipulated that if during the life of the contract the scheduled wage increase were less than the consumer price increase, then wages would be adjusted automatically in accordance with the cost of living. This type of agreement was signed, again in the printing industry, in Elmira, New York in 1922 (Carr 1925: 206). In contrast to the Seattle and Chicago contracts, this agreement called for complete real wage protection. In fact, since there were scheduled wage increases in the contract, real wages would rise if prices remained stable. This type of contract occurs with some frequency today. In effect, it guarantees that real wages will not fall, and if prices are fairly stable, then real wages will rise.

More intricate Colas than the Elmira agreement gave a schedule relating wages to specific values of the BLS's cost-of-living index. For example, in the Spokane printing industry agreement of 1922, such a schedule was set. Each December the BLS's index was recorded, and wages were adjusted to the appropriate level. The contract gave a schedule of wages corresponding to different inflation rates. For example, if prices fell below their 1913 level, day shift weekly wages would be set at $34.50. However, if prices rose by no more than 9.2 percent, wages would rise to $36. For inflation rates between 9.2 and 24.4 percent, wages would be $37.50. Wages under the contract would continue to rise as new intervals of inflation were reached up to a 100.4 percent price rise. For inflation rates greater than or equal to this figure, wages would be fixed at $45. Thus, the 1922 Spokane Cola placed upper and lower limits on wages and gave far less than complete indexation. For example, under this contract, if prices doubled from the 1913 level during the life of the contract, wages would rise by only about 20 percent (Carr 1925: 206).

Unlike the automatic Colas just described, several contracts during this period had wage reopeners. Some reopeners called for renegotiation if a particular CPI figure was reached by a certain date (e.g., some printing industry contracts in Chicago and Detroit) or if a "material increase" in living costs occurred by a given date. An arbitrator was called in to determine whether a material increase had occurred. Such contracts were reminiscent of federal arbitration boards in World War I and occurred in the street-railway industry in San Francisco, the New York building trades, and the Rochester, New York garment industry (Carr 1925: 206–15).

The use of voluntary arbitration in settling wage disputes was quite common in the 1919–23 period in a variety of industries. Arbitrators almost always took cost-of-living figures into account in making their decisions. Some of the arguments made by labor and management illustrate both sides' concerns over cost-of-living adjustments. Employers often argued that cost-of-living-related wage increases should be applied only to the increase in the cost-of-living budget rather than the wage. Under this doctrine, all workers would get the same number of dollars as compensation for rising living costs; the higher paid workers would thus get smaller percentage increases. Today, most Colas are of the same type — equal, across-the-board cents-per-hour increases. In addition, employers argued on occasion that standards of living were rising and that further wage increases were thus not necessary. Further, employers argued for wage cuts when consumer prices fell, especially in the 1920–22 period, when the CPI fell about 16 percent (Table 2–1). Finally, employers argued against pay raises after periods of rising prices because a period of falling prices was anticipated (Carr 1925: 270). Thus, employers expressed a desire to not be locked into high rates of pay. This concern has appeared again during the 1970s and 1980s as many employers do not want wages tied to an index that might not reflect their own prices.

During these arbitration proceedings, unions argued in favor of cost-of-living-based wage increases and against pay cuts during periods of falling prices. They argued that prices would remain high or even rise further, implying that a wage increase was needed to keep pay from lagging behind inflation (Carr 1925: 287). This concern lies behind unions' current defense of uncapped Cola plans (Nag and O'Boyle 1982). In arguing against wage cuts, unions argued that there was a tendency toward higher prices. Again, the prospect of being "left behind" inflation was a motivating factor. In addition, workers argued that wages did not keep up with inflation in the past, so that cuts in pay were not justified (Carr 1925: 322–23). Similar reasoning has been used to explain the high rates of wage inflation even in the face of the 1970–71 recession (Kennedy 1970). Finally, the workers argued against wage cuts on the grounds that real wages (living standards) should be rising. The same rationale underlies the UAW-initiated "annual improvement factor" — a scheduled wage increase beyond Cola adjustments to permit a rising standard of living (Bortz 1948).

In summary, automatic escalator clauses in union contracts during 1915–23 appear to be limited to the printing industry. However, some reliance on the CPI was widespread in collective bargaining, reflecting an increased awareness of the problem of inflation. Further, several features of Colas initiated during this period characterize indexation in the 1980s.

Individual Companies, 1921–22

In 1921 and 1922 the BLS sampled about 7,000 companies to determine the degree to which they used cost-of-living figures in setting wages. Just over 2,300 responded, implying a response rate of about 33 percent (Carr 1925: 339). Table 2–4 illustrates the varying degrees with which cost-of-living figures were used.

The percentage of firms that had genuine Colas was small; the category of firms using cost-of-living figures regularly in a definite way includes 1.3 percent of firms and 3.7 percent of workers. Of these plans, some were discretionary and resembled wage reopeners in union contracts. The other categories consist exclusively of discretionary

Table 2–4. Use of Cost-of-Living Data by Private Companies, 1921–22 Survey.

	Number of Employers	Percentage of Employers in Each Category Relative to Total Making Wage Adjustments	Number of Workers	Percentage of Workers in Each Category Relative to Total Getting Adjustments
Employers using own cost-of-living figures	41	2.2%	106,676	6.6%
Employers using existing cost-of-living figures:				
a) Regularly in definite way	25	1.3%	60,306	3.7%
b) In definite way on specific occasions	41	2.2%	205,830	12.7%
c) In general way, considerable influence	623	33.5%	605,198	37.3%
d) In general way, little influence	640	34.4%	531,330	32.7%
Employers making no use of cost-of-living figures but who made wage adjustments	491	26.4%	114,621	7.1%
Total	1,861		1,623,961	
Employers making no wage adjustments	399		—	

Source: Carr 1925: 339.

plans. Thus, the 1.3 percent and 3.7 percent figures are likely to be upper bounds for automatic Cola coverage. However, some companies in this category did institute automatic Colas. For example, a New York City bank in 1919 devised a formula whereby salaries would rise or fall by 5 percent for each point rise or fall in Bradstreet's quarterly living costs index. Since the index at this time was 17.53, this plan represented nearly complete indexation because wages would rise (fall) 5 percent for each 5.7 percent rise (fall) in prices (Carr 1925: 383).[7]

A high percentage of companies making wage adjustments referred in some way to cost-of-living figures in setting wages. About 74 percent referred to such figures, and these firms employed 93 percent of the workers getting adjustments. In contrast, only 11 to 38 percent of firms in 1975 were influenced by the CPI in making wage and salary decisions, according to the National Industrial Conference Board (NICB) (Weeks 1976). Although we have no information on the ways in which the CPI was used in these cases, the larger percentage of firms using cost-of-living figures in 1921–22 demonstrates the concern for inflation in the World War I era. This comparison is especially noteworthy because the rapid inflation of 1973–74 (Table 2–7) would have been expected to increase firms' and workers' awareness of the CPI. Although most of the firms in the 1921–22 or 1975 studies relying on the CPI did not have automatic Colas, use of the CPI might be a kind of "informal indexation" in which workers come to expect wage adjustments based on inflation (Carr 1925; Weeks 1976).

Larger firms in the 1921–22 survey were more likely to have Colas or to use cost-of-living figures than were smaller firms. This can be seen by noting that the percentages of workers for whom cost-of-living figures were used is greater than the percentage of firms that used these figures. This firm-size relationship might reflect the need for large bureaucracies to establish impartial rules for determining wages and salaries (Reynolds 1982). As our data from the 1970–81 period show, there is a positive relationship between bargaining unit size and the presence and strength of wage indexation in collective bargaining agreements (Hendricks and Kahn 1983). This finding mirrors that of Table 2–4.

Firms in the 1921–22 survey that used their own cost-of-living figures deserve special mention. These companies averaged about 2,600 employees apiece, compared to the sample average of only about 900 (see Table 2–4). Such firms regularly surveyed their own employees to determine their cost of living. This method presumably had the ability to produce a more accurate picture of inflation as it affected each company's workers. However, it is important to note that these plans were initiated by the companies themselves. In a collective bargaining context, the parties need to refer to figures that neither side can manipulate. For this reason, all Colas in union contracts now use published government statistics. However, just as labor and management argued in the 1920s over the degree to which BLS figures showed rising or falling living costs, such controversies continue today (*Business Week,* February 21, 1983).

1923–World War II

Interest in the Cola principle diminished in the 1920s and 1930s. Table 2–1 shows a period of price stability from 1923 (CPI = 51.1) to 1929 (CPI = 51.3). Prices dropped sharply during the Depression to a low of 38.8 in 1933. From 1933 until U.S. entry into World War II, there was modest inflation in most years, with small CPI declines in 1938 and 1939. With this price behavior, workers' purchasing power was not abruptly attacked the way it was during 1915–20. Observing U.S. companies' wage-setting policies in 1929, W. Jett Lauck believed that since 1923, living costs were no longer used in adjusting workers' wages (1929: 92).

Until World War II, only the federal government, a small number of large companies, and a few unions showed any interest in applying the cost-of-living principle to wage setting. The Economy Act of 1933 authorized the president to reduce federal workers' salaries by as much as 15 percent, based on BLS living cost data. The six-month interval ending June 1928 was the base period for such adjustments. President Roosevelt ordered a 15 percent salary cut in April 1933 and continued the cut through June 1934 (*Monthly Labor Review,* February 1934; Lowenstern 1974). Although a 15 percent salary cut seems severe, consumer prices were about 24 percent lower in 1933 than in the base period. Thus, even under Roosevelt's executive order, real federal salaries were higher in 1933 than in 1928.

In 1933 prices began to rise moderately: From 1933 to 1937 the CPI rose by a compounded average of 2.5 percent per year. At the same time, unionism in the United States was expanding due in part to such New Deal legislation as the National Industrial Recovery Act of 1933 and the Wagner Act of 1935 (Pelling 1960). From 1933 to 1939, union members as a percentage of nonfarm employment rose from 11.3 percent to 28.6 percent. It is likely that some combination of the effects of renewed inflation and union growth induced some large companies to institute Colas. For example, on May 27, 1935 Standard

Oil of New Jersey announced a 5 percent Cola payment effective June 1, 1935 for its 46,000 employees. Further, Standard Oil pledged to base future wage adjustments on BLS cost-of-living figures (Princeton University Industrial Relations Section 1939: 10). In 1936 the General Electric Company (GE) began a plan whereby employees' wages would rise automatically by the same percentage as the BLS index up to a limit of 10 percent. If prices rose by 10 percent, GE stated that it would reconsider the plan. An interesting feature of GE's scheme was to include downward wage adjustments when prices fell but to guarantee that wages would never fall below the level prevailing at the start of the contract. An analogous provision characterized the trend-setting GM–UAW contract of 1948, as discussed below. In the year that GE instituted its Cola, U.S. Steel announced a similar plan (Princeton University Industrial Relations Section 1939: 8–9, 11, 12).

Despite Cola plans in such large companies, these were the exception. In 1936 the NICB surveyed 1895 companies and found that only 3 percent of the companies had automatic Cola plans. These companies employed 12 percent of the workers in the sampled firms, providing another piece of evidence linking wage indexation and firm size (NICB 1937: 9–14). The union sector also had little provision for Cola adjustments. A 1939 study of the BLS file on 7,000 contracts found that only 5 percent allowed for wage adjustments during the life of the contract. Most of these adjustments were based on the cost of living (Kuntze and Wilde 1948: 68; *Monthly Labor Review,* January 1940: 6–15). According to an NICB survey, most Colas during this time preserved existing wage differentials by giving equal percentage (rather than cents-per-hour) wage increases when prices rose (NICB 1941). The large nonunion plans of GE and U.S. Steel appeared to set a pattern for other plans. As noted before, most Colas in union contracts today call for wage compression by giving equal cents-per-hour Cola increases. The fact that nonunion Colas were more likely to preserve existing wage differentials is consistent with recent evidence that unions in general lead to a narrowing of pay differentials through standard rate policies (Freeman 1980, 1982).

The period just preceding World War II saw less reliance on cost-of-living figures in setting wages than the 1915–23 era, due to greater price stability in the 1930s. In addition, the problems of Depression unemployment and the struggles for union representation played center stage in labor–management relations during the 1930s (Pelling

1960). However, by 1941 the NICB anticipated that the impending war would greatly increase the use of automatic Colas (NICB 1941: 21).

WORLD WAR II

The major effects of World War II on wage indexation came from the acceleration of inflation during the war and the imposition of wartime wage and price controls. Table 2-1 shows an acceleration of inflation during the war, especially in the 1940–43 period. In these three years, prices rose by a compounded annual average of about 7.2 percent; from 1933 to 1940 prices had risen at only a 1.1 percent annual rate. After 1943, prices continued to rise during the war, but at a slower rate (an annual inflation rate of 2 percent from 1943 to 1945), possibly reflecting the impact of wage and price controls instituted in October 1942 [National War Labor Board (NWLB) 1945]. Although inflation did accelerate during the early war years, this change was much less rapid than that of World War I.

The labor movement responded to the new inflation of the early World War II period by calling for increased wage reopening provisions. By 1942 roughly 40 percent of manufacturing contracts had reopeners. One-third of these based wage adjustments on consumer prices; a small number based wage adjustments on profits, other wages, or the economy in general. However, most had no criteria for reopening (Bortz 1948).

Colas in the early World War II period applied mostly to the ship-building industry. Such clauses, calling for semiannual adjustments based on the BLS cost-of-living index, were adopted in 1941 and covered the major U.S. shipyards. However, on May 2, 1942, President Roosevelt urged the Shipbuilding Wage Stabilization Conference in Chicago to give up Colas and the conference acceded to his request (NWLB 1945: 40).

The Wage Stabilization Program in effect during the war suspended most wage reopeners from 1942 on. On October 3, 1942 President Roosevelt issued the Economic Stabilization Order (Executive Order 9250) which froze most wages in the United States at their May 1942 levels (NICB 1951: 18, Lowenstern 1974: 23). The NWLB subsequently issued General Order No. 22, which applied the wage freeze to escalator clauses. This order outlawed any Cola that would raise wages by more than 15 percent over their January 1, 1941 levels and was applied beginning October 3, 1942 (NICB 1951: 18).

The 15 percent limit was established by the "Little Steel" formula case of July 1942. In this instance, the NWLB allowed steelworkers a 15 percent raise based on the 15 percent rise in the BLS cost-of-living index from January 1941 to May 1942 (NWLB 1945).

In most cases, the NWLB did not allow any escalator increases that pushed wages beyond the limits set up by the Little Steel formula. However, there were a few interesting exceptions to this rule. For example, if a Cola adjustment were due before October 3, 1942 (the date of the wage freeze), the NWLB approved the payment even if the increase exceeded the 15 percent limit. In addition, the board allowed some escalator increases to correct inequities. For example, in one case the board allowed a Cola increase to one plant of the Babcock and Wilcox Company because a similar adjustment had been allowed to another of the company's plants (NICB 1951: 19).

The Little Steel formula stood throughout the war, even though prices rose by more than 15 percent over the January 1941 levels. In March 1943 this added inflation spurred the American Federation of Labor (AFL) to petition the NWLB to amend the Little Steel formula. Although the AFL pointed out that the BLS cost-of-living index showed a 22 percent rise from January 1941 to March 1943, the board denied the AFL's request. This denial led the AFL to attack the BLS figures as understatements of the true increase in living costs (Kuntze and Wilde 1948: 20–21). The AFL and Congress of Industrial Organizations (CIO) claimed, for example, that the cost of living had risen 43.5 percent from January 1941 to December 1943 instead of the BLS's 22.8 percent figure (Kuntze and Wilde 1948: 21). With such controversy, there was pressure for a revision of the BLS index. Much of the disagreement centered around the temporary adjustments made by the BLS in weights for food, fuel, transportation, and other items affected by rationing or shortages. In 1946 the index was revised to reflect prewar weights and more precise weighting methods (Shiskin 1974: 6).

POSTWAR INFLATION AND THE 1948 AND 1950 GM–UAW AGREEMENTS

The immediate postwar period witnessed an unprecedented outbreak of strikes in the United States. In 1946, for example, an estimated 1.43 percent of work time was lost in the private, nonfarm sector — by far the highest value that this measure has ever taken. The next highest

Table 2-5. Real Annual Earnings per Full-Time Employee (in 1914 dollars), Selected Years and Industries.

	Industry		
Year	Manufacturing	Mining	Transportation
1914	$ 696.00	$ 666.00	$ 695.00
1915	654.46	708.91	703.96
1916	691.53	818.60	707.18
1917	692.01	891.85	693.57
1918	738.99	933.91	844.46
1919	751.31	796.05	785.59
1920	768.69	844.96	825.39
1921	755.76	986.52	860.75
1922	769.18	779.38	875.90
1923	826.27	1073.03	873.97
1940	1026.52	994.98	1258.78
1941	1128.33	1077.82	1286.69
1942	1248.00	1107.96	1346.70
1943	1364.90	1256.25	1448.58
1944	1437.46	1427.18	1529.98
1945	1405.36	1463.43	1526.52
1946	1295.42	1399.38	1530.11
1947	1256.41	1400.36	1425.55
1948	1268.48	1417.95	1448.02

Source: U.S. Bureau of the Census 1975: 166, 210–11.

value for this statistic was 0.61 in 1959, the year of a major steel strike (U.S. Bureau of the Census 1975: 179; Kochan 1980). In 1946 major strikes took place in most organized industries (Pelling 1960: 185–86). Tables 2–1, 2–5, and 2–6 give an idea as to why these strikes occurred as well as providing some interesting comparisons between the periods after World Wars I and II.

Table 2–1 indicates a sharp acceleration of inflation after World War II. From 1945 to 1948, its annual rate was 10.2 percent; the figure for 1943–45 was 2 percent. In addition, Tables 2–5 and 2–6 show declines in living standards after World War II. In particular, during World War II, despite wage controls, real hourly wages rose, as did real annual income; the same can be said about World War I. How-

Table 2-6. Real Hourly Earnings of Production Workers in Manufacturing (in 1914 dollars), Selected Years.

Year	Average Real Hourly Earnings
1914	$.22
1915	—
1916	—
1917	—
1918	—
1919	$.27
1920	$.28
1921	$.29
1922	$.29
1923	$.31
1940	$.47
1941	$.50
1942	$.52
1943	$.56
1944	$.58
1945	$.57
1946	$.56
1947	$.55
1948	$.56

Source: U.S. Bureau of the Census 1975: 169–70, 210–11.

ever, after the second war, reductions in real hourly wages (due to inflation) and cuts in hours of work led to declining real incomes.[8] These cuts in real living standards contrast markedly with the post–World War I situation. First, prices dropped sharply two years after World War I, and they continued to rise steadily after World War II.[9] Second, real living standards (of employed workers) continued to rise after World War I despite sustained inflation through 1920 and the decline of unionism after 1921 (Table 2–3).

Concern with inflation and living standards in the years immediately following World War II led to a marked increase in the number of collective bargaining agreements with reopeners. A 1946 study of ninety-nine pattern-setting contracts showed that seventy-one agreements covering 72 percent of the workers had reopeners (*Monthly Labor Review,* November 1946). In addition, some contracts in the

1946–47 period had escalator clauses. For example, the International Shoe Company (1947), Atlantic Richfield (1946), Massachusetts shoe firms (1946), and the International Brotherhood of Paper Makers in New England (1946) all had automatic escalator clauses (Ruben 1974: 43–44; NICB 1948). The latter agreement is noteworthy because, like some of the earlier agreements we have discussed from the 1920s and 1930s, it placed a maximum on the allowable Cola increase. According to Ruben (1974), Colas after World War II but before the 1948 GM agreement were rare because they froze workers' real wages — an undesirable effect from labor's point of view (Ruben 1974: 44).

Although it was generally not imitated at the time, the 1948 GM–UAW agreement was of historic proportions because it anticipated future developments. First, the duration of the agreement was to be two years, making it a pioneer of multiyear contracts. The two-year duration was important to GM because it gave the company a reasonable assurance that there would be no companywide strikes over the life of the contract (Garbarino 1962). Since this agreement, there has been a strong tie between Colas and long-term contracts. Second, it called for an automatic Cola with quarterly adjustments based on the CPI. One cent would be added or subtracted from wages for every 1.14-point change in the CPI with no maximum increase and a five-cent maximum pay cut. The 1.14-point figure was chosen to keep average hourly real wage rates constant. These adjustments were relatively rapid and were across-the-board cents-per-hour wage changes, thus narrowing wage differentials. The Cola raised low-paid workers' living standards relative to that of high-paid workers. Most Colas today provide similar across-the-board increases. Further, quarterly Cola adjustments have become quite common. Third, in addition to the Cola, an extra wage increase was given to restore purchasing power to the 1940 level. This added wage increase was determined to be eight cents per hour — a 5.4 percent raise for the average hourly wage of $1.485 at the time of the signing of the agreement. Finally, an "annual improvement factor," three cents per hour, of scheduled wage increases was included to provide rising real wages during the life of the contract. This clause met labor's objection that Colas froze real wages. The three-cent figure (about 2 percent) was based on the idea that the worker's real wage should grow with productivity (BNA 1950).

Although the 1948 GM–UAW agreement was a significant breakthrough in collective bargaining, few companies or unions showed any interest at the time in Colas. A 1948 NICB study showed that about 86 percent of leading executives were not willing to use Colas. The most often quoted reason for rejecting Colas was the feeling that wages had already outstripped the cost of living (Lowenstern 1974: 24). In addition, a study in New Jersey showed that 88 percent of managers and 79 percent of unions opposed automatic Colas. Employers did not wish to risk the unlimited wage gains implied by an uncapped Cola, and unions did not wish to use 1940 as a base for wages, as was the case in the GM–UAW contract. Evidently, union leaders thought any Cola they negotiated would use the GM agreement as the pattern. In fact, wages in other industries had risen faster since 1940 than those in the automobile industry (Lowenstern 1974: 24).

Experience with the GM–UAW Cola nearly led the UAW to abandon the Cola principle. After a Cola payment of three cents in September 1948, the CPI remained stable for three months, leading to no Cola adjustment in December 1948. However, the CPI then fell, triggering a two-cent wage cut in March 1949. The UAW took further pay cuts of one cent in June and September 1949 and a two-cent cut in March 1950. The net effect of the contract was a three-cent accumulated Cola raise and nine cents added to the base rate, totaling twelve cents per hour. Many UAW members were upset about the pay cuts entailed by the Cola, although the union pointed out that these were not cuts in real wages. Despite the UAW's efforts, many union members were demanding the discontinuation of the Cola as the 1948 contract was due to expire. After nearly two months of negotiations, an agreement was reached on May 23, 1950. The UAW gained a modified union shop, pensions, and group insurance; the Cola was retained; and the annual improvement factor was raised to four cents per hour, representing a 2.5 percent productivity increase. The agreement had a five-year duration, which the GM management hailed as a guarantee of five years' labor peace. It is significant that the GM contract was negotiated while the UAW was carrying out a 100-day strike against Chrysler (NICB 1951: 7, 10). The Cola was evidently not viewed by GM as problematic because of the anticipated inflation associated with the impending Korean War — prices could be raised to cover the wage increases. Because prices were not expected to fall, the wage floor provision of the Cola had no harmful anticipated effects to the union (Lowenstern 1974: 24–25).

INDEXATION IN THE 1950s

The decade of the 1950s was the first period during which automatic Colas became widely established in U.S. collective bargaining agreements. A new round of inflation caused by the Korean War as well as the pattern-setting GM–UAW contract paved the way for wage indexation, which by the end of the decade covered about half of major (i.e., covering over 1,000 workers) collective bargaining agreements (Table 2-7). Since the 1950s at least 20 percent of workers in such agreements have had Colas, mid-1980s figures being in the 55 to 60 percent range. Thus the 1950s inaugurated a sustained period of Cola usage.

The Korean War mobilization effort had a major impact on the development of Colas in the early 1950s. It is clear that most parties expected rising inflation during this period. This notion is borne out by the second column of Table 2-7, which refers to the expected inflation rate. This rate was calculated from a survey of economists taken every six months in which the respondents were asked about their expectations concerning future inflation rates.[10] In December 1949 (before the growth of active combat in Korea) the survey respondents on average expected a 2.2 percent fall in the CPI; however, by December 1950 fighting in Korea was underway, and on average a 4 percent rise in prices over the coming year was expected. In addition, Table 2-7 shows that during 1950, the actual inflation rate (6.7 percent) was 8.9 percent above what was anticipated. Although no data are available on the price expectations of unions and management, the survey data appear to be an intuitively reasonable approximation of these expectations.

Anticipation of rising prices is, however, not enough by itself to generate a demand for wage indexation. For example, if unions expected a 5 percent inflation rate over the coming year, they could ask for a 5 percent wage increase. It is the fear of being left behind (risk aversion) that helps generate the demand for Colas. In the previous example, workers expecting a 5 percent inflation rate might prefer a Cola to a fixed 5 percent raise if they felt inflation could easily be higher than 5 percent. In the Korean War context, the combination of unexpectedly high inflation rates and the nature of President Truman's wage control program greatly increased union demands for Colas. Table 2-7 shows an increase in workers covered by Colas from

800,000 in September 1950 to 3 million by September 1951. The Truman wage stabilization program endorsed the Cola principle: On September 9, 1950 he declared that workers should ask for wage increases no higher than the inflation rate (BNA 1950: 61).

Despite this position, many unions felt that a wage stabilization program including a wage freeze was around the corner. These unions often felt that a Cola would allow them to circumvent a wage freeze (NICB 1951: 13). If this were true, then a Cola might be the only means by which workers' wages would not be left behind wartime inflation. Indeed, in December 1950 (before the creation in 1951 of the Wage Stabilization Board) a wage freeze was ordered in the auto industry that recognized the existing Colas in the contracts; in addition, at the same time, the government sanctioned the escalator in the railroad industry (NICB 1951: 13). These actions encouraged unions to demand Colas.

The operation of the Wage Stabilization Board in 1951 gave further endorsement of the Cola principle but tried to eliminate inequities between workers with and without Colas. The board issued two regulations concerning escalators. General Wage Regulation No. 6 outlawed wage increases greater than 10 percent above January 1950 levels. However, Colas in contracts signed before January 1951 were considered in force until June 30, 1951 even where wage increases were greater than 10 percent. General Wage Regulation No. 8 allowed Colas in effect on January 25, 1951 to continue until June 30 of that year. Again, the 10 percent limit could be exceeded in these cases. For contracts signed after January 25, 1951, Cola increases could not exceed the 10 percent limit. However, Regulation No. 8 was amended to allow workers without a formal plan to get semiannual cost-of-living increases restoring any loss in real wages from January 25, 1951 to the date of the increase. By not allowing any increases in real wages, the board hoped to achieve more stable prices than could otherwise have been sustained (Staller and Solnick 1975: 73–74).

The rapid increase in Colas during the Korean War period reflected in part workers' desire to keep up with inflation. On the employer side, management found that the regular wage adjustments of Colas were a convenient method of keeping pace with industry or area wages during a tight labor market. More importantly, as was the case for GM, companies that granted Colas with annual improvement factors felt that they were achieving labor peace. For example, the NICB in 1951 took a random sample of 229 contracts. Of the 23 that

Table 2-7. Unemployment, Inflation, Expected Inflation, and Cola Coverage in Major Collective Bargaining Agreements, 1948–84.

Year	Percentage[a] Increase in CPI	Expected[a] Increase in CPI	Unexpected (actual minus expected) Increase in CPI	Number[b] Covered by Escalation on January 1 (millions)	Percentage of Workers Covered by Escalation	Unemployment Rate (civilian labor force)
1948	2.6%	−0.6%	+3.2%	0.25	—	3.8%
1949	−2.3	−2.7	+0.4	—	—	5.9
1950	6.7	−2.2	+8.9	0.8[c]	—	5.3
1951	5.8	4.0	+1.8	3.0[c]	—	3.3
1952	0.8	2.0	−1.2	3.5	—	3.0
1953	0.9	−0.8	+1.7	—	—	2.9
1954	−0.5	−1.1	+0.6	—	—	5.5
1955	0.3	0.0	+0.3	1.7	22.7%	4.4
1956	2.9	0.5	+2.4	—	—	4.1
1957	3.1	1.1	+2.0	3.5	44.8	4.3
1958	1.7	0.2	+1.5	4.0	50.0	6.8
1959	1.5	0.8	+0.7	4.0	50.0	5.5
1960	1.6	1.1	+0.5	4.0	49.4	5.5
1961	0.5	0.7	−0.2	2.7	33.3	6.7
1962	1.1	1.2	−0.1	2.5	31.3	5.5
1963	1.7	1.1	+0.6	1.9	24.4	5.7
1964	1.1	1.0	+0.1	2.0	25.6	5.2
1965	2.0	1.3	+0.7	2.0	25.3	4.5
1966	3.3	1.7	+1.6	2.0	20.0	3.8

Year						
1967	3.1	2.2	+0.9	2.2	20.8	3.8
1968	4.7	2.8	+1.9	2.5	23.6	3.6
1969	6.1	2.9	+3.2	2.7	25.0	3.5
1970	5.5	3.6	+1.9	2.8	25.9	4.9
1971	3.4	3.8	−0.4	3.0	27.8	5.9
1972	3.4	3.2	+0.2	4.3	40.6	5.6
1973	8.8	3.5	+5.3	4.1	39.4	4.9
1974	12.2	5.4	+6.8	4.0	39.2	5.6
1975	7.0	7.4	−0.4	5.3	51.5	8.5
1976	4.8	6.0	−1.2	6.0	59.4	7.7
1977	6.8	5.4	+1.4	6.0	61.2	7.0
1978	9.0	6.3	+2.7	5.8	60.4	6.0
1979	13.3	7.1	+6.2	5.6	58.9	5.8
1980	12.4	9.6	+2.8	5.4	58.1	7.1
1981	8.9	10.3	−1.4	5.3	58.2	7.6
1982	3.9	7.2	−3.3	5.1	56.7	9.7
1983	3.8	5.1	−1.3	4.9	57.6	9.5
1984	—	5.6	—	4.5	57.3	—

[a] All inflation figures refer to the period from December of the previous year to December of the current year.

[b] Contracts covering at least 1,000 workers in private sector. Before 1966, construction, service, finance, insurance, and real estate industries were not included.

[c] September figures.

Sources: Monthly Labor Review (MLR), various issues for inflation and unemployment data; Livingston Survey tapes for price expectations data; Davis 1983; Lacombe and Conley 1984; LeRoy 1977, 1978, 1981, 1982; Levin 1979; Mills 1978; U.S. Bureau of the Census 1975: 135; Wasilewski 1980.

had a three-year duration, 8 contained Colas plus annual increases; however, of the 15 that had durations of five years (the duration of the 1950 GM–UAW agreement), 12 had both Colas and annual wage increases (NICB 1951: 17–18). Both of these reasons for Colas are related to the idea of negotiation costs. In the first instance, Colas presumably eliminated the need for detailed wage comparisons and thus saved labor and management a good deal of time. Second, by combining Colas with long-term agreements, the fixed costs induced by a strike threat could be reduced by decreasing the union's opportunities to strike. These costs include shutdown and startup considerations and the loss of business as customers who anticipate a strike try to find alternative sources of supply (Jacoby and Mitchell 1983). In fact, the absence of a strike threat may well explain the lower incidence of Colas in the nonunion sector compared to those in the union sector. Nonunion wages are adjusted at intervals typically no longer than one year (Flanagan 1976), reducing the attractiveness to employees of a Cola compared to that of a multiyear contract. Indeed, in 1978 the percentages of one-, two-, and three-year major agreements with Colas were, respectively, 3, 17, and 71 (Sheifer 1979). As we will discuss in Chapter 5, the stronger unions (those with more credible strike threats) appear to have longer contracts and greater incidence of Colas. The low incidence of Colas among one-year contracts and among nonunion workers suggests that the costs of adjusting wages are low enough or company resistance is strong enough in these situations to overcome any employee desires for indexation.

From its peak value in 1952 of 3.5 million workers covered, Cola coverage fell precipitously to 1.7 million workers by 1955. During the Korean War, the largest numbers of workers covered by Colas had been in the automotive and related industries or in railroads. For example, in 1951 about 800,000 UAW members and 300,000 railway workers had Colas, constituting over one-third of total U.S. Cola coverage (NICB 1951: 13; Table 2–7). Other large groups of workers covered by Colas were found in the textile, aircraft, and flat glass sectors (Douty 1975). However, after the Korean War, the popularity of Colas declined. For example, by August 1954 escalation had been abandoned by all railroad unions. George M. Harrison, president of the Brotherhood of Railway Clerks, told his membership that the Cola had been adopted in 1951 only temporarily; prices were expected to rise, and a Cola would help insure wages from the effects of a pay freeze (David and Helm 1955).

According to the BLS, there were three main reasons behind the trend away from Colas after 1953.[11] First, unions did not historically wish to fix real wages — as a Cola presumably does, in the absence of an improvement factor. Second, Colas could lead to wage cuts if prices were to start falling after the Korean War ended. The problem of falling wages, as we have seen, has influenced workers' attitudes toward Colas since World War I. In fact, there was a 0.5 percent decline in the CPI from December 1953 to December 1954. Perhaps more importantly, as Table 2-7 shows, starting in December 1952, for two consecutive years, prices were expected to fall, reinforcing workers' fears about wage cuts under Colas (to the extent that these expectations were widespread). Third, the BLS argued that the decline in Colas did not actually begin until early 1953, when it was clear that prices would not accelerate with the ending of controls (David and Helm 1955: 316). This idea is again borne out by the inflation expectations figures in Table 2-7. Further, the sizes of the prediction errors in forecasting inflation were getting smaller by 1954 and 1955, suggesting smaller inflationary or deflationary "surprises" during these years. In such an environment, workers without Colas had a smaller chance of falling behind inflation than in a period of more uncertain prices; on the other hand, firms' resistance to Colas may be less during a period of "validated" price expectations. However, unions are the initiators of the demand for Colas, as illustrated by the fact that automatic Colas are much less common for nonunion workers.

Although the presence of Colas declined sharply from 1953 to 1955, the incidence of indexation rose just as precipitously over the next three years. From 1955 to 1958, the number of workers with Colas rose from 1.7 million (22.7 percent of workers in major agreements) to 4 million (50 percent of such workers). This increase occurred during the acceleration of inflation between 1955 and 1957; further, the price expectations figures in Table 2-7 suggest that this increase in inflation was largely unanticipated. Workers without Colas were presumably left behind by the rise in prices. The rebound in Cola coverage by the end of the decade might have been aided by the renewal in 1955 of long-term agreements with Colas in the automobile industry (for three years) and by the new five-year General Electric indexed contract (David and Helm 1957). Colas had been negotiated for the first time in basic steel and meatpacking. In addition, by 1957 Colas had returned to the railroad industry (David and Helm 1958).

Characteristics of Colas in the 1950s

Automatic escalators can take many forms. The particular features of Colas themselves have become negotiating items and can have a large influence over workers' incomes and firms' costs. Colas vary along four major dimensions. First, some call for monthly or quarterly reviews; others call for annual reviews. Although the review period does not affect the base wage in the long run, longer review periods save companies money and cost workers money. For example, a delay of three months in a twenty-cent-per-hour Cola payment (a common figure for the 1970s and 1980s) in a bargaining unit of 100,000 workers (a UAW-sized unit) will save a company $10 million and cost each worker $100 (assuming a forty-hour work week). Second, formulas relating consumer prices to wages vary greatly. The majority, for example, give across-the-board cents-per-hour raises (narrowing wage differentials), and others give equal percentage Cola increments (preserving wage differentials). Some formulas are vastly more generous than others. For example, some currently give one cent for each 0.3-point rise in the CPI; others give one cent for each 0.6-point rise in the CPI. In this instance, the first Cola would give double the yield of the second. Third, many Colas have maximum or minimum adjustments. In periods of rapid inflation, caps on a Cola can greatly reduce the workers' protection from inflation while saving companies a great deal of money. The effect of caps is investigated in our statistical analyses in later chapters. Finally, the choice of the particular index of prices to use can have important implications. For example, most bargaining units use national figures; however, a significant minority use local CPIs, which can diverge from the national CPI. From August 1976 to May 1982, for example, the U.S. city average CPI rose from 171.9 to 286.5 (1967 = 100); however, in San Diego the index went from 172.1 to 323.3 during this period (BNA 1982: LRX174f, s). A typical Cola calling for one cent per hour for each 0.3-point increase in the CPI would have yielded raises of $3.82 per hour over this period based on the national CPI and $5.04 per hour based on the San Diego CPI. Further, the choice of base year can be important as well. A CPI of 100 using 1967 as the base period would be 116.3 using 1957–59 as the base (*Monthly Labor Review,* January 1974). Thus, a given formula (e.g., one cent per 0.3 points) gives 16.3 percent higher adjustments when 1957–59 is the base than when 1967 is the base.

In the 1950s the characteristics of Colas were strongly influenced by the 1950 GM–UAW agreement. For example, a 1951 study of Colas found that 90 percent used the national CPI (the one used in the GM–UAW contract), and 95 percent of the workers with quarterly adjustments had Cola formulas in one of two categories: one cent per hour for each 1-point change in the CPI and one cent per hour for each 1.14-point change (the GM formula). A few agreements, covering about 6 percent of the workers with Colas, gave equal across-the-board percentage raises. Construction contracts with Colas, though rare, most often were of this type (Kramer and Nix 1951). It is interesting to note that this outcome in construction has continued and is evident in our current data. It is likely that construction contractors and unions prefer to maintain existing intercraft wage differentials by using this type of Cola.

The use of long-term contracts inaugurated by GM and the UAW in 1948 also spread to other bargaining units. For example, the percentage of contracts with length of two or more years went from 25 percent in 1948 to 55 percent in 1950 to 69 percent in 1952 to 81 in 1957 (Stieber 1959).

Although the 1950 GM–UAW contract was supposed to last five years, the wage formula was changed before 1955. The alterations in the contract made during its reopening in 1953 also became pattern setters for U.S. collective bargaining. In 1953 the UAW requested a reopening of its five-year contracts, due mainly to the unanticipated inflation of 1951 and early 1952. After initial opposition by the major auto makers, they agreed to a new package in May 1953. Among the new contract provisions were the following: a liberalization of the Cola formula to one cent per hour for each 0.6-point change in the CPI (from one cent for each 1.14 points), a raise in the annual improvement factor to five cents from four cents, a roll-in of nineteen cents of the twenty-four cents of the existing accumulated Cola into base wage rates, a special increase for skilled workers of ten to twenty cents per hour, and liberalization of pension plans (Goldberg 1954; *Monthly Labor Review,* August 1955). The new Cola formula became a pattern for Colas later in the 1950s, as did the rolling in of Cola payments into the base wage. This latter feature of the new contract was important because various benefits such as overtime pay are calculated on base wage rates. The UAW was able to change the Cola formula to one cent per 0.5-point CPI change in the 1955 agreements (*Monthly Labor Review,* August 1955). Finally, the added increase for skilled workers addressed a problem facing many industrial unions:

the effects on union cohesiveness of the narrowing of skill differentials (Weber 1963).

As the 1950s proceeded, some of the characteristics of Colas underwent changes. First, perhaps following the lead of the UAW, formulas became more liberal by the end of the decade. In 1959 the most frequent formulas were one cent per 0.5 points (the UAW's formula) or two cents per 0.9 points (David and Helm 1958). At the same time, however, in 1958 and 1959 several contracts were signed that called for a ceiling provision or cap on the size of the Cola adjustments. For example, some agreements signed in late 1958 or 1959 in the auto parts industry had ceilings (David and Benny 1959).

Developments in the steel industry's Colas were particularly noteworthy and foreshadowed later events in this sector. The October 1959 agreement between Kaiser Steel and the United Steelworkers (USW) called for semiannual Cola payments during the twenty-month contract that were not to exceed three cents apiece. Further, in the major steel companies' October 17, 1959 proposal to the USW, a demand was made to eliminate Cola payments in the first year of a three-year contract and to limit payments to three cents (David and Benny 1959: 1328).[12] The 1959 contract negotiations in the steel industry resulted in a long strike. Although nonwage issues were important, management had hoped to eliminate Cola payments from the final settlement (Garbarino 1962). This effort continued into the 1960s and remains a concern of steel companies today. An important development in the steel agreement was the diversion of a Cola payment in exchange for company assumption of the cost of voluntary insurance (Garbarino 1962). This principle has been widely applied today as the costs of fringe benefits have risen dramatically (see below). The practice of diverting Cola payments allows workers to retain the Cola concept while saving companies a great deal of money.

A second change in Colas during the 1950s concerned the timing of reviews. Although quarterly reviews remained the dominant form of timing (by a slight margin), semiannual reviews became much more popular after 1956 (David and Helm 1957: 52). By 1959 quarterly adjustments predominated in autos, farm equipment, aircraft, and electrical equipment; semiannual reviews prevailed in trucking, meat-packing, steel, aluminum, and railroads (David and Benny 1959). The lengthening of review period intervals can be seen as a method to cut the costs of Cola payments.[13]

COLAS IN THE 1960s

The 1960s saw a sharp decline in the incidence of Colas in the early part of the decade and a gradual increase in their presence during the latter part of the decade. From 1960 to 1963, the number of workers under major agreements with Colas fell from 4 million to 1.9 million and the percentage of workers covered by Colas fell from 49.4 percent in 1960 to 20 percent in 1966. However, by 1969, 2.7 million (25 percent of workers) had escalators.

The early 1960s were characterized by recession and stable prices. Actual inflation never reached 2 percent until 1965. In addition, the Livingston price expectations data show that these forecasts of inflation during the 1960–65 period were usually realized. Unanticipated inflation over this period ranged from −0.2 percent to +0.7 percent. With moderately high unemployment (compared to the 1950–57 period) and with few inflationary surprises, workers felt less ability and less need to press for Colas than under other economic circumstances. In addition, the Kennedy–Johnson wage guideposts strongly opposed wage escalation. Although economists have disputed the impact of the guideposts due to their voluntary nature, wage and price inflation were lower in the early 1960s than could otherwise have been expected.[14]

The Council of Economic Advisers' 1962 wage and price guidelines based on productivity increases were the first instance of peacetime wage and price government policy (Groom 1963). Contracts with Colas were treated the same as those without Colas. Even when prices accelerated in 1967, the Council of Economic Advisers declined to change the wage guideposts. The council argued that linking wages to prices would perpetuate a wage-price spiral:

> If on the average [wage settlements] should exceed productivity by the amount of the recent increase in living costs, price stability could never be restored. . . . Arrangements which automatically tie wage rates to changes in consumer prices will contribute to inflation. (David 1972: 337)

The guideposts soon collapsed under the inflationary pressures of the late 1960s (David 1972). However, during the early 1960s the guideposts might have restrained some bargaining units from negotiating Colas.

Much of the sharp downturn in Cola coverage was associated with the abandonment of escalation in the railroad, electrical equipment, and steel industries (Garbarino 1962; Ruben 1962). As noted earlier, railroad workers had had a history of discontinuance and reinstatement of their Colas; thus, the industry and its unions were usually on the margin between acceptance and rejection of the Cola principle. The stable price environment of the early 1960s pushed them toward rejection. The abandonment of Colas in the electrical equipment industry came about after a bitter strike in 1960 against General Electric. Although it is doubtful that escalation was a major issue in the strike, GE, which was widely acknowledged as having won the strike, eliminated the Cola in favor of an eighteen-month wage reopening provision (Northrup 1963). A similar contract was signed at Westinghouse with no strike. The railroad and electrical equipment contracts accounted for a fall of about 1 million workers covered by Colas (Helm and Seefer 1960), or about 80 percent of the 1.3 million worker decline in Colas from 1960 to 1961 (Table 2-7).

The major basic steel companies and the USW discontinued their Cola in 1962. This step was a logical progression from the industry's success after the 1959 strike in placing a six-cent cap on Cola payments (see above). A total of about 550,000 workers under the related steel, aluminum, and container contracts simultaneously abandoned their Colas, accounting for over 90 percent of the 600,000-worker decline in Cola coverage from 1962 to 1963 (Ruben 1962; Table 2-7; *Monthly Labor Review,* December 1961). Economic security was the major concern of the USW in 1962. According to Marvin Miller, assistant to the union's president, steelworker unemployment was about 20 percent and the overall rate was 6 percent at that time (Cunningham 1962: 1226). The relationship between wage indexation and job security became, as we will show, of vital concern to many unions in the late 1970s and 1980s.

Following the acceleration of inflation in 1965 and 1966, Cola coverage began to increase gradually throughout the rest of the decade. According to the Livingston surveys, much of this inflation was unanticipated, as actual inflation outran expected inflation by 0.9 percent to 3.2 percent in the 1966-70 period (Table 2-7). In addition, the labor market was tightening during these years as the Vietnam War accelerated: The civilian unemployment rate fell from 4.5 percent in 1965 to 3.5 percent in 1969 (Table 2-7). Reduced unemployment may well have put management in more of a mood to grant Colas during this period.

In the early 1960s Colas were concentrated mainly in the automobile, farm and construction equipment, aerospace, meatpacking, and trucking industries (Ruben 1962). However, by the late 1960s a number of Colas were negotiated for the first time or reinstated in several instances. For example, by 1967 the machinists in the airline industry had negotiated their first Cola, covering 38,000 workers. By this time, escalation was reestablished in the electrical equipment industry for 210,000 workers (Ward and Davis 1966). The ILGWU also negotiated Colas in 1966 (*Monthly Labor Review,* September 1966). Other additions included the glass container industry, the tobacco industry, and the Pacific Coast shipbuilding industry in 1968 (Ward and Davis 1969).

Characteristics of Colas in the 1960s

Although the incidence of wage indexation was on the rise by the end of the 1960s, management at the same time attempted to limit the cost of Colas in two major ways. First, the period between reviews generally lengthened, and second, caps were increasingly applied to Cola formulas. As a result, Colas appeared to provide less protection against inflation by the late 1960s than in the early 1960s. These conclusions are borne out by the data in Tables 2-8, 2-9, and 2-10.

According to Table 2-8, after 1967 the fraction of reviews that were on a quarterly basis fell sharply while the extent of annual reviews rose sharply. Much of this change is due to the 1967 auto contracts which changed the Cola from quarterly to annual reviews (Ward and Davis 1968). However, the trend toward longer review intervals began earlier in the decade. In 1961 the trucking industry's Cola review period was changed from semiannual to annual, and the steel industry agreements called for ten-month review intervals—an increase from the six-month period in the previous contract (Garbarino 1962; Seefer 1961). The trend started by these contracts and accelerated by the 1967 auto agreements resulted in annual review coverage of 78 percent of workers getting Cola reviews in 1969. As late as 1964, only 5.2 percent of workers getting reviews had annual reviews. Over the same period, the incidence of quarterly reviews fell from 85.2 to 16 percent.

The review interval by itself doesn't affect the wage rate in the long

Table 2-8.   Frequency of Cola Reviews in Major Agreements, 1964-84.

Year	Percentage of Indexed Contracts Having Reviews in a Given Year	Percentage of Reviews that Were:		
		Quarterly	Semiannual	Annual
1964	76.3%	85.2%	9.8%	5.2%
1965	–	–	–	–
1966	95.0	68.4	5.3	26.3
1967	–	60.0	–	–
1968	–	–	–	65.0
1969	95.0	16.0	3.9	78.0
1970	94.3	14.2	6.6	75.8
1971	83.3	7.1	16.7	73.3
1972	90.7	43.6	1.1	51.3
1973	98.8	46.9	0.9	51.9
1974	75.0	63.3	3.1	32.9
1975	86.8	43.5	6.2	47.8
1976	76.7	50.1	17.3	29.5
1977	61.5	41.7	19.7	33.4
1978	76.8	41.5	6.6	50.0
1979	73.3	50.4	12.0	36.4
1980	66.5	49.6	35.1	13.1
1981	85.6	39.9	28.2	30.2
1982	67.4	54.3	9.2	35.0
1983	59.2	57.0	17.1	23.9
1984	86.0	38.8	15.9	43.9

Sources: Bornstein and Bolton 1971; Davis 1983; Gurney 1974; Kuhmerker 1976; Lacombe and Conley 1984; Larson 1973; LeRoy 1977, 1978, 1981, 1982; Levin 1979; Ruben 1965a, 1965b; Sparrough and Bolton 1972; Spring 1970; Ward and Davis 1968, 1969; Wasilewski 1975, 1980.

run. Rather, the length of the review period affects the speed with which successive increases or decreases in wages (usually the former in the case of Colas) is achieved. This speed clearly does affect annual income and labor costs (see above). In contrast, the presence of minimum or maximum payment provisions can have a direct effect on wages in the long run as well as in the short run. In their drive to limit the costs of providing Colas in the late 1960s, companies were

Table 2-9.   Incidence of Minimum and Maximum Cola
Payments in Indexed Major Agreements, 1966-83.

	Minimum Payments		Maximum Payments ("Caps")	
	Thousands of Workers Covered	Coverage by Minimum Payment Colas as a Percentage of Cola Coverage	Thousands of Workers Covered	Coverage by Capped Colas as a Percentage of Cola Coverage
1966	–	–	50	2.5%
1967	–	–	–	–
1968	–	–	1,500	60.0
1969	–	–	1,900	70.4
1970	1,100	39.3% [a]	1,800	64.3
1971	221	7.4	1,210	40.3
1972	189	4.4	1,089	25.3
1973	800	19.5	1,230	30.0
1974	1,400	35.0	1,000	25.0
1975	1,100	20.8	1,400	26.4
1976	1,100	18.3	2,100	34.4
1977	395	6.6	1,600	26.7
1978	290	5.0	1,500	25.9
1979	500	8.9	1,300	22.0
1980	635	11.8	1,200	22.2
1981	300	5.7	1,200	22.6
1982	547	10.7	1,100	21.6
1983	350	7.1	1,100	22.4

[a] Percentages might add to more than 100 because some contracts have minimum and maximum Cola payments.

Sources: Bornstein and Bolton 1971; Davis 1983; Gurney 1974; Kuhmerker 1976; Lacombe and Conley 1984; Larson 1973; LeRoy 1977, 1978, 1981, 1982; Levin 1979; Ruben 1965a, 1965b; Sparrough and Bolton 1972; Spring 1970; Ward and Davis 1968, 1969; Wasilewski 1975, 1980.

successful in negotiating caps in Cola payments during this period. Table 2-9 shows that in 1966 such caps were quite rare: Only 50,000 workers, or 2.5 percent of those with escalators, were covered by ceilings in Cola adjustments. By 1968 the figure had reached 1.5 million workers (60 percent of those with Colas), and this trend continued into 1969, with 1.9 million workers having capped Colas, about 70

Table 2-10.   Estimated Average Yield of Colas in Major Agreements, Compared to Inflation, 1958–82.

(1) Year	(2) Average Cola[a] Yield (dollars/hr)	(3) Average Union Hourly Wage in Manufacturing (dollars/hr)	(4) (2)/(3) ×100	(5) (4)/ Rate of Increase in CPI (×100)	(6)[b] Average of Cola Yield as a Percentage of Hourly Pay/ Rate of Increase of CPI (×100)
1958	$.064/hr	$3.03/hr	2.1%	123.5%	–
1959	.023	3.13	0.7	46.7	–
1960	.034	3.23	1.1	68.8	–
1961	.025	3.33	0.8	160.0	–
1962	.024	3.41	0.7	63.6	–
1963	.033	3.50	0.9	52.9	–
1964	.033	3.57	0.9	81.8	–
1965	.040	3.70	1.8	90.0	–
1966	.083	3.82	2.2	66.7	–
1967	.058	3.97	1.5	48.4	–
1968	.049	4.18	1.2	25.5	34.0%
1969	.055	4.39	1.3	21.3	26.2
1970	.056	4.65	1.2	35.3	67.3
1971	.112	4.94	2.3	67.6	91.2
1972	.088	5.20	1.7	50.0	58.8
1973	–	–	–	–	46.6
1974	–	–	–	–	47.5
1975	–	–	–	–	68.6
1976	–	–	–	–	72.9
1977	–	–	–	–	57.4
1978	–	–	–	–	–
1979	–	–	–	–	56.0
1980	–	–	–	–	66.0
1981	–	–	–	–	75.0
1982	–	–	–	–	75.0

[a] Average Cola yield in column (2) is for contracts with Colas in force the entire year.

[b] Cola yield for column (6) is average Cola yield for those receiving adjustments, as a percentage of hourly wages for the bargaining unit, all expressed relative to the inflation rate. CPI is measured from December of the previous year to December of the current year.

Sources: Davis 1983; Douty 1975; Larson and Bolton 1973; LeRoy 1977, 1981, 1982; Wasilewski 1980; *MLR,* various issues for price data; Robert Flanagan kindly provided *Current Wage Developments* data for wages.

percent of total Cola coverage. Much of this rapid increase in ceilings was associated with key bargaining units, as was the case with the lengthening of review intervals. For example, in 1967 negotiations in the trucking industry set a four-cent-per-hour annual Cola ceiling; in the auto and related industries (auto parts and farm and construction equipment), eight-cent annual caps were negotiated (Ward and Davis 1968). The automobile Cola also had a minimum payment of three cents an hour every year (Talbot 1968).[15] The 1968 aerospace industry settlements adopted the auto industry's minimum and maximum provisions as well as the change from quarterly to annual reviews. Over the contract period, the cap in the basic auto agreements was effective in that the formula, if uncapped, would have yielded forty-two cents per hour instead of the sixteen cents per hour allowed by the cap (Bornstein and Bolton 1971).

Although the cap in the 1967 UAW Cola clause set the pattern for many other units, 1966 contracts in the electrical equipment industry (GE and Westinghouse) incorporated Colas for the first time since 1960 and also capped the adjustments. In these agreements there were to be two annual adjustments. In each case, wages would rise by a minimum of 0.5 percent if the CPI fell, remained constant, or increased by less than 2 percent in the previous twelve months. Wages would rise up to a limit of 1.75 percent if inflation were 3.5 percent or above (Ruben 1967). Since inflation for the two years that the Cola was in force was 2.8 percent and 4.3 percent respectively, the Cola presumably returned a small portion of inflation, and the cap was effective in the second year.[16]

The examples of the auto and electrical equipment contracts suggest that the caps were effective in limiting the yield of Colas in those industries. Table 2-10 provides further evidence on the yield of Colas relative to inflation. Columns 2 through 5 give indirect information on this question for 1958-72. For these years, data are available on average Cola yield in indexed contracts on a cents-per-hour basis only (column 2). However, column 3 presents the average union wage in manufacturing, which is essentially a weighted average of wages under both escalated and nonescalated contracts. The Cola yield figures, though theoretically covering all sectors, reflect mostly manufacturing, which contained most of the nation's Colas (Larson and Bolton 1973). Thus, column 5 is an estimate of the average percentage of consumer price inflation that was recovered in a given year by the typical Cola. This percentage has been termed by some the "degree of indexation."[17] If, for example, it were to equal 100 percent, we would conclude that Colas give workers on average complete protection against inflation. Column 5 of Table 2-10 shows relatively high estimated degrees of indexation up to 1965 with a sharp downturn by 1969. In these four years, the figure fell from 90 percent to 21.3 percent.

The estimates of the degree of indexation for 1958–72 in column 5 are indirect because we do not know the wage levels of the contracts with Colas. However, column 6 provides direct estimates of the degree of indexation for 1968–82 based on Cola yield and wage level information for indexed contracts. The years 1968–72, when the data for the two methods of computing the degree of indexation overlap, provide a check on the indirect method of column 5. Although the values in columns 5 and 6 are different for 1968–72 (especially 1970 and 1971), the direction of change is always the same in the two columns. This similarity gives us some confidence that the degree of indexation was lower in the late 1960s than in the early to mid-1960s. In particular, the direct estimate in column 6 shows a decline from 1968 to 1969, as does column 5.

A likely interpretation of the decline in the degree of indexation in the late 1960s is that management intended this to happen to some extent (and labor grudgingly acquiesced) by pushing for the rapid expansion of caps in Cola adjustments. The increase in unexpected inflation in the 1965–69 period added to this effect. Presumably, unions agree to a certain cap in their Cola with some notion of what inflation is likely to be over the life of the contract. The more unexpected inflation that occurs during the life of the contract, the less inflation protection a Cola with a cap will give. Thus, the unanticipated inflation of the late 1960s was bound not only to raise workers' desires for Colas but also to cause demands for more liberal Colas in the 1970s.

INDEXATION IN THE 1970s AND 1980s

The 1970s and 1980s have offered a far more unpleasant economic climate than the 1940–69 period. Unemployment and inflation have been substantially higher during these recent years. We have experienced two bouts of rapidly expanding inflation, each related to oil price increases: 1973–74 and 1979–80. As Table 2-7 shows, those episodes of inflation reached levels above 10 percent and were largely unanticipated. There were severe recessions in 1974–75 and 1982 following each outbreak of inflation. These two periods of economic downturn are widely regarded as the most serious since the Great Depression (Scheuch 1981; Ruben 1982). It is doubtful that the severity of these recessions was anticipated by most people. Thus, the 1970s and 1980s have been periods of great economic uncertainty over prices and unemployment. In addition, high levels of unemployment have meant hardship for many workers and have served to restrain union demands (see below). Further, inflation has put a squeeze on workers' real purchasing power.

Tables 2–11 and 2–12 illustrate the pressure that the inflation of the 1970s and 1980s has put on real earnings and living standards. Real weekly and hourly earnings as well as real family incomes progressed steadily from 1950 to 1969. Real growth rates were positive during these years, although they slowed down during the inflation of the late 1960s. However, in the 1970–79 period, real weekly earnings fell, real hourly earnings remained virtually the same, and the growth rate of family income slowed sharply.[18] During the inflation of 1979–81, real earnings and family income fell sharply. Thus, by 1981 real weekly and hourly earnings were below their 1964 and 1967 levels, respectively, and 1981 real family income had declined to below its 1968 level.[19]

Inflation uncertainty was undoubtedly important in causing a large increase in workers' demands for Colas in the 1970s. In addition, few unions seemed willing to give up or water down their Cola provisions as employers began demanding concessions in the late 1970s and early 1980s. The demands were caused by the worsening fortunes of many industries due in part to rising labor costs, increased foreign competition, and the recessionary condition of the economy. In many cases, workers did make concessions, but Colas were usually retained in favor of eliminating other benefits. Further, there were two periods of federal intervention in wage setting: the Nixon controls of 1971–74 and the Carter guidelines of 1978–81. In each of these instances, the government prescribed different treatment for workers with Colas from that for workers without escalators. As it turned out, government policy favored those with Colas. In the early 1980s inflation finally decelerated sharply, but the experience of the post-1965 period has produced a lasting concern among workers over inflationary surprises. This concern is reflected in the tenacity with which workers hold onto their Colas.

Table 2–11.   Real Average Weekly and Hourly Earnings for Production and Nonsupervisory Workers, Private Nonfarm Sector, 1950–81 (in 1967 dollars).

Year	Real Average Weekly Earnings	Real Average Hourly Earnings	Median Real Family Income
1950	$ 73.69	$1.85	$4603
1951	74.37	1.86	4767
1952	76.29	1.91	4893
1953	79.60	2.01	5285
1954	80.15	2.05	5184
1955	84.44	2.13	5512
1956	86.90	2.21	5876
1957	86.99	2.24	5897
1958	86.70	2.25	5874
1959	90.24	2.31	6205
1960	90.95	2.36	6336
1961	92.19	2.39	6403
1962	94.82	2.45	6574
1963	96.47	2.49	6815
1964	98.31	2.54	7071
1965	101.01	2.60	7362
1966	101.67	2.63	7749
1967	101.84	2.68	7933
1968	103.39	2.74	8284
1969	104.38	2.77	8591
1970	103.04	2.78	8484
1971	104.95	2.84	8494
1972	109.26	2.95	8887
1973	109.23	2.96	9070
1974	104.78	2.87	8751
1975	101.45	2.81	8525
1976	102.90	2.85	8788
1977	104.13	2.89	8836
1978	104.30	2.91	9043
1979	101.02	2.83	9025
1980	95.18	2.70	8533
1981	93.72	2.66	8233

Sources: Monthly Labor Review, various issues for wage and price data; U.S. Bureau of the Census 1975: 297; U.S. Bureau of the Census 1984: 463.

Table 2-12.   Average Annual Rates of Growth: Average Real Weekly Earnings, Real Hourly Earnings, and Family Income, 1950-81.

Years	Annual Growth Rates[a]		
	Real Average Weekly Earnings	Real Average Hourly Earnings	Median Real Family Income
1950-60	2.05%	2.46%	3.25%
1960-70	1.26%	1.65%	2.96%
1970-79	-0.36%	0.20%	0.69%
1979-81	-3.68%	-3.05%	-4.49%

[a] Percentages computed from Table 2-11.

From 1969 to 1977, the number of workers in major agreements covered by Colas rose from 2.7 million (25 percent of all workers under major contracts) to an all-time high of 6 million (61.2 percent of workers under major contracts). Since 1977 the number covered has fallen to its 1984 value of 4.5 million. However, since the number of workers under major contracts has also fallen, the probability that workers in such agreements have Colas has dwindled only slightly to its 1984 level of 57.3 percent.

There have been two periods of particularly rapid increase in Cola coverage: 1971-72 and 1974-76. The increase of 1.3 million workers covered by Colas from 1971 to 1972 was due primarily to the 1971 steel and communications industry contracts. The Cola had been eliminated from the steel industry in 1962 during a period of high perceived unemployment among steelworkers. By 1970 the USW began to regret this decision, as the inflation of the late 1960s had outrun their scheduled wage increases (Sparrough and Bolton 1972). By making escalation a top priority among its bargaining demands, the union was able to regain its Cola in the 1971 contract (Gurney 1970; Abel 1973). This Cola had no maximum adjustments and was, as our data sample of collective bargaining contracts shows, established in USW contracts in the aluminum and can industries (Abel 1973). The main agreement in basic steel alone added about 400,000 workers to the list of those with Colas (Bornstein and Bolton 1971). This Cola has proved to be quite generous to the steelworkers, to the consternation of the steel companies, and has been watered down but not capped in the 1983 agreement. The 1971 Bell System agreement, covering about 500,000 employees, added escalation for the first time. The Cola provision called for annual Cola payments with no floor or ceiling and gave special allowances for workers in areas with a high cost of living such as New York, Chicago, and San Francisco (Sparrough and Bolton 1972; Knobloch 1972). This latter provision was part of an increasing trend in the 1970s toward making Colas reflect local rather than national living costs (see below).

Shortly after the steel and communication industry settlements, Cola incidence dropped slightly. From 1972 to 1974, coverage fell from 4.3 million to 4 million workers, representing a small drop from 40.6 percent of all workers under major agreements to 39.2 percent. This decline has been attributed to the abatement of inflation during the Nixon controls period (David 1972). Indeed, Table 2-7 shows inflation rates for 1971 and 1972 of 3.4 percent in each year — a decline from the 5.4 percent average annual rate that characterized the December 1967–December 1970 period. Further, the table indicates that inflationary expectations were being realized in 1971–72 — unexpected inflation was −0.4 percent to +0.2 percent in these years compared to an average annual inflationary surprise of +2.3 percent from December 1967 to December 1970. Since the Cola coverage figures in Table 2-7 refer to January 1, any change in coverage, for example, from 1972 to 1973 reflects 1972 negotiations and presumably the 1972 environment. In fact, since most major contracts by the 1970s had three-year duration (as shown by our sample of contracts), Cola coverage as of January 1973 reflects contracts that were negotiated in the 1970–72 period. Thus, the Cola coverage figures will tend to lag one to three years behind the data on inflationary surprises. In particular, Cola coverage continued to drop as of January 1, 1974, despite the unexpected acceleration of inflation in 1973.

There is some debate over the degree to which the Nixon controls were effective.[20] However, there is no doubt that for 1971 and 1972, which included the initial controls period of August 15, 1971 to December 31, 1972 (Phases I and II), prices significantly stabilized, lessening workers' incentives for indexation. This stabilization was evidently strong enough to offset favorable treatment given to contracts with Colas by administrators of the Nixon controls. The program began with the ninety-day wage and price freeze of Phase I, initiated on August 15, 1971. On November 14 of that year, the Phase

II period of strict controls on wages and prices began and lasted until the end of 1972. During Phase II, the price inflation goal was a 2.5 percent annual rate of increase, and the wage standard was a 5.5 percent rate, reflecting an expected 3 percent annual productivity increase (Staller and Solnick 1975).

Two regulations of Phase II at least indirectly affected Cola negotiations. First, a 7 percent limit for pay raises negotiated before August 14, 1971 was allowed; second, Cola increases were time weighted. For example, if a Cola adjustment that was paid on June 30, 1972 raised wages 2 percent, it would count as a 1 percent annual raise (Staller and Solnick 1975). Thus, base wages for workers with Colas could rise by more than the pay standard. For newly negotiated contracts with Colas, the controls administrators (the Pay Board) estimated the time-weighted value of the Cola payments by assuming a 2.5 percent inflation rate. Since inflation exceeded this figure, Colas returned an added bonus. Although the parties in such a case were required to notify the Pay Board, during Phase II the board never reduced an escalator payment—despite the fact that inflation was over 2.5 percent (Staller and Solnick 1975). In Phases III and IV (lasting until April 30, 1974) each bargaining situation was evaluated on its own merits. As with Phase II, no escalator increase was reduced (Staller and Solnick 1975).

During the latter stages of and after the Nixon controls period, prices began to rise rapidly. The food and oil price increases of 1973 and 1974 helped lead to the acceleration of inflation during these years.[21] In addition, Table 2–7 shows that the majority of this inflation was unanticipated, and Table 2–12 shows steady declines in real wages from 1973 to 1975. This unexpected loss of purchasing power led to increased worker demands for cost-of-living escalators. Coverage by Colas rose from 4 million to 6 million workers in the 1974–76 period, signifying a rise from 39.2 percent to 59.4 percent Cola coverage. During these years, indexation spread to new areas in collective bargaining. For example, the United Mineworkers, who had previously opposed Colas, demanded one in the 1974 negotiations with the Bituminous Coal Operators Association.[22] The union obtained a quarterly Cola as well as scheduled wage increases (Defina 1975). In the same period, after a nationwide strike, the Amalgamated Clothing Workers were also able to secure a Cola (Defina 1975).

The Cola principle continued to spread in 1975 and 1976. The return of indexing in the railroad industry in 1975 was the first time

Table 2-13.   Importance of Factors Influencing Salary Decisions, 1975.

Employee Category	Percentage of Firms Influenced by Cost-of-Living Index	Percentage Influenced by Area Wage Surveys	Percentage of Firms Influenced by Financial Results
Executives	11%	33%	51%
Exempt salaried	34	51	41
Nonexempt salaried	38	58	33
Nonunion hourly	25	38	20
Union hourly	32	16	15

[a] "Exempt" employees are those not covered by the provisions of the Fair Labor Standards Act. They are generally higher paid, managerial, and professional workers.

Source: Weeks 1976: 11, 15. Reproduced with permission of the Conference Board, Inc., New York, New York.

since 1960 that these workers had Colas (Defina 1976). The United Rubber Workers struck the major tire companies for four months in 1976. The union sought wage increases to allow a catching up to UAW levels and the introduction of a Cola. The resulting contract contained an unlimited escalator with similar features to the UAW's (Bornstein 1977).

The inflation of 1973 and 1974 affected nonunion workers and employees as well as those in the union sector. A 1976 NICB study based on a 1975 survey of companies found substantial nonunion concern with inflation in wage setting (Weeks 1976), although this concern was less than that following World War I. This survey, conducted on a random sample of 480 private sector companies, asked firms about the factors influencing their compensation policies. Table 2–13 illustrates the relative importance of living costs, area wage standards, and financial performance in affecting executives' decisions about pay for various employee groups. The cost of living influenced comparable percentages of firms for the various occupational groups except executives (for whom the CPI was a less often cited factor in salary determination). However, the cost of living was cited more frequently for union hourly workers relative to area wage standards and financial results than was the case for other employee groups.

Table 2-14.   Types of Pay Increases Given, 1974-75.

	Type of Increase			
	(Percentage of Firms Employing a Given Type of Worker Providing a Given Type of Increase)			
Employee Class	*General*	*Merit*	*Cola*	*Longevity*
Union hourly	87%	10%	39%	27%
Nonunion hourly	69	49	10	17
Nonexempt salaried	49	88	11	7
Exempt salaried	41	87	9	3
Officers	25	91	4	1

Source: Weeks 1976: 21. Reproduced with permission of the Conference Board, Inc., New York, New York.

Table 2-14 compares the types of pay increases actually given to each of the employee groups in the NICB sample. The percentage of union hourly workers with Cola increases was 39 percent, substantially higher than for the other groups. This figure is close to the 39.2 percent Cola coverage estimate in Table 2-7 for major agreements, although the NICB sample might have included smaller agreements (which, as our data show, are less likely to be indexed). On the whole, then, the sample might be representative of union agreements, at least regarding the incidence of Colas. Although the nonunion workers were less likely to have Colas than the union hourly workers, a non-negligible percentage (roughly 10 percent) of the nonunion hourly and salaried workers did have some kind of Cola adjustment. We have no way of knowing whether these nonunion plans were discretionary. However, the fact that employers called the adjustments Colas, as well as the reliance on the CPI as shown in Table 2-13, illustrates the concern in the nonunion sector with the inflation of 1973-74.[23] Even if a company's plan is discretionary, by labeling an increase as a Cola adjustment bearing some relationship to the CPI, the firm might bring about an expectation among its employees that future CPI increases will be met with "Cola" raises.

The severe recession following the 1973-74 inflationary episode helped cause a sharp deceleration of inflation in 1975 and 1976. By the latter year, a relatively modest inflation rate of 4.8 percent was reached. Further, in 1975 and 1976 the Livingston inflation forecasts overshot the actual inflation rate, suggesting that people were surprised by the extent of its deceleration. However, the inflation picture soon turned around, and the CPI accelerated from 1976 to 1980. From 1976 to 1978, the movement was gradual, though not completely anticipated. Then, from 1978 to 1980, led by rising oil prices, the CPI shot up at a 12.8 percent annual rate, a sizable portion of which was not expected.[24] Following 1980, prices sharply decelerated, reaching a 3.8 percent rate for 1983, following a severe recession. Not only was this the lowest inflation rate in eleven years, but the magnitude of the fall in inflation was substantially underpredicted. The unemployment that was associated with the fall in inflation averaged 9.7 percent in 1982, its highest average since the 1941 rate of 9.9 percent (U.S. Bureau of the Census 1975: 126; Table 2-7). Thus, the 1974-82 period was characterized by high degrees of inflation uncertainty (as measured by unexpected inflation in Table 2-7) on the up and down sides and by periodic severe recession.

During 1978, in the midst of the 1976-80 acceleration of inflation, the Carter administration embarked on a voluntary wage and price guidelines program. This program lasted until President Reagan abolished it in January 1981 (BNA 1981b). Although the program's administrators claimed initial success in reducing wage inflation, it was obvious that the guidelines could not prevent prices from rising at a rapid pace in 1979 and 1980 (Katzen 1981).

The Carter guidelines gave apparent, though inadvertent, favoritism to indexed contracts. The initial guideline for wages and benefits was a 7 percent annual rate of increase while Colas were costed at 6 percent inflation. Thus, if inflation went over 6 percent, as it did, workers with Colas could get raises over 7 percent and still be in compliance with the guidelines (Katzen 1981). To remedy the disparity between indexed and nonindexed contracts, the guidelines administrators (Council on Wage and Price Stability—COWPS) allowed a 1 percent catch-up raise for workers without Colas. Because inflation was proceeding at a rate of 12 to 13 percent per year at this time, workers with Colas were still in practice favored (BNA 1979). Although in the second year of the program, COWPS raised the inflation assumption to 7.5 percent and adopted a new guideline of 7.5 to 9.5 percent for wages, the high inflation gave workers with Colas a large advantage (BNA 1981a).

The inflation uncertainty of the post-1974 period and the Carter guidelines affected all workers. However, the economic slowdown of the 1980s had an especially strong effect on some of the industries where Colas were most strongly entrenched — automobiles, steel, and trucking (Ruben 1983). In particular, in 1982 the UAW, the USW, and the Teamsters together represented 1.96 million workers with Colas, or about 38 percent of the workers in major agreements who had indexation (LeRoy 1982). These opposing forces on the incidence of indexation — Carter guidelines, increasing inflation uncertainty, and severe downturn in heavily indexed industries — appear to have approximately canceled each other out. From 1976 to 1984, the percentage of workers in major agreements having Colas remained fairly stable, declining from 60 percent to 57.3 percent. During these years, relatively few important bargaining units actually abandoned indexation, although there were strong pressures from management to water down the provisions of existing Colas.

Two unions, the Glass Bottle Blowers in 1977 and the Mineworkers in 1978, settled for generous deferred wage increases in return for abandoning their Colas. However, these settlements covered only 35,000 (Glass Bottle Blowers) and 127,000 (Mineworkers), or only about 3 percent of workers covered by Colas at the time (LeRoy 1977, 1978; Bornstein 1978; Table 2-7). This 3 percent amounts to 1.8 percent of workers under major agreements, accounting for nearly the entire fall in Cola coverage percentage by 1979. The continued slow decline until the present is most likely due to the disproportionate losses in employment in the heavily indexed steel, auto, and trucking industries (relative to the decline in workers under major agreements). For example, Table 2-15 shows that the declines in production worker employment for trucking, motor vehicles, and basic steel from November 1979 to November 1982 were, respectively, 16, 32.1, and 43.1 percent. In contrast, for the private sector as a whole, the decline was only 3.3 percent and for workers covered by major contracts the decline was only 5.3 percent.

Characteristics of Colas in the 1970s and 1980s

Since 1970, Cola provisions have become more liberal, although the trend is not uniform. Review intervals among contracts with reviews

Table 2-15. Production Worker Employment in Heavily Indexed Industries and Total Private Sector, November 1979 and November 1982, and Major Agreement Coverage, January 1979 and January 1982.

| | Number of Production Workers | | |
Industry	November 1979	November 1982	Percentage Change
Trucking	1,157,000	971,600	−16.0%
Motor vehicles and equipment	692,300	470,300	−32.1%
Blast furnace and basic steel products	430,600	244,100	−43.1%
Total private sector	61,291,000	59,254,000	−3.3%

	Number of Production and Nonproduction Workers		
	January 1979	January 1982	
Workers covered by major agreements (all sectors)	9,500,000	9,000,000	−5.3%

Sources: LeRoy 1982; USBLS, *Employment and Earnings,* January 1980 and January 1983.

have gotten shorter, although a smaller fraction of indexed agreements now get a review in any given year. Perhaps more importantly, there has been a noticeable trend away from ceiling provisions in Cola adjustments. Even during the 1980s period of concession bargaining, coverage by capped Colas as a fraction of total Cola coverage has not risen. Workers, wary of inflationary surprises, have been more willing to make other concessions to management than to cap their Cola payments. In addition, the formulas themselves have gradually become more liberal. As a result, Colas gave more complete protection against inflation in the early 1980s than in early to mid-1970s or late 1960s.

The frequency of Cola reviews shows a mixed path over the post-1970 period. Following the readoption of quarterly reviews in the 1970 UAW contracts (to start in 1972), there was a sharp upturn in the extent of such reviews (Ruben 1974; Table 2-8). The fraction of reviews that are quarterly has fluctuated between roughly 40 and 60 percent since the UAW agreement. Semiannual reviews became more popular by 1980. However, in 1981 the Teamsters agreed to annual reviews as part of a concessionary package (BNA 1982b). The major group with annual reviews since the mid-1970s has been the Communications Workers in the Bell System.

Although a larger proportion of reviews in 1983 were either semiannual or quarterly than at most times in the past, there has been a countervailing trend toward a smaller likelihood of a review during any given year. In the late 1960s and in 1970, over 90 percent of contracts with Colas had at least one review in any given year. This figure reached a high of 98.8 percent in 1973 and has generally fallen since then. After a relatively high review percentage of 85.6 percent in 1981, the extent of reviews among contracts with Colas fell sharply to 59.2 percent in 1983 (the smallest level ever). This decline in the frequency of reviews might reflect one aspect common to many concession bargains in financially troubled industries: the deferral of Cola payments. For example, as part of its 1980 and 1981 concession package, Chrysler workers agreed first to roll back and then to discontinue Cola payments until September 1982 (BNA 1980, 1981a). In the 1982 Ford, GM, and American Motors settlements, the UAW agreed to defer several Cola payments for eighteen months in each case (BNA 1982c, d, e). Similar provisions were negotiated in 1980–83 in meatpacking, tires, and steel (BNA 1981c, 1982g; *Business Week,* March 14, 1983). In 1984, however, more workers with Colas were getting reviews (86%), but more of these reviews were annual (43.9%) than in the recent past.

The trend toward uncapped Cola payments, as well as the trend toward quarterly reviews, was started by the 1970 UAW agreements (Ruben 1974). The incidence of maximum adjustment provisions among contracts with Colas fell sharply from 1970 to 1972. Table 2-9 shows a drop in the extent of caps from 64.3 percent to 25.3 percent during this time. This percentage rose in 1976 due to the negotiation of capped Colas in the railroad industry (Defina 1976), which had been without indexation since 1960. From 1976 to 1979, the extent of caps dropped from 34.4 percent to 22 percent and has remained at about 22 percent ever since. In the trucking and electrical equipment industries, for example, unions in 1976 were successful in eliminating the caps from their escalator provisions (Bolton 1978).

Even during the 1979–83 period of concession bargaining, unions with uncapped Colas have, when necessary, generally given up other benefits and have kept their unlimited indexation plans. Such concessions have often involved the deferral, with eventual resumption, of Cola payments. In addition, two other kinds of Cola-related concessions have been popular: giving up scheduled wage increases and occasional diversion of Cola payments to fund other benefits. For example, workers at Chrysler, Ford, GM, and American Motors all gave up scheduled wage increases (BNA 1982c, e, i). Teamsters, meatpackers, and rubber workers also gave up general wage increases but kept their Colas (BNA 1981, 1982f, g). Finally, the recent agreement between the USW and the steel industry includes the following major concessions by the union: $1.70-per-hour cuts in wages and benefits, cancellation of six quarterly Cola payments, and limitations on Cola adjustments until 1986, when the Cola again becomes unlimited (*Business Week,* March 14, 1983). The steel industry sought major concessions in this period because of the depressed state of the industry. At the time the 1983 contract was negotiated, the industry was operating at 50 percent of capacity. The steel companies particularly wanted to reduce the yield of the Cola, which had raised wages by $5.17 per hour since 1972 (*Business Week,* March 14, 1983). For many unions making concessions, Cola payments have been diverted to other uses. In the aircraft industry, for example, in some contracts one cent from each Cola payment would be withheld to pay for improved retirement benefits (Wasilewski 1980). In addition, Teamsters have diverted Cola adjustments to pay for pension and health and welfare funds (BNA 1982b).

These settlements all took place in depressed industries, as the employment figures in Table 2–15 suggest. In the auto, steel, and trucking industries, in many cases at least 20 to 40 percent of the work force was on layoff during negotiations.[25] However, in each case, the bargain included a return to an uncapped Cola at a future point. Workers in these bargaining units are extremely reluctant to be left behind by the next bout of unexpected inflation, which at some level seems to be "anticipated" by all.

In addition to a steadfast defense of uncapped Colas, unions in the 1970s have negotiated more liberal formulas. An indication of the generosity of a particular formula per se (as opposed to the effects of caps) can be obtained by computing the degree of inflation protection afforded by the formula if it were uncapped. For contracts negotiated in 1971, our sample of agreements shows that the dominant Cola formula was a one-cent-per-hour raise for each 0.4-point rise in the U.S. 1957–59 base CPI: 89.3 percent of Colas negotiated in 1971 were of this type. Since the 1971 CPI (base 1957–59) averaged 141, a 10 percent rise in prices would yield about a thirty-five-cent-per-hour raise under this formula if it were uncapped (*Monthly Labor Review*, April 1972). This raise is about 10 percent of our sample average 1972 base wage for janitors and laborers of $3.49, implying a 100 percent degree of indexation for these workers. However, by 1973, 65.7 percent of new contracts with Colas (in our sample) had a formula of one cent per 0.3 points using the 1967 base U.S. CPI. Under an uncapped formula of this type, a 10 percent rise in prices in 1973 would yield a forty-four-cent-per-hour Cola adjustment, since the 1973 CPI averaged 133.1 on a 1967 base (*Monthly Labor Review*, April 1973). Since base wages for janitors and laborers with Colas in 1973 and 1974 averaged $3.72 and $4.07 respectively, the new formula would have given greater inflation protection than the old one if both were uncapped. This change is due to the fact that, although prices were 16.3 percent higher in 1967 than 1957–59 (see above), implying that a change to base 1967 would reduce Cola adjustments 16.3 percent, this reduction was outweighted by the change from one cent per 0.4 to one cent per 0.3 points, base 1967. By 1979 the dominant formula was still one cent per 0.3, base 1967. A 10 percent rise in prices in 1979 would yield seventy-three cents per hour under this formula if uncapped (the CPI was 217.7 — *Monthly Labor Review,* January 1982). Since 1979 and 1980 base wages for janitors and laborers with Colas averaged $6.30 and $7.41, the dominant formula yielded about the same degree of inflation protection as that in 1971 but less than the one for 1973. Finally, the 1979 UAW and Rubber Workers' contracts stipulated that in 1981 the Cola formula would change to one cent per 0.26 base 1967 (LeRoy 1982). To the extent that the UAW remains a pattern setter, this formula could become the model for other unions. In 1982 a 10 percent rise in prices under this formula would yield $1.12 if it were uncapped (the CPI for 1982 was about 290 — *Monthly Labor Review,* January 1983). The 1982 base wage in our sample for janitors and laborers averaged $8.58, implying a sharp increase in Cola protection afforded by the new formula. Even the one-cent-per-0.3, base 1967 formula would yield ninety-seven cents under a 10 percent 1982 inflation.[26] Thus, the prevailing Cola formulas in the early 1980s were more generous, assuming they were uncapped, than those in the early 1970s.

The dominant Colas all serve to narrow wage differentials by giving equal cents-per-hour increases to everyone. The major instance of an approximately differential-preserving Cola occurs in the contract for the 600,000 Communications Workers in the Bell system. Their Cola guarantees a fifty-five-cent-per-week raise and raises wages 0.65 percent for each 1 percent rise in the CPI. This Cola was liberalized in 1981 from its 1980 provisions of fifty cents per week plus 0.6 percent raise for each 1 percent CPI increase (Wasilewski 1980; LeRoy 1981, 1982).

The net effect of the reduction over the 1970s and 1980s in caps and the liberalization of formulas has been an increase in inflation protection afforded to those with Colas. Table 2–10 shows that by 1982 the average Cola raised wages by 75 percent of the rise in prices, an increase in inflation protection relative to the mid-1970s. Workers with indexation seem in no mood to give it up or to weaken its provisions. This inclination might change if the recent deceleration of prices leads to a low, stable inflation rate. However, it would take a long period of price stability to make workers forget the uncertainties of the 1970s and 1980s.

New Developments in Cola Provisions

Two issues have recently emerged as important considerations in the design of Colas: the use of city-specific CPIs and the growth of escalated pensions. These issues have implications for wage differentials as well as labor costs in general.

In 1969 the number of workers in major indexed agreements using a city price index was about 90,000, or 3 percent of those with Colas (Talbot 1969; Table 2–7). The example of San Diego discussed earlier shows that inflation in one city can diverge from the national average. In part due to the disparity in inflation rates across cities, the number of workers with Colas tied to city price indexes rose to 500,000 in 1975 (about 9 percent of those with Colas), and by 1979 the figure had reached about 728,000 (13 percent of workers with Colas).[27] An increasing reliance on city price indexes implies a less rigid national nominal wage structure and presumably a smaller disparity in purchasing power across workers in different cities. However, city-specific

Colas provide disincentives for firms to expand operations in areas where the cost of living is rapidly expanding relative to other areas.

The issue of escalated pensions has become a crucial public policy issue, especially in the area of Social Security and federal pensions, and has also touched private pensions. In the Social Security system, the introduction in 1972 of indexation of benefits and the rising percentage of the population of retirement age put great financial strain on the system. Federal pensions are also indexed, putting pressure on the federal budget (Munnell 1977). Among private sector pension plans, a Conference Board survey showed that in 1975 about 6.8 percent of companies with pension plans had formulas with cost-of-living escalators (Weeks 1976). However, the study concluded that future inflation uncertainty prevents many benefits planners from advocating pension indexation schemes for their companies (Weeks 1976: 55). The study did not make clear whether the escalator clauses were automatic or discretionary.

Pensions under collective bargaining agreements generally do not have automatic escalators but rather have benefit structures that are subject to periodic renegotiation in response to inflation. For example, such adjustments have occurred in recent years in the basic steel and auto industry agreements (Defina 1975; Ruben 1980). Interestingly, in 1974 the USW established an automatic pension escalator in the aluminum and container industries that called for a rise in pension benefits in 1976 and 1977 by 65 percent of inflation. However, the provision was terminated in 1977 (Defina 1975; Bornstein 1978).

The issue of escalated pensions for union workers could become particularly explosive if inflation picks up again and employment in union industries continues to shrink. In such a case, retirees will have an increasing share of political influence in unions, and a greater demand for escalated pensions is likely. However, employers might present stiff resistance to this increasing demand because rising pension costs would be out of their control. Cola payments for current workers can be controlled somewhat by layoffs; payments to retirees are less easily affected.

CONCLUSIONS

This review of the history of wage indexation in the United States has uncovered several regularities, some of which will be tested more rigorously in later chapters. First, wage escalation appears to grow during periods of rapid, unanticipated inflation: World War I, the Korean War, and the inflationary surprises of the 1970s and 1980s. Second, unions that are typically categorized as being relatively powerful (e.g., the UAW, USW, and Teamsters) tend to account for a large portion of workers covered by Colas. Third, government wage and price controls programs in the 1970s favored contracts with Colas by "costing" them out at unrealistically low levels of inflation. Fourth, Colas typically do not raise wages by as much as prices rise, and they cover a relatively small portion of the total work force. These features of Colas must be kept in mind as we proceed to evaluate their impact on inflation. Finally, Colas tend to be associated with long-term agreements guaranteeing industrial peace for a number of years. To the extent that strikes cost society lost output or inconvenience, this potential impact of Colas can be of social benefit.

Currently, formal indexation plans cover at most a small minority of the U.S. work force, since only 20 to 25 percent of workers are unionized. However, even in the troubled 1980s, workers with Colas have generally been able to hold onto them. A substantial new outbreak of unanticipated inflation would undoubtedly rekindle union demands for Colas as well as nonunion demands for catch-up increases or even Colas. Indeed, the extreme volatility of prices in other countries such as Israel or Brazil has left a legacy of systems of generalized wage indexation in these countries (Cukierman 1977).

NOTES

1. For more on this agreement see Bortz (1948), the February 1949 issue of the *Review of Economics and Statistics,* and Merkin (1982).

2. Systems in which wages are adjusted to fluctuations in the price of the good produced (sliding-scale systems), though very rare in the United States, originated in the 1860s in the iron and steel and coal industries (*Monthly Labor Review,* July 1951). It is likely that such plans resulted from employer initiative in industries with volatile and especially falling prices, the latter of which occurred in the post–Civil War period (U.S. Bureau of the Census 1975). Such plans clearly did not adjust wages to changes in workers' living costs and are thus not what we normally think of as Colas. An early form of indexation occurred in the American Revolution as Massachusetts linked its soldiers' wages to an index based on beef, corn, wool, and leather prices (Arak 1978).

3. The reader should be cautioned that the pre-1912 data in Table 2–1 are estimates. The BLS did not publish cost-of-living figures until 1919 (covering the post-1912 period) with regular publication since February

1921 (U.S. Bureau of the Census 1975: 191). Thus, the pre–World War I data might not be comparable to the later figures. However, even allowing for substantial measurement error, Table 2–1 yields a conclusion of considerable price stability from 1880 to 1914 followed by a period of rapidly rising prices.

4. The following table illustrates the unemployment situation during these years:

Year	Unemployment as a Percentage of the Civilian Labor Force
1918	1.4%
1919	1.4
1920	5.2
1921	11.7
1922	6.7

Source: U.S. Bureau of the Census 1975: 126.

5. This is obviously in great contrast to modern-day Colas such as the UAW's, which raises wages one cent per hour for each 0.26-point increase in the CPI.

6. See note 3.

7. The banking industry had a history of reliance on cost-of-living figures. During 1915 and 1916, several banks and trust companies gave out Christmas bonuses to compensate employees for inflation. In addition, the Bankers' Trust Company of New York used Bradstreet's data to compute a rise in living costs of 21 percent from 1915 to 1916. This 21 percent was multiplied by the portion of salaries that was used for basic living necessities, as determined by a local survey of the New York area (Fisher 1918).

8. The following table illustrates the decline in the work week following the war:

Year	Average Weekly Hours of Production Workers in Manufacturing, 1940–48
1940	38.1 hours
1941	40.6
1942	43.1
1943	45.0
1944	45.2
1945	43.5
1946	40.3
1947	40.4
1948	40.0

Source: U.S. Bureau of the Census 1975: 169.

9. Some have attributed the persistent inflation we have experienced since World War II to expansionary government policies designed to reduce unemployment (mandated by the Full Employment Act of 1946); others believe that the presence of unions (largely organized during the 1930s and 1940s) prevents downward flexibility of wages and thus prices. For a discussion of these views, see Scheuch (1981).

10. These surveys were taken by Joseph Livingston of the *Philadelphia Inquirer*. For a discussion of these data, see Carlson (1977).

11. For further discussion of these reasons, see David and Helm (1955: 315–16).

12. Kaiser adopted these provisions as did the Pacific Coast shipbuilding industry (David and Benny 1959).

13. See the example described above on the effect of a three-month delay in a Cola payment.

14. See Hamermesh (1971) for some discussion and analysis of alternative hypotheses regarding controls and inflation in the early 1960s.

15. In the auto contracts, both sides agreed that if the CPI should rise by more than anticipated, the 1970 negotiations would reflect this (Ward and Davis 1968).

16. The inflation figures are taken from the January 1967, January 1968, and January 1969 issues of the *Monthly Labor Review*.

17. See, for example, Card (1983).

18. Real family income growth does not slow down as much as real earnings because in the 1960–79 period an increasing percentage of the population (particularly women) was employed, as illustrated in the following table.

Civilian Employment and Labor Force
as a Percentage of the Population
(over 16 years of age), various years

Year	Employment	Labor Force
1950	55.2%	58.3%
1955	55.1	57.7
1960	54.9	58.1
1965	55.0	57.6
1970	56.1	59.0
1975	55.3	60.4
1979	59.2	62.9
1981	58.3	63.1

Source: Monthly Labor Review 106, no. 1 (January 1983): 71.

In fact, some have suggested that stagnation in real incomes, due to inflation, has been a cause of rising female labor force participation and total employment rates (relative to population). See Reynolds (1982).

19. Progressive taxes added to the squeeze that inflation put on real income. For example, if a family's before-tax income and the CPI were constant in a given year, then real before-tax and after-tax income also were the same. However, if before-tax income and the CPI rose 10 percent, then real after-tax income fell because taxes rose by more than 10 percent due to the progressive tax rate structure (in the absence of tax bracket indexation, which begins in 1985).

20. Although there is some evidence that wages decelerated during the control periods of Phases I through IV, when controls were lifted wages "exploded," reflecting pent-up inflationary pressures. Thus, the total effect of the Nixon controls must be measured by examining the postcontrols (i.e., 1974 and beyond) period. For further discussion, see Reid (1981).

21. From November 1972 to August 1973, the wholesale price index for farm products rose 65.6 percent (an annual rate of 95.9 percent); from January 1973 to February 1974, the index for crude petroleum rose 75.9 percent (an annual rate of 68.4 percent). See the *Monthly Labor Review,* April 1973 and August 1974.

22. In 1939 John L. Lewis, president of the United Mineworkers and the CIO, addressed the CIO convention and argued against the linking of wages to living costs. His reasoning was that Colas tend to freeze real wages (*BLS* 1966: 2).

23. We are assuming that the salaried employees are, by and large, nonunion workers. Table 2–14 shows that union workers are much more likely than others to get nondiscretionary across-the-board raises (general increases, Colas, and longevity increases). This finding is consistent with Freeman's (1980, 1982) research indicating that unions lead to a narrowing of pay differentials through standard rate policies.

24. From May 1978 to May 1980, the wholesale price index for crude petroleum rose at an average annual rate of 35.2 percent. See the *Monthly Labor Review,* July 1979 and July 1980.

25. See BNA (1982b, h, i).

26. About 51 percent of workers under major agreements with Colas in 1983 were covered by either of these two formulas. This figure is from data in LeRoy (1982); the *Monthly Labor Review,* May 1982; and the following issues of the BLS's *Current Wage Developments:* January, February, and April 1981, and April 1982.

27. See Wasilewski (1975), Levin (1979), and Table 2–7.

REFERENCES

Abel, I. W. 1973. "Basic Steel's Experimental Negotiating Agreement."
Monthly Labor Review (*MLR*) 96, no. 9 (September): 39–42.

"Adjustment of Federal Salaries to the Cost of Living." 1934. *MLR* 57,
no. 2 (February): 367–79.

"Adjustment of Wages According to Changes in the Cost of Living." 1937.
Supplement to Conference Board Service Letter (February 11): 9–14.

"Adjustment of Wages to Changes in the Cost of Living." 1946. *MLR* 69,
no. 11 (November): 733–43.

Arak, Marcelle V. 1978. "Indexation of Wage and Retirement Income in the
United States." *FRBNY Quarterly Review* (Autumn): 16–23.

"Bad News Blasts Steelworkers." 1983. *Business Week*. (February 14): 41.

Bolton, Lena W. 1978. "Heavy Bargaining Returns in 1979." *MLR* 101,
no. 12 (December): 15–24.

Bornstein, Leon, and Lena W. Bolton. 1971. "Calendar of Wage Increases
and Negotiations for 1971." *MLR* 94, no. 1 (January): 31–37.

Bornstein, Leon. 1977. "Industrial Relations in 1976: Highlights of Key
Settlements." *MLR* 100, no. 1 (January): 27–35.

———. 1978. "Industrial Relations in 1977: Highlights of Key Developments." *MLR* 101, no. 2 (February): 24–31.

———. 1979. "Industrial Relations in 1978: Some Bargaining Highlights."
MLR 102, no. 1 (January): 58–64.

Bortz, Nelson M. 1948. "Cost-of-Living Wage Clauses and UAW-GM
Pact." *MLR* 71, no. 7 (July): 1–7.

Bureau of National Affairs (BNA). 1950. *Tying Wages to the Cost of Living*.
Washington, D.C.: The Bureau of National Affairs.

———. 1979. *Daily Labor Report* (*DLR*) no. 187 (September 26).

———. 1980. *DLR* no. 244 (December 17).

———. 1981a. *DLR* no. 10 (January 15).

———. 1981b. *DLR* no. 19 (January 29).

———. 1981c. *DLR* no. 243 (December 18).

———. 1982a. *DLR* no. 11 (January 16).

———. 1982b. *DLR* no. 23 (February 3).

———. 1982c. *DLR* no. 50 (March 15).

———. 1982d. *DLR* no. 55 (March 22).

———. 1982e. *DLR* no. 75 (April 19).

———. 1982f. *DLR* no. 76 (April 20).

———. 1982g. *DLR* no. 85 (May 3).

———. 1982h. *DLR* no. 109 (June 7).

———. 1982i. *DLR* no. 139 (July 20).

———. 1982j. *Labor–Management Reporter*.

Card, David. 1983. "Cost-of-Living Escalators in Major Union Contracts." *Industrial and Labor Relations Review* 37, no. 1 (October): 34–48.

Carlson, John. 1977. "A Study of Price Forecasts." *Annals of Economic and Social Measurement* 6, no. 1 (Winter): 27–56.

Carr, Elma B. 1925. *The Use of Cost-of-Living Figures in Wage Adjustments* (Bureau of Labor Statistics Bulletin No. 369). Washington, D.C.: U.S. Government Printing Office.

Cukierman, Alex. 1977. "General Wage Escalator Clauses and the Inflation Unemployment Tradeoff." *Economic Inquiry* 15, no. 1 (January): 67–84.

Cunningham, Maurice. 1962. "The 11th Convention of the United Steelworkers." *MLR* 85, no. 12 (December): 1226–28.

"Comments on the G.M.–U.A.W. Wage Contract of 1948." 1949. *Review of Economics and Statistics* 31, no. 1 (February): 1–14.

Davey, Harold W.; Mario F. Bognanno; and David L. Estenson. 1982. *Contemporary Collective Bargaining,* 4th ed. Englewood Cliffs, N.J.: Prentice-Hall.

David, Lily Mary. 1972. "Cost-of-Living Escalation in Collective Bargaining." In *Hearings on Price and Wage Control: An Evaluation of Current Policies,* Joint Economic Committee, 92nd Congress, 2nd Session, pp. 332–41. Washington, D.C.: U.S. Government Printing Office.

David, Lily Mary, and Ruth Benny. 1959. "Deferred Wage Increases and Escalator Clauses." *MLR* 82, no. 12 (December): 1324–28.

David, Lily Mary, and Donald L. Helm. 1955. "Wage Escalation—Recent Developments." *MLR* 78, no. 3 (March): 315–18.

———. 1957. "Deferred Wage Increases in 1957 and Wage Escalator Clauses." *MLR* 80, no. 1 (January): 50–52.

———. 1958. "Deferred Increases and Escalator Clauses." *MLR* 81, no. 12 (December): 1362–65.

Davis, William. 1983. "Collective Bargaining in 1983: A Crowded Agenda." *MLR* 106, no. 1 (January): 3–16.

Defina, Catherine C. 1975. "Labor and the Economy in 1974." *MLR* 98, no. 1 (January): 3–16.

———. 1976. "Labor and the Economy During 1975." *MLR* 99, no. 1 (January): 3–15.

Douty, H. M. 1975. "Cost-of-Living Escalator Clauses and Inflation." Prepared for the Council on Wage and Price Stability. Washington, D.C.: U.S. Government Printing Office.

"Escalator Wage Adjustments Based on Price of Product." 1951. *MLR* 74, no. 7 (July): 48–49.

Fisher, Irving. 1918. "Adjusting Wages to the Cost of Living." *MLR* 41, no. 11 (November): 1–5.

Flanagan, Robert. 1976. "Wage Interdependence in Unionized Labor Markets." *Brookings Papers on Economic Activity* No. 3, pp. 635–73. Washington, D.C.: The Brookings Institution.

Freeman, Richard. 1980. "Unionism and the Dispersion of Wages." *Industrial and Labor Relations Review* 34, no. 10 (October): 3–23.

———. 1982. "Union Wage Practices and Wage Dispersion Within Establishments." *Industrial and Labor Relations Review* 36, no. 1 (October): 3–21.

Garbarino, Joseph W. 1962. *Wage Policy and Long-Term Contracts.* Washington, D.C.: The Brookings Institution.

Goldberg, Joseph. 1954. "A Review of American Labor in 1953." *MLR* 77, no. 2 (February): 121–27.

Groom, Phyllis. 1963. "American Labor in 1962; a Retrospect." *MLR* 86, no. 1 (January): 14–23.

Gurney, John L. 1970. "United Steelworkers of America." *MLR* 93, no. 12 (December): 33–34.

———. 1974. "Calendar of Wage Increases and Negotiations for 1974." *MLR* 97, no. 1 (January): 3–8.

Hamermesh, Daniel. 1970. "Wage Bargains, Threshold Effects and the Phillips Curve." *Quarterly Journal of Economics* 84, no. 3 (August): 501–17.

Helm, Donald L., and Richard G. Seefer. 1960. "Deferred Wage Increases and Escalator Clauses." *MLR* 83, no. 12 (December): 1268–71.

Hendricks, Wallace. 1981. "Unionism, Oligopoly and Rigid Wages." *Review of Economics and Statistics* 63, no. 2 (May): 198–205.

Hendricks, Wallace, and Lawrence M. Kahn. 1983. "Cost of Living Clauses in Union Contracts: Determinants and Effects." *Industrial and Labor Relations Review* 36, no. 3 (April): 447–60.

Jacoby, Sanford M., and Daniel J. B. Mitchell. 1983. "Are Long-Duration Contracts Insurance Against Strikes?" *MLR* 106, no. 4 (April): 28–29.

Katzen, Sally. 1981. "The Status of the Wage Guidelines." In *Proceedings of NYU 33rd Annual National Conference on Labor,* pp. 211–19. New York: Matthew Bender.

Kennedy, Thomas. 1970. "Freedom to Strike is in the Public Interest." *Harvard Business Review* 48, no. 4 (July–August): 45–57.

Knobloch, Merv. 1972. "Labor and the Economy in 1971." *MLR* 95, no. 1 (January): 15–27.

Kochan, Thomas. 1980. *Collective Bargaining and Industrial Relations.* Homewood, Ill.: Irwin.

Kramer, Lucy M., and James Nix. 1951. "Wage Escalators and the CPI." *MLR* 74, no. 5 (May): 509–13.

Kuhmerker, Peter. 1976. "Scheduled Wage Increases and Escalator Provisions in 1976." *MLR* 99, no. 1 (January): 42–48.

Kuntze, Ramona, and Louise Wilde. 1948. "The BLS Consumers' Price Index and Its Application to Wage Problems." *Wisconsin Commerce Reports* 2 (July): 1–70.

Lacombe II, John J., and James R. Conley. 1984. "Collective Bargaining Calendar Crowded Again in 1984." *MLR* 107, no. 1 (January): 19–32.

Larson, David, and Lena Bolton. 1973. "Calendar of Wage Increases and Negotiations for 1973." *MLR* 96, no. 1 (January,): 3–16.

Lauck, W. Jett. 1929. *The New Industrial Revolution and Wages.* New York and London: Funk and Wagnalls.

Leroy, Douglas R. 1977. "Scheduled Wage Increases and Escalator Provisions in 1977." *MLR* 100, no. 1 (January): 20–26.

———. 1978. "Scheduled Wage Increases and Escalator Provisions in 1978." *MLR* 101, no. 1 (January): 3–8.

———. 1981. "Scheduled Wage Increases and Cost-of-Living Provisions in 1981." *MLR* 104, no. 1 (January): 9–14.

———. 1982. "Scheduled Wage Increases and Cost-of-Living Provisions in 1982." *MLR* 105, no. 1 (January): 16–20.

Levin, Beth A. 1979. "Scheduled Wage Increases and Escalator Provisions in 1979." *MLR* 102, no. 1 (January): 20–25.

Lewis, H. Gregg. 1963. *Unionism and Relative Wages in the United States.* Chicago: University of Chicago Press.

Lowenstern, Henry. 1974. "Adjusting Wages to Living Costs: A Historical Note." *MLR* 97, no. 7 (July): 21–26.

"Major Agreement Expirations and Reopenings in 1962." 1961. *MLR* 84, no. 12 (December): 1309–18.

Merkin, Steven B. 1982. "The Evolution of COLA in the United States' System of Collective Bargaining." Unpublished manuscript, University of Illinois.

Mills, D. Quinn. 1978. *Labor–Management Relations.* New York: McGraw-Hill.

Munnell, Alicia. 1977. *The Future of Social Security.* Washington, D.C.: The Brookings Institution.

Nag, Amal, and Thomas O'Boyle. 1982. "USW's Rejection of a 3-Year Wage Freeze is Likely to Result in More Plant Closings." *Wall Street Journal.* (August 2).

National Industrial Conference Board (NICB). 1941. *Problems in Wage Adjustment,* Studies in Personnel Policy, No. 13. New York: NICB.

———. 1948. "Conference Board Management Record" (September).

———. 1951. *Cost of Living Provisions in Union Contracts,* Studies in Personnel Policy, No. 113. New York: NICB.

National War Labor Board. 1945. *Wage Report to the President on the Wartime Relationship of Wages to the Cost of Living.* Washington, D.C.: U.S. Government Printing Office.

Northrup, Herbert. 1963. "The Case for Boulwarism." *Harvard Business Review* 41, no. 5 (September–October): 86–97.

Pelling, Henry. 1960. *American Labor.* Chicago: University of Chicago Press.

Princeton University, Industrial Relations Section. 1939. "Changes in the Cost of Living and Wage Adjustments—A Selected List of References with Excerpts from Certain Studies." *Bibliographical Series No. 61,* (December, with Supplement to June 15, 1942): 1–22.

Reid, Frank. 1981. "Control and Decontrol of Wages in the United States." *American Economic Review* 71, no. 1 (March): 108–20.

Reynolds, Lloyd. 1982. *Labor Economics and Labor Relations,* 8th ed. Englewood Cliffs, N.J.: Prentice-Hall.

Ruben, George. 1962. "Deferred Wage Increases Due in 1963 and Wage Escalation." *MLR* 85, no. 12 (December): 1343–46.

———. 1965a. "Developments Under Major Bargaining Agreements, 1964." *MLR* 88, no. 10 (October): 1189–95.

———. 1965b. "Deferred Increases Due in 1965 and Wage Escalation." *MLR* 88, no. 12 (December): 1381–84.

———. 1967. "Wage Developments in Manufacturing, 1966." *MLR* 90, no. 8 (August): 31–38.

———. 1974. "Major Collective Bargaining Developments—A Quarter-Century Review." *Current Wage Developments* (February): 42–54.

———. 1982. "Organized Labor in 1981: A Shifting of Priorities." *MLR* 105, no. 1 (January): 21–28.

———. 1983. "Collective Bargaining in 1982: Results Dictated by Economy." *MLR* 106, no. 1 (January): 28–37.

Sachs, Jeffrey. 1980. "The Changing Cyclical Behavior of Wages and Prices." *American Economic Review* 70, no. 1 (March): 78–90.

Scheuch, Richard. 1981. *Labor in the American Economy.* New York: Harper & Row.

Seefer, Richard. 1961. "Deferred Wage Increases and Escalator Clauses." *MLR* 84, no. 12 (December): 1319–23.

Sheifer, Victor J. 1979. "Cost-of-Living Adjustment: Keeping Up With Inflation?" *MLR* 102, no. 6 (June): 14–17.

Shiskin, Julius. 1974. "Updating the Consumer Price Index—An Overview." *MLR* 97, no. 7 (July): 3–20.

Sparrough, Michael E., and Lena W. Bolton. 1972. "Calendar of Wage Increases and Negotiations for 1972." *MLR* 95, no. 1 (January): 3–8.

Spring, H. Charles. 1970. "Collective Bargaining Calendar for 1970." *MLR* 93, no. 1 (January): 13–19.

Staller, Jerome M., and Loren M. Solnick. 1975. "Treatment of Escalators Under Wage and Price Controls." In *Wage and Price Controls: The U.S. Experiment,* edited by J. Kraft and B. Roberts, pp. 70–79. New York: Praeger.

"Steel's Big Labor Savings Are Still Ahead." 1983. *Business Week* (March 14): 29, 33.

Stieber, Jack. 1959. "Evaluation of Long-Term Contracts." In *New Dimensions in Collective Bargaining,* edited by H. Davey, H. Kaltenborn, and S. Rutterban, pp. 137–53. New York: Industrial Relations Research Association.

Talbot, Joseph E. 1968. "Major Wage Developments in 1967." *MLR* 91, no. 7 (July): 9–16.

———. 1969. "An Analysis of 1968 Changes in Wages and Benefits." *MLR* 92, no. 7 (July): 43–48.

"The CPI's Confusing New Split Personality." 1983. *Business Week* (February 21): 39.

"The 1955 Ford and General Motors Union Contracts." 1955. *MLR* 78, no. 8 (August): 875–81.

"The Prevalence of Escalator Clauses and Experience with Them in the Past 20 Years." 1966. *MLR* 89, no. 9 (September): III–IV.

U.S. Bureau of Labor Statistics (USBLS). 1966. *Deferred Wage Increases and Escalator Clauses.* Bulletin No. 1925-4. Washington, D.C.: U.S. Government Printing Office.

———. 1980. *Employment and Earnings* (January).

———. 1981a. *Current Wage Developments* (January).

———. 1981b. *Current Wage Developments* (February).

———. 1981c. *Current Wage Developments* (April).

———. 1982. *Current Wage Developments* (April).

———. 1983. *Employment and Earnings* (January).

———. The following issues of the *Monthly Labor Review* were used as data sources:

    January, 1940 (vol. 63, no. 1)

    January, 1950 (vol. 73, no. 1)

    January, 1951 (vol. 74, no. 1)

    January, 1967 (vol. 90, no. 1)

    January, 1968 (vol. 91, no. 1)

    January, 1969 (vol. 92, no. 1)

    January, 1970 (vol. 93, no. 1)

    April and July, 1972 (vol. 95, nos. 4 and 7)

    April and July, 1973 (vol. 96, nos. 4 and 7)

    January and August, 1974 (vol. 97, nos. 1 and 8)

    July, 1979 (vol. 102, no. 7)

    July, 1980 (vol. 103, no. 7)

    January and May, 1982 (vol. 105, nos. 1 and 5)

    January, February and March, 1983 (vol. 106, nos. 1, 2, and 3)

    March, 1984 (vol. 107, no. 3)

    Every June issue from 1950 through 1982 (vols. 73–105, no. 6)

U.S. Bureau of the Census. 1975. *Historical Statistics of the United States, Part 1.* Washington, D.C.: U.S. Government Printing Office.

———. 1984. *Statistical Abstract of the United States, 1984.* Washington, D.C.: U.S. Government Printing Office.

Ward, Cordelia, and William Davis. 1966. "The Wage Calendar for 1967." *MLR* 89, no. 12 (December): 1339–46.

———. 1968. "The Wage Calendar for 1968." *MLR* 91, no. 1 (January): 20–27.

———. 1969. "Negotiations and Wage Calendar for 1969." *MLR* 92, no. 1 (January): 52–59.

Wasilewski, Edward. 1975. "Scheduled Wage Increases and Escalator Provisions in 1975." *MLR* 98, no. 1 (January): 43–48.

———. 1980. "Scheduled Wage Increases and Escalator Provisions in 1980." *MLR* 103, no. 1 (January): 9–13.

Weber, Arnold. 1963. "The Craft-Industrial Issue Revisited: A Study of Union Government." *Industrial and Labor Relations Review* 16, no. 3 (April): 381–404.

Weeks, David A. 1976. *Compensating Employees: Lessons of the 1970s.* New York: The Conference Board, Inc.

Williams, Leroy D., and Alfred B. Holt. 1919. "Cost of Living in Relation to Wage Adjustments — A Research Made at the Holt Manufacturing Company, Inc., Peoria, Ill." *Bulletin of the Taylor Society* (October): 29–46.

Chapter 3

Current Characteristics of Colas

The previous chapter described and analyzed the history of wage indexation in U.S. collective bargaining. It was primarily concerned with the presence or absence of Colas and their average characteristics in the aggregate for various time periods. This chapter makes a more detailed study of Colas' characteristics during recent years. It begins with a description of the unique data base used in this and subsequent chapters. The data are then used to examine Cola characteristics along a number of dimensions (such as Cola incidence, types of formulas, timing of Cola reviews, and minimum and maximum adjustments), as well as to compare these traits in various settings. The importance of these factors has been noted in Chapter 2. These characteristics are then broken down by factors such as union, industry, and bargaining structure in order to provide some information on the locus of various types of indexation.

THE DATA BASE

Our data on Cola provisions in individual collective bargaining agreements come from four major sources. The primary source is the collective bargaining agreement file kept by the U.S. Bureau of Labor Statistic (BLS) in Washington, D.C.[1] This file contains copies of all agreements covering over 1,000 workers ("major" contracts). Until recently, the file also contained a large number of nonmajor (under

1,000 workers) contracts. Luckily, we were able to obtain a great deal of information on these latter contracts before they were excluded from the file.

The major advantage of using actual agreements is that all provisions of Colas can be gathered. These provisions include the timing of adjustments; the formula used; floors, ceilings, or "corridors" applicable to the Cola; the particular CPI used (e.g., U.S. 1967 = 100 or Los Angeles 1957–59 = 100); as well as any changes in the provisions over the life of the contract. In addition, starting and ending dates are available to compute length as well as associated time series variables from other data sources. These agreements also typically contain wage level information (manufacturing only) which is crucial in some stages of our analysis. In all, data were obtained on 3,588 collective bargaining relationships in both manufacturing (2,638 union–management pairs) and nonmanufacturing (950 pairs) over the period of 1967–82. The data base yielded information on 7,797 individual negotiations in manufacturing and 3,270 in nonmanufacturing. In addition, the BLS has provided certain additional information about each bargaining relationship (e.g., number of workers covered, union, bargaining unit type, four-digit industry Standard Industrial Classification (SIC) code). This information is used directly in our analysis and also allows matching to other data sets.

Our second source of Cola and wage data is the *Daily Labor Report* of the Bureau of National Affairs (BNA). The BNA provides varying information on Colas and wage changes for contracts on a biweekly basis. This information covers a large number of contract relationships but does not identify the detailed industry, does not provide wage level data by detailed occupation, and only rarely gives full Cola information. Company and union names, dates of the contract, and region of the country are matched with the BLS information. The BNA information allows us to fill in gaps in our BLS data and to update continually the original data source. Our third source is the *Wage Chronologies* series published by the BLS. These provide ready access to all the necessary information but are available on only a small number of bargaining relationships. Finally, the BLS's *Current Wage Developments* series allows us to expand the sample.

Wage and Cola information from these sources is augmented in several ways using other data sources. Our first augmentation is the attachment of a variety of industry and demographic characteristics to each contract by using the four-digit SIC code. Industry characteristics include market structure variables, such as concentration ratio (manufacturing only) and degree of unionization as well as occupational, demographic, and regional variables associated with workers in the industry. A final industry characteristic is time series data on wholesale prices for the industry (manufacturing only).

REPRESENTATIVENESS OF THE CONTRACTS IN OUR SAMPLE

Since our sample represents the only available information on a number of characteristics of Colas, it is worthwhile to compare some of its characteristics to available data sources to determine if it is representative of U.S. collective bargaining in the private sector.

Summary statistics on union contracts are collected by the BLS for major agreements only. Although there are no corresponding data sources with which to compare the nonmajor contracts of our sample, we can compare the characteristics of major agreements in our sample with those in published sources. In several respects, our sample is quite similar to the BLS's random sample of major agreements, although our file has wage and Cola information not found anywhere else. First, according to the BLS (1977), among major private sector agreements in 1975, 53.8 percent of contracts and 53.1 percent of workers were in manufacturing. When our total sample is restricted to major agreements, the corresponding figures are 54 percent of agreements and 54.7 percent of workers—figures quite close to those of the BLS.[2]

Second, and most important, is the comparison of Cola coverage and characteristics among contracts in our sample (Table 3-1) with the BLS figures given in Table 2-7. Table 3-1 breaks Cola coverage down by year and sector, for all contracts in our sample and for major contracts only. Each entry is the percentage of workers who, as of January of a given year, had Cola coverage, the same figure computed by the BLS (Table 2-7). Workers in manufacturing are substantially more likely than those in nonmanufacturing to have Colas. In addition, Cola coverage is slightly higher among major agreements than among our entire sample, suggesting that large bargaining units are more likely to have Colas. This hypothesis is tested in more detail in Chapter 6. Finally, comparison of Table 3-1 for major agreements and the BLS's figures in Table 2-7 shows a remark-

Table 3-1. Cola Coverage by Year for Existing Contracts (as of January of each year).

		All Contracts Percentage of Workers with Colas			
Year	Manufacturing	Number of Contracts	Nonmanufacturing	Number of Contracts	Total
1971	42.4%	(736)	3.7%	(25)	41.1%
1972	43.4	(948)	47.3	(167)	44.2
1973	60.6	(1,087)	51.6	(321)	57.7
1974	59.0	(1,330)	41.5	(479)	52.2
1975	61.5	(1,704)	39.3	(645)	51.9
1976	68.4	(2,215)	44.8	(787)	57.4
1977	67.9	(2,445)	44.4	(862)	56.9
1978	71.2	(2,494)	45.4	(869)	59.0
1979	71.2	(2,154)	44.1	(873)	58.0
1980	72.0	(1,811)	42.7	(862)	57.4
1981	77.2	(1,375)	41.9	(844)	59.3
1982	79.2	(1,034)	40.1	(790)	59.4

		Major Agreements Only[a] Percentage of Workers with Colas			
Year	Manufacturing	Number of Contracts	Nonmanufacturing	Number of Contracts	Total
1971	43.7%	(463)	2.8%	(24)	42.2%
1972	44.6	(564)	47.3	(156)	45.1
1973	62.4	(588)	51.7	(299)	58.8
1974	61.1	(639)	41.7	(444)	53.2
1975	64.1	(695)	39.6	(587)	52.9
1976	72.0	(788)	45.1	(715)	58.6
1977	71.7	(811)	44.8	(777)	58.1
1978	76.1	(794)	45.7	(779)	60.5
1979	75.6	(757)	44.3	(785)	59.4
1980	75.3	(759)	42.9	(776)	58.4
1981	79.5	(733)	42.1	(765)	59.8
1982	80.4	(672)	40.4	(722)	59.7

[a] Major Agreements are those covering at least 1,000 workers.

Source: Authors' data base.

Table 3–2. Characteristics of Existing Colas by Year in Major Contracts.

Year	Percentage of Reviews that were:			Percentage of Colas with:	
	Quarterly	Semiannual	Annual	Minimum	Maximum
1971	28.8%	11.9%	55.1%	34.7%	72.4%
1972	30.5	10.3	54.6	18.0	61.5
1973	51.9	6.3	39.6	25.4	30.3
1974	52.6	6.7	37.4	23.3	28.5
1975	46.8	8.3	35.3	26.2	34.0
1976	48.1	11.6	37.2	11.8	34.6
1977	48.6	12.3	35.6	11.7	35.9
1978	48.1	12.0	36.5	7.2	27.8
1979	47.6	10.6	38.5	7.0	22.6
1980	48.3	9.8	39.1	7.6	20.8
1981	48.3	18.6	30.6	7.2	20.0
1982	48.5	18.8	30.1	6.6	18.8

Note: Percentages might add to more than 100 because some contracts have both a minimum and a maximum Cola payment.

Source: Authors' data base.

able similarity in the percentage of workers with Colas, especially in the years with the largest sample sizes.

Our sample of contracts with Colas appears representative in its characteristics as well. Table 3–2 shows the incidence of two of these characteristics for major contracts in our data. It is directly comparable to the BLS data on major contracts depicted in Tables 2–8 and 2–9. Our sample and the BLS estimates show the same shift from annual to quarterly reviews over the 1970s and early 1980s. The orders of magnitude of the various review periods are also similar in the two samples.[3] Further, the incidence of minimum and maximum Cola payments in our data falls over the 1970s and 1980s, as do the BLS figures in Table 2–9. In both samples the incidence of minimums falls from 30 to 40 percent to less than 10 percent and that of maximum adjustments falls from about 70 percent to about 20 percent. The close correspondence over time of the Cola characteristics increases our confidence of having collected a representative sample of contracts.

The third test of representativeness is a comparison of other aspects of our sample of contracts with published BLS sources. For example, in our sample of major agreements, the average numbers of workers covered in manufacturing and nonmanufacturing were, respectively, 4,727 and 4,609. In the BLS sample of 1975 major contracts, the corresponding figures were 4,602 and 4,748 (BLS 1977). In addition, in our data for major contracts, roughly 13 percent of manufacturing and 69 percent of nonmanufacturing agreements were multiemployer; the BLS figures for 1975 are 19 percent and 71 percent. Again, the representativeness of our data base is underscored.

CHARACTERISTICS OF THE DATA – COLA INCIDENCE

Table 3-3 shows the incidence of Colas and reopeners by sector and year of negotiation. For example, the table indicates that 68.7 percent of manufacturing contracts negotiated in 1980 had Colas and 1.5 percent had reopeners. Unlike published BLS data, or the figures in Table 3-1, these data portray changes at the margin. Each year's negotiations are depicted.

The percentage of workers with Colas is almost invariably larger than the percentage of indexed contracts, again reflecting a positive association between bargaining unit size and wage indexation. The incidence of Colas is also much greater in manufacturing industries. This difference in coverage will be discussed further when indexation across particular industries is compared.

These figures show a general rising trend, although the increase is not monotonic. In particular, there is a much higher incidence of Colas for the years 1967, 1970-71, 1973-74, 1976-77, and 1979-80 than for the other years. This pattern undoubtedly reflects the bargaining calendars of the United Auto Workers (UAW), United Steelworkers (USW), and Teamsters. The UAW negotiated its basic agreements in 1967, 1970, 1973, 1976, and 1979; the other two unions each signed three-year contracts for 1968, 1971, et cetera. The low 1968 Cola incidence for manufacturing is due to the fact that the USW did not reintroduce their Cola until the 1971 contract (see Chapter 2). The overall pattern is also evident for nonmanufacturing industries. This

Table 3–3. Incidence of Colas by Year of Negotiation (all contracts, regardless of size).

Year of Negotiation	Manufacturing					Nonmanufacturing				
	Total Contracts	Percentage of Contracts with Cola	Percentage of Contracts with Reopener	Percentage of Workers with Cola	Percentage of Workers with Reopener	Total Contracts	Percentage of Contracts with Cola	Percentage of Contracts with Reopener	Percentage of Workers with Cola	Percentage of Workers with Reopener
1966	21	33.3%	0.0%	48.6%	0.0%	—	—	—	—	—
1967	165	24.8	0.5	69.2	0.1	—	—	—	—	—
1968	366	24.6	1.6	21.5	1.0	1	0.0%	0.0%	0.0%	0.0%
1969	266	18.0	5.3	19.4	8.0	20	10.0	5.0	4.6	2.8
1970	314	30.9	3.8	63.7	1.3	135	26.7	3.7	52.9	1.6
1971	618	45.3	10.0	62.2	3.9	158	31.7	3.8	56.0	5.1
1972	402	26.9	2.0	29.1	2.8	198	5.6	7.1	15.2	9.0
1973	775	37.5	7.7	63.7	3.6	289	21.5	5.9	44.8	5.0
1974	1,067	58.0	0.5	80.3	0.5	412	30.8	1.9	50.1	1.2
1975	769	29.9	7.2	35.6	6.8	294	12.2	4.8	22.7	9.4
1976	790	41.5	1.6	71.1	4.1	330	24.9	2.4	46.5	5.1
1977	928	49.5	5.0	74.8	2.4	376	31.4	1.1	46.2	0.7
1978	295	44.7	3.4	52.9	5.1	289	14.5	1.7	17.7	4.2
1979	365	50.7	16.4	78.1	6.8	256	28.1	0.8	50.1	0.2
1980	453	68.7	1.5	85.4	1.3	329	30.1	1.5	43.2	1.1
1981	202	46.0	7.4	43.8	5.6	181	11.6	1.7	11.0	1.0
1982	0	—	—	—	—	2	0.0	0.0	0.0	0.0
Total	7,796	42.6	4.1	63.6	3.1	3,270	23.2	2.8	40.0	3.3

Note: The entries in this table refer to contracts negotiated in a given year.

Source: Cola data base compiled by the authors (see text).

similarity is due in part to the fact that the USW and Teamsters have many nonmanufacturing contracts and in part may be due to some pattern-following behavior on the part of nonmanufacturing unions. Unlike the Cola pattern, the incidence of reopeners shows no obvious patterns over time or for the contracts–workers comparison. Reopeners are far less frequent than Colas or contracts with no Cola or reopener. In later analyses, contracts with reopeners are treated as being nonindexed because wage adjustments in these contracts are discretionary.

Tables 3–4 and 3–5 illustrate Cola coverage by industry and by union, respectively. In addition, Table 3–4 contains data on reopeners by industry. The tables permit several conclusions. First, in manufacturing, indexation is concentrated in metal industries, machinery, and transportation equipment. Of the 3,319 contracts with Colas, 2,446 (73.7 percent) were in these industries. These sectors are relatively highly unionized and have high product market concentration and large firm size. In nonmanufacturing, several interesting findings emerge. The largest number of contracts in this sector comes from construction: 1,446 of the 3,270 (44.2 percent) of the nonmanufacturing contracts are in construction. Yet only 63 (i.e., 4.4 percent) construction constracts have Colas, accounting for only 8.4 percent of the Colas in nonmanufacturing. Construction is characterized by many multiemployer contracts with several unions involved. In nonmanufacturing, Cola coverage is not as concentrated as it is for manufacturing, with sectors such as trucking, communications, and food stores accounting for the largest numbers of Colas. These three industries also have a relatively high incidence of indexation. Second, in manufacturing, reopeners are most frequent in petroleum, where 59 percent of the contracts had reopeners. Coincidentally, 59 percent of the reopeners in our manufacturing sample were in petroleum. Among nonmanufacturing industries, reopeners are more common in retail trade and services than in other sectors.

Third, Cola incidence by union (Table 3–5) follows that for industries. In manufacturing, the Machinists, UAW, and USW together account for 52.2 percent of the Colas. In nonmanufacturing, Cola coverage is more spread out across unions (as it was for industries), with the Teamsters carrying the largest share (23.2 percent) of the Colas.

It is interesting to note that our findings regarding the incidence of Colas in the United States are similar to results from a study of

1968–75 Canadian collective bargaining agreements. Wilton (1979) examined a sample of 1,405 individual Canadian contract negotiations over this period and obtained similar results to those of our larger sample of U.S. agreements. In his sample the percentage of workers with Colas under newly signed contracts rose steadily from 15.9 percent in 1968 to 62 percent. Table 3–3 shows a similar rise for the United States over these years except for low figures in 1972 and 1975 (and 1978 and 1981 as well). Evidently, in the United States there is a stronger correlation between Cola incidence and the bargaining calendar than in Canada, with 1972, 1975, 1978, and 1981 being off years for the United States. Of course, an overall similarity between the two countries might be expected, since unions such as the UAW and USW have many Canadian contracts (Card 1983).

COMPARISON OF INDEXED AND NONINDEXED CONTRACTS

Table 3–6 compares various characteristics of contracts with Colas and those without Colas. Some important differences between indexed and nonindexed contracts emerge from the table. As expected, a typical indexed contract covers far more workers than a typical contract with no Cola: The ratios for average size of indexed relative to nonindexed contracts are 2.36 in manufacturing and 2.21 in nonmanufacturing. The size of nonmanufacturing agreements in our sample is much larger than for manufacturing, reflecting the greater coverage in the latter sector of nonmajor agreements.[4] Indexed bargaining units also are less likely to be located in the South or outside large SMSAs (standard metropolitan statistical areas) than those without Colas, are more likely than those without Colas to be negotiated with a single employer or to be negotiated in industries organized by only one union, and occur in industries with higher concentration ratios than contracts without Colas.

Indexed agreements have four to five months longer average duration than nonindexed contracts. Canadian data show a similar discrepancy between the contract lengths of agreements with Colas and that of nonindexed agreements. Wilton (1979) found that among newly signed agreements in each year between 1968 and 1975, except 1974, average duration for contracts with Colas was 4.6 to 10.4 months

Table 3-4.   Cola Incidence by Two-Digit SIC Code 1966-81.

Manufacturing

SIC Code	Industry	Percentage of Contracts with Cola	Percentage with Wage Reopener	Number of Contracts
20	Food and kindred products	31	2	819
21	Tobacco manufactures	74	4	54
22	Textile mill products	16	10	120
23	Apparel and other finished products	9	19	200
24	Lumber and wood products, except furniture	9	0	213
25	Furniture and fixtures	34	2	131
26	Paper and allied products	4	2	750
27	Printing and publishing	28	0	69
28	Chemicals and allied products	24	6	539
29	Petroleum, refining	1	59	374
30	Rubber and miscellaneous plastics products	34	2	151
31	Leather and leather products	5	5	65
32	Stone, clay, glass, and concrete products	47	1	415
33	Primary metal industries	70	.2	899
34	Fabricated metal products	49	.3	459
35	Machinery, except electrical	66	1	902
36	Electrical machinery	64	0	704
37	Transportation equipment	79	1	692
38	Measuring instruments	25	0	133
39	Miscellaneous manufacturing industries	18	8	108
	Total	43	5	7,797

Nonmanufacturing

SIC Code	Industry	Percentage of Contracts with Cola	Percentage with Wage Reopener	Number of Contracts
1	Agricultural crop production	100	0	2
9	Fishing, hunting, and trapping	0	0	2
10	Metalmining	80	0	55
11	Anthracite mining	100	0	3
12	Bituminous coal, lignite	33	0	3
14	Mining, nonmetallic minerals	0	0	10
15	Building construction (general)	3	2	575
16	Construction (other)	7	1	353

Table 3-4. (Continued)

Nonmanufacturing (continued)

SIC Code	Industry	Percentage of Contracts with Cola	Percentage with Wage Reopener	Number of Contracts
17	Construction — special trade	4	.4	518
19	Ordnance	71	0	52
41	Local and suburban transit and interurban highway passenger transit	43	0	30
42	Trucking, warehousing	89	0	168
44	Water transport	6	0	51
45	Air transport	33	0	3
48	Communications	67	0	213
49	Electric, gas, and sanitary	10	5	329
50	Wholesale trade — durable	41	0	41
52	Retail trade — building materials	100	0	2
53	General merchandise stores	38	0	45
54	Food stores	51	2	324
55	Automotive dealers, service	4	24	25
56	Apparel and accessory stores	0	0	13
58	Eating and drinking places	3	21	75
59	Miscellaneous retail	6	20	15
60	Banking	0	0	3
62	Security, commodity brokers	100	0	3
63	Insurance carriers	27	4	26
65	Real estate	39	4	28
70	Hotels, lodging	0	10	61
72	Personal services	0	4	24
73	Business services	20	2	56
75	Auto repair, services, garages	0	0	7
76	Miscellaneous repair services	33	0	9
78	Motion pictures	6	4	49
79	Amusement, recreation	14	5	21
80	Health services	21	12	61
82	Education services	0	0	5
86	Membership organizations	0	0	2
89	Miscellaneous services	25	25	8
	Total	23	3	3,270

Source: Authors' data base (see text).

Table 3-5.   Cola Incidence by Union, 1966-81.

Manufacturing[a]

Code	Union	Number of Contracts	Percentage with Cola
107	Allied Industrial Workers (AIW)	141	74
108	Bakery Workers	174	9
119	Carpenters	153	26
121	Chemical Workers	124	23
127	Brotherhood of Electrical Workers (IBEW)	352	55
134	Ladies' Garment Workers (ILGWU)	143	3
135	Glass Bottle Blowers	103	59
155	Meat Cutters (Retail Clerks)	220	57
218	Machinists (IAM)	725	58
231	Paperworkers	443	5
333	Rubber Workers	136	32
335	Steelworkers (USW)	1167	63
337	Clothing and Textile Workers ((AC)TWU)	126	14
347	Electrical, Radio and Machine Workers (IUE)	213	47
357	Oil, Chemical and Atomic Workers (OCAW)	444	12
527	Western Pulp and Paper	127	0
531	Teamsters	344	24
553	Auto Workers (UAW)	669	86

Nonmanufacturing[b]

Code	Union	Number of Contracts	Percentage with Cola
100	Two or more AFL-CIO unions	43	9
112	Boilermakers	36	8
115	Bricklayers	61	0
116	Ironworkers	89	8
118	Service Employees	122	19
119	Carpenters	313	2
127	Electrical Workers (IBEW)	356	15
129	Engineers, Operating	178	4
143	Laborers	299	4
145	Hotel and Restaurant Employees	120	0
155	Meat Cutters[c]	135	46
162	Musicians	26	0

Table 3-5. (Continued)

Nonmanufacturing (continued)

Code	Union	Number of Contracts	Percentage with Cola
164	Painters	41	17
168	Plasterers and Cement Masons	20	0
170	Plumbers	155	1
184	Retail Clerks[c]	183	53
187	Sheet Metal Workers	45	9
218	Machinists	44	57
239	Longshoremen's Association	34	0
332	Retail Wholesale and Department Store Union	32	16
335	Steelworkers (NSW)	56	70
342	Utility Workers	28	36
346	Communications Workers	90	72
500	National Federation of Independent Unions	49	24
516	Telephone Unions; Independent	27	100
531	Teamsters	313	56
600	Two or more unions – different affiliations	68	28
903	Nurses	24	21

[a] For manufacturing unions with greater than 100 contracts listed.

[b] For nonmanufacturing unions with at least 20 contracts listed.

[c] Meat Cutters and Retail Clerks have merged.

Source: Authors' data base (see text).

longer than in nonindexed contracts. In 1974 the latter actually had 2.6 months longer duration than contracts with Colas. The corresponding differential in our data (1968–75) ranged from 2.6 months in 1969 to 6.4 months in 1968 and 1974. Overall, computations we performed using Wilton's (1979) reported data showed an average duration of 27.8 months for indexed contracts and 24.9 months for contracts without Colas – smaller duration averages than our U.S. figures in Table 3-6. Finally, Wilton's data indicated a decline in duration from 1968 to 1975 for contracts with Colas (duration fell

Table 3-6. Average Characteristics of Indexed and Nonindexed Contracts, 1966–81.

Variable	Manufacturing		Nonmanufacturing	
	Without Cola	With Cola	Without Cola	With Cola
SIZE[a]	1482.8	3501.6	3307.9	7295.4
SOUTH[b]	.223	.124	.146	.108
MULTI[c]	.119	.054	.754	.488
%UNION[d]	.723	.773	.500	.474
CR8[e]	.496	.589	—	—
CONSOL[f]	.556	.589	.460	.673
CRAFT[g]	.255	.280	.389	.181
OPER[h]	.569	.574	.089	.245
SMSA[i]	.345	.391	.310	.344
MAR[j]	.791	.781	.681	.695
MALE[k]	.803	.833	.821	.748
WHITE[l]	.874	.865	.907	.911
ED[m]	11.4	11.5	12.0	12.1
EXP[n]	23.7	23.0	19.9	20.1
CHILD[o]	1.27	1.29	.986	1.023
DURATION[p]	30.983	35.280	30.387	35.236
WAGE[q]	4.153	5.198	—	—

Note: For nonmanufacturing, the variables CRAFT through CHILD are computed for all workers in the industry due to insufficient numbers of union workers in these industries.

[a] SIZE = number of workers covered by the contract (as of 1975).

[b] SOUTH = dummy variable referring to location of the bargaining unit in the South.

[c] MULTI = dummy variable referring to multiemployer bargaining units.

[d] % UNION = fraction of the three-digit industry's workers covered by collective bargaining.

[e] CR8 = eight-firm concentration ratio for the four-digit SIC.

[f] CONSOL = fraction of union workers in the three-digit industry organized by the largest union.

[g] CRAFT = fraction of the three-digit industry's union workers who are craftsmen.

[h] OPER = fraction of the three-digit industry's union workers who are operators.

[i] SMSA = fraction of the three-digit industry's union workers who live in the thirty-four largest SMSAs.

from 34.1 to 28.4 months), as well as for nonindexed agreements (23.7 months to 19.6 months). Our data also show a slight decline in duration from 1968 to 1975 that had reversed itself by 1981. For example, duration in our U.S. sample behaved as follows over the period: For contracts with Colas, duration figures were 36.1 months (1968), 34.9 months (1975), and 35.8 months (1981); the corresponding figures for contracts without Colas were 33.9 months (1968), 28.7 months (1975), and 31.9 months (1981).

The occupational and demographic data do not show strong patterns, with the exceptions of *CRAFT, OPER,* and *MALE* in the nonmanufacturing sector. For this sector, contracts with Colas are more likely to be in industries with smaller percentages of craftsmen, larger percentages of operators, and smaller percentages of men. Finally, in manufacturing, wage levels for indexed contracts are about 25 percent higher than those in contracts without Colas.

Tables 3-7 and 3-8 give a more detailed comparison of wages in indexed and nonindexed contracts. The first of these tables indicates that while nominal wages have risen substantially from 1969 to 1981, real wages were on average about the same in 1981 as in 1969. Recall

---

Notes to Table 3-6 (continued).

[j] *MAR* = fraction of the three-digit industry's union workers who are married, spouse present.

[k] *MALE* = fraction of the three-digit industry's union workers who are male.

[l] *WHITE* = fraction of the three-digit industry's union workers who are white.

[m] *ED* = average grades of school completed by the three-digit industry's union workers.

[n] *EXP* = average of (age–ED–5) for the three-digit industry's union workers.

[o] *CHILD* = average number of children for the three-digit industry's union workers.

[p] *DURATION* = duration of the agreement in months.

[q] *WAGE* = hourly wage level for janitors or laborers (including Cola payments) at the end of the previous contract.

Sources: SIZE, SOUTH, MULTI, WAGE, CONSOL, and *DURATION* are all taken either directly from the contracts or from the BLS tape summarizing the contract information. *CONSOL* is an estimate of the true figures because of incomplete coverage by industry. Concentration data come from U.S. Department of Commerce *1972 Census of Manufactures* 1972. Unionization is computed from Freeman and Medoff 1979 and the BLS *Industry Wage Series* (various issues). Data for the rest of the variables for manufacturing were provided by Medoff's computation using the 1973-1975 *Current Population Surveys.* For nonmanufacturing, we obtained the 1979 *Current Population Survey* tapes to compute these variables.

Table 3-7. Average Nominal and Real Hourly Wage by Year of Negotiation and Cola Status, Manufacturing Only.

| Year of Negotiation | Wage Level | | | | |
| | Cola (1) | | No Cola (2) | | |
	Nominal	Real	Nominal	Real	(1)/(2)
1969	$3.32	$3.02	$2.75	$2.50	1.207
1970	3.26	2.80	2.67	2.30	1.221
1971	3.49	2.88	3.08	2.54	1.133
1972	3.61	2.88	3.02	2.41	1.195
1973	4.27	3.21	3.51	2.64	1.217
1974	4.51	3.05	3.51	2.37	1.285
1975	4.37	2.71	3.84	2.38	1.138
1976	4.94	2.90	4.02	2.36	1.229
1977	5.99	3.30	4.77	2.63	1.256
1978	6.56	3.36	5.08	2.60	1.291
1979	7.28	3.35	5.85	2.69	1.244
1980	7.22	2.92	6.21	2.52	1.163
1981	7.88	2.89	7.10	2.61	1.110
Total	5.20	3.08	4.15	2.50	1.252 (nominal) 1.232 (real)

Note: Wages are for janitors and laborers and are measured as of the expiration of the previous contract. Any Cola payments from the previous contract are included in the wage. Real wages are in 1967 dollars. For any year, the ratio of nominal wages for contracts with Colas to that for contracts without Colas equals the ratio for real wages. The average real and nominal wages differ because the number of contracts negotiated varies by year.

Source: Authors' data base.

from Table 2-11 that average real hourly wages for production and nonsupervisory workers in the United States (union and nonunion) *fell* from $2.77 to $2.66 (1967 dollars) during this period. In addition, newly negotiated contracts with Colas have had 11 to 29 percent higher wage levels than nonindexed contracts, although the differential appeared to be declining from 1978 to 1981. Table 3-8 breaks down wages by industry and Cola status. For each industry except lumber, wages in contracts with Colas were higher than in nonindexed agreements. The industries with the largest wage differentials are tobacco, leather, metals, machinery, and transportation equipment.

Table 3-8. Average Nominal and Real Hourly Wage by Industry and Cola States, Manufacturing, 1969-81.

Industry	Nominal Wage Level Cola (1)	No Cola (2)	(2)/(3)	Real Wage Level (1967 dollars) Cola (4)	No Cola (5)	(4)/(5)
20 Food	$5.65	$4.40	1.284	$3.38	$2.58	1.310
21 Tobacco	5.27	2.37	2.224	2.85	1.47	1.939
22 Textiles	3.99	2.90	1.376	2.30	1.78	1.292
23 Apparel	3.09	2.61	1.184	1.71	1.64	1.043
24 Lumber	4.09	4.40	0.930	2.51	2.59	0.969
25 Furniture	4.34	3.30	1.315	2.37	1.94	1.222
26 Paper	5.00	4.69	1.066	2.87	2.68	1.071
27 Printing	4.58	3.95	1.159	2.73	2.19	1.247
28 Chemicals	5.42	4.64	1.168	3.07	2.76	1.112
29 Petroleum	6.67	5.01	1.331	3.91	3.16	1.237
30 Rubber	6.20	3.78	1.640	3.30	2.61	1.264
31 Leather	6.68	2.54	2.630	3.43	1.64	2.091
32 Stone, glass, clay, concrete	5.22	3.81	1.370	3.02	2.38	1.269
33 Primary metal	5.01	3.92	1.278	3.18	2.38	1.336
34 Fabricated metal	5.13	3.82	1.343	3.04	2.35	1.294
35 Machinery, except electrical	5.41	3.82	1.416	3.11	2.23	1.395
36 Electrical machinery	4.61	3.29	1.401	2.65	2.19	1.210
37 Transportation equipment	5.71	4.27	1.337	3.38	2.46	1.374
38 Measuring instruments	4.19	3.80	1.103	2.61	2.21	1.181
39 Miscellaneous manufacturing	4.04	3.02	1.338	2.34	1.85	1.265
Total	5.20	4.15	1.252	3.08	2.50	1.232

Note: See note to Table 3-7. Ratios of real and nominal wages are not identical in this case because each industry's negotiations are pooled across years.

Source: Authors' data base.

The data in Tables 3-6, 3-7, and 3-8 are not intended to test any hypotheses about the determinants of indexation. Rather, they are included to give the reader a picture as to the locus of wage indexation. In Chapter 6 these hypotheses are tested using multivariate analyses.

CHARACTERISTICS OF COLAS

This data base allows a closer look at the characteristics of Colas. As already indicated, there is substantial variety in the types of wage indexation. For example, the presence of minimum or maximum adjustments, the timing of reviews, and the properties of the formulas themselves can have major effects on the yield of Colas.

The presence of a minimum or maximum Cola adjustment provision can greatly influence the inflation protection a Cola gives. Maximum adjustments are a way of limiting the response of wages to prices beyond some level of inflation. On the other hand, minimum adjustments assure workers of wage increases even in the absence of inflation. Triggers or corridors can be viewed as a compromise between labor and management. For example, many Colas in our sample do not yield payments until inflation has reached a certain level (trigger). Workers' wages are insured only for that portion of inflation above the trigger. A corridor is a range for inflation such that there is no Cola yield in that interval (e.g., 7 to 9 percent in some electrical equipment contracts). Triggers and corridors can be a method for causing the degree of inflation protection offered by a Cola to change over the life of a contract. Caps and delays in Cola reviews can serve this purpose as well.

Table 3–9 illustrates the incidence of various Cola characteristics by year of contract negotiation and sector. Nonmanufacturing has a slightly lower frequency of caps but a substantially higher incidence of triggers and corridors than manufacturing. These findings are very close to those in the Canadian data described earlier. Between 1968 and 1975, in Canadian manufacturing, 38.1 percent of the Colas had caps and 8.9 percent had triggers; for nonmanufacturing the figures were 27.8 percent with caps and 22.8 percent with triggers (Card 1983). In addition, manufacturing in our sample has a slightly lower extent of minimum adjustments than nonmanufacturing. Further, Table 3–9 shows a gradually declining incidence of caps, particularly in manufacturing, since 1975. In Canada there was a sharp decline from 1972 to 1975 (Card 1983).

Table 3–10 illustrates the incidence of minimum and maximum adjustments among Colas by industry of negotiation. Maximum adjustment provisions appear especially common in the light manufacturing and service industries, with additional concentrations in trucking; stone, clay, glass, and concrete; chemicals; and electrical

Table 3-9. Characteristics of Colas by Year of Negotiation.

Manufacturing

Year	Number of Contracts with Cola	Percentage with No Maximum or Minimum	Percentage with Minimum	Percentage with Maximum	Percentage with Trigger or Corridor
1966	7	0.0%	14.3%	14.3%	0.0%
1967	41	29.3	31.7	39.0	2.4
1968	90	10.0	28.9	56.7	6.7
1969	48	8.3	12.5	60.4	0.0
1970	97	59.8	8.3	33.0	4.1
1971	280	46.4	32.5	18.6	6.1
1972	108	50.9	11.1	42.6	12.0
1973	291	52.9	9.3	42.6	7.2
1974	619	64.9	4.4	31.8	4.4
1975	230	45.7	9.1	49.6	11.3
1976	328	65.6	4.9	32.9	14.0
1977	459	75.2	4.1	20.5	3.9
1978	132	59.1	14.4	29.6	9.1
1979	185	76.8	3.2	17.3	18.4
1980	311	83.9	2.9	14.8	10.9
1981	93	67.7	8.6	28.0	18.3
Total	3,319	61.3	9.3	30.3	8.3

Nonmanufacturing

Year	Number of Contracts with Cola	Percentage with No Maximum or Minimum	Percentage with Minimum	Percentage with Maximum	Percentage with Trigger or Corridor
1969	2	100.0%	0.0%	0.0%	100.0%
1970	36	22.2	0.0	77.8	25.0
1971	50	86.0	6.0	8.0	18.0
1972	11	63.6	0.0	36.4	18.2
1973	62	32.3	54.8	66.1	17.7
1974	127	75.6	11.8	19.7	22.8
1975	36	63.9	8.3	36.1	33.3
1976	82	86.6	8.5	12.2	15.9
1977	118	78.0	10.2	17.0	14.4
1978	42	69.1	4.8	31.0	35.7
1979	72	73.6	8.3	23.6	18.1
1980	99	76.8	11.1	18.2	19.2
1981	21	52.4	14.3	42.9	14.3
Total	758	70.1	12.7	26.7	20.3

Note: Percentages might add to more than 100 because some Colas have more than one of the indicated provisions.

Source: Authors' data base.

Table 3-10. Characteristics of Colas by Industry, 1966-81.

		Manufacturing			
	Industry	Number of Contracts with Cola	Percentage with No Maximum or Minimum	Percentage with Minimum	Percentage with Maximum	Percentage with Trigger or Corridor
20	Food	233	63.2%	5.6%	28.4%	11.6%
21	Tobacco	33	37.5	2.5	45.0	7.5
22	Textiles	17	47.4	0.0	42.1	31.6
23	Apparel	18	22.2	11.1	77.8	83.3
24	Lumber	18	36.8	0.0	57.9	5.3
25	Furniture	41	40.9	4.6	52.3	9.1
26	Paper	28	65.6	6.3	31.3	21.9
27	Printing	19	84.2	5.3	10.5	26.3
28	Chemicals	122	55.8	7.0	39.5	12.4
29	Petroleum	2	0.0	0.0	100.0	0.0
30	Rubber	48	72.6	3.9	23.5	5.9
31	Leather	3	0.0	66.7	33.3	0.0
32	Stone, clay, glass, concrete	190	49.2	4.1	45.1	28.7
33	Primary metal	618	72.4	15.1	14.1	3.2
34	Fabricated metal	217	62.0	8.5	30.8	6.7
35	Machinery, except electrical	556	60.7	7.5	30.1	5.3
36	Electrical machinery	433	53.5	7.1	40.8	5.1
37	Transportation equipment	527	66.4	12.4	27.2	4.9

38	Measuring instruments	32	36.4	24.2	54.6	21.2
39	Miscellaneous manufacturing	16	42.1	0.0	42.1	42.1
	Total	3,319	61.3%	9.3%	30.3%	8.3%

Nonmanufacturing

1	Agriculture	2	100.0%	0.0%	0.0%	0.0%
10	Metal mining	44	84.1	11.4	4.5	6.8
11	Anthracite mining	3	0.0	33.3	100.0	0.0
12	Bituminous coal	1	0.0	0.0	100.0	0.0
15	General construction	16	62.5	37.5	25.0	31.3
16	Other construction	24	66.7	33.3	0.0	16.7
17	Special trade construction	20	65.0	25.0	10.0	15.0
19	Ordnance	37	73.0	10.8	27.0	2.7
41	Transit	13	92.3	7.7	0.0	0.0
42	Trucking	150	59.3	23.3	40.6	0.0
44	Water transport	3	100.0	0.0	0.0	0.0
45	Air transport	1	0.0	0.0	100.0	0.0
48	Communications	143	94.4	0.0	5.6	3.5
49	Electric, gas, and sanitary	32	81.3	0.0	18.7	37.5
50	Wholesale trade—durable	17	64.7	5.9	29.4	58.8
52	Retail trade—building materials	2	0.0	0.0	100.0	50.0
53	General merchandise	17	11.8	0.0	88.3	17.7
54	Food stores	165	73.3	17.0	26.1	35.2
55	Automative dealers, service	1	0.0	0.0	100.0	0.0
58	Eating and drinking	2	50.0	0.0	50.0	100.0
59	Miscellaneous retail	9	77.8	0.0	22.2	100.0

Nonmanufacturing (continued)

Industry	Number of Contracts with Cola	Percentage with No Maximum or Minimum	Percentage with Minimum	Percentage with Maximum	Percentage with Trigger or Corridor
62 Securities	3	0.0%	0.0%	100.0%	100.0%
63 Insurance	7	57.1	0.0	42.9	0.0
65 Real estate	11	18.2	9.1	72.7	72.7
73 Business services	11	54.5	0.0	45.5	100.0
76 Miscellaneous repair	3	0.0	33.3	66.7	0.0
78 Motion pictures	3	33.3	0.0	66.7	66.7
79 Amusement	3	66.7	0.0	33.3	100.0
80 Health services	13	30.8	0.0	69.2	69.2
89 Miscellaneous services	2	0.0	0.0	100.0	100.0
Total	758	70.1	12.7	26.7	20.3

Note: Percentages might add to more than 100 because some Colas have more than one of the indicated provisions.
Source: Authors' data base.

machinery. Triggers and corridors are especially common in textiles; apparel; stone, clay, glass, and concrete; utilities; food stores; and services. Card (1983) finds similar patterns for caps and triggers in the Canadian food products, electrical equipment, and auto industries as our U.S. data show for these sectors.

The particular formula a contract uses on which to base Cola payments is of obvious importance in the study of wage indexation. In our sample, many formulas appear, covering a range of levels of generosity. The vast majority of them provide equal cents-per-hour raises for the entire bargaining unit, thus narrowing wage differentials within the unit. For example, suppose one worker earns ten dollars an hour, another earns fifteen dollars an hour, and they each receive a one-dollar-per-hour Cola payment. If inflation is 10 percent, the lower paid worker's real wage is constant and the higher paid worker's real wage falls. Thus, the Cola narrows the absolute and relative real wage differential. In contrast to this type of adjustment, a minority of contracts in our sample provide equal *percentage* Cola raises, thus preserving wage differentials within the bargaining unit.

Among the formulas that provide equal cents-per-hour increases, the formulas range in generosity from one cent per hour for each 0.1-point change in the CPI to one cent for each point—a tenfold difference in Cola payments. A few formulas (about 3.8 percent) give one cent for each percentage (e.g., 0.3 percent) change in the CPI, again narrowing wage differentials. Another small minority of formulas (2.9 percent) change during the life of a particular contract. However, the dominant equal cents-per-hour adjustments are one cent per 0.3 point and one cent per 0.4 point. Of the Colas that provide equal percentage adjustments, the formulas range from 0.25 percent to 1 percent wage increases for each 1 percent price increase.

Tables 3–11 and 3–12 describe the incidence of various Cola formulas by industry and by year of contract negotiation. Several interesting findings emerge from these tables. First, nonmanufacturing Colas are much more likely to give equal percentage raises (26 percent) than those in manufacturing (5.4 percent). These kinds of contracts are especially common in construction, communications, trade, and services among nonmanufacturing and in printing and publishing among manufacturers. Second, the two formulas of one cent per 0.3 and one cent per 0.4 are especially common in metal industries, machinery, transportation equipment, food, tobacco,

Table 3-11.   Incidence of Various Cola Formulas by Industry, 1966–81.

Manufacturing

	Industry	Percentage of Formulas of Type:			
		1¢/0.3 pt.	1¢/0.4 pt.	1%/1%	x%/1% (x≠1)
20	Food	28.4%	47.0%	3.9%	0.4%
21	Tobacco	21.2	78.8	0.0	0.0
22	Textiles	0.0	33.3	33.3	0.0
23	Apparel	0.0	5.6	11.1	0.0
24	Lumber	0.0	5.6	5.6	0.0
25	Furniture	9.8	26.8	4.9	2.4
26	Paper	9.4	21.9	0.0	15.6
27	Printing	21.1	26.3	36.8	10.5
28	Chemicals	18.5	31.9	5.0	0.8
29	Petroleum	100.0	0.0	0.0	0.0
30	Rubber	10.2	10.2	0.0	0.0
31	Leather	0.0	100.0	0.0	0.0
32	Stone, glass, clay, concrete	27.0	21.7	0.0	0.0
33	Primary metal	55.2	33.6	1.0	1.6
34	Fabricated metal	24.4	52.1	1.4	0.9
35	Machinery, except electrical	27.0	48.2	3.2	2.5
36	Electrical machinery	13.6	29.2	0.0	12.7
37	Transportation equipment	32.4	43.2	1.0	0.4
38	Measuring instruments	0.0	38.7	25.8	0.0
39	Miscellaneous manufacturing	12.5	18.8	31.3	0.0
	Total	29.7	38.1	2.5	2.9

Nonmanufacturing

1	Agriculture	0.0%	100.0%	0.0%	0.0%
10	Metal mining	63.6	27.3	2.3	4.5
11	Anthracite mining	0.0	100.0	0.0	0.0
12	Bituminous coal	0.0	100.0	0.0	0.0
15	General construction	0.0	0.0	43.8	6.3
16	Other construction	0.0	0.0	41.7	0.0
17	Special trade construction	0.0	15.0	25.0	0.0

Table 3–11. (Continued)

Nonmanufacturing (continued)

Percentage of Formulas of Type:

	Industry	*1¢/0.3 pt.*	*1¢/0.4 pt.*	*1%/1%*	*x%/1% (x ≠ 1)*
19	Ordnance	29.7	54.1	2.7	0.0
41	Transit	0.0	0.0	23.1	0.0
42	Trucking	70.7	24.0	0.0	0.0
44	Water transport	0.0	0.0	0.0	100.0
45	Air transport	0.0	100.0	0.0	0.0
48	Communication	0.0	0.7	3.5	73.4
49	Electric, gas, and sanitary	21.9	31.3	3.1	9.4
50	Wholesale trade— durable	29.4	29.4	17.6	0.0
52	Retail trade— building materials	0.0	50.0	50.0	0.0
53	General merchandise	64.7	17.6	17.6	0.0
54	Food stores	8.5	52.7	7.8	0.0
55	Automotive dealers, service	0.0	0.0	100.0	0.0
58	Eating and drinking	0.0	0.0	50.0	50.0
59	Miscellaneous retail	0.0	0.0	77.8	22.2
62	Securities	0.0	0.0	100.0	0.0
63	Insurance	42.9	0.0	0.0	0.0
65	Real estate	0.0	0.0	36.4	0.0
73	Business services	0.0	0.0	54.5	0.0
76	Miscellaneous repair	0.0	0.0	0.0	0.0
78	Motion pictures	0.0	0.0	66.7	33.3
79	Amusement	0.0	0.0	66.7	0.0
80	Health services	0.0	38.5	38.5	15.4
89	Miscellaneous services	0.0	0.0	0.0	0.0
	Total	24.7	25.1	10.2	15.8

[a] 1¢/0.3 pt. means a one-cent-per-hour raise for everyone for each 0.3-point increase in the CPI.

[b] 1%/1% means a 1 percent raise for each 1 percent increase in the CPI.

Source: Authors' data base.

mining, ordnance, and trucking. Finally, over the 1970s and early 1980s there has been a shift from the one-cent-per-0.4 to the one-cent-per-0.3 formula, though no pattern emerges for the incidence of

Table 3-12.   Incidence of Cola Formulas by Year of
Negotiation.

		Manufacturing			
		Percentage with Formula of Type:			
Year	Number of Colas	1¢/0.3 [a]	1¢/0.4	1%/1% [b]	x%/1% (x ≠ 1)
1967	26	0.0%	92.3%	0.0%	0.0%
1968	36	0.0	58.3	2.8	0.0
1969	12	0.0	33.3	0.0	0.0
1970	79	6.3	50.6	2.5	0.0
1971	249	2.8	80.7	1.2	0.8
1972	96	5.2	56.3	5.2	0.0
1973	282	18.8	42.9	3.9	2.5
1974	611	36.2	35.5	1.8	2.3
1975	226	26.5	42.0	3.1	0.4
1976	324	23.8	34.0	4.6	2.5
1977	446	43.7	33.4	1.1	5.6
1978	131	38.9	35.9	3.1	0.8
1979	180	22.2	16.7	3.9	4.4
1980	309	50.2	15.2	1.9	7.4
1981	92	55.4	22.8	0.0	1.1
		Nonmanufacturing			
1970	36	72.2%	16.7%	8.3%	0.0%
1971	50	0.0	32.0	12.0	0.0
1972	11	0.0	45.5	27.3	9.1
1973	62	64.5	6.5	9.7	0.0
1974	127	15.7	22.0	12.6	26.8
1975	36	5.6	36.1	27.8	11.1
1976	82	4.9	57.3	8.5	1.2
1977	118	18.6	21.2	5.1	32.2
1978	42	19.0	38.1	16.7	2.4
1979	72	56.9	15.3	4.2	4.2
1980	99	21.2	12.1	7.1	35.4
1981	21	14.3	33.3	4.8	14.3

[a] 1¢/0.3 pt. means a one-cent-per-hour raise for everyone for each 0.3 point increase in the CPI.

[b] 1%/1% means a 1 percent raise for each 1 percent increase in the CPI.

Source: Authors' data base.

differential-preserving Colas (Table 3-12). As mentioned earlier, the UAW's and Rubberworkers' Cola formulas were changed in 1982 to one cent per 0.26 point. Perhaps this change will be the start of a trend.

Although caps and the actual formula used receive most of the attention in the press, the CPI base and the time delay before the Cola starts can also have a significant effect on wages. Some examples of this effect were discussed in Chapter 2. The base year for most of our sample started in the late 1960s at 1957-59 = 100. However, in 1971-73, it switched over to 1967 = 100. By 1981 about 94 percent of Colas negotiated that year were on a 1967 = 100 basis. Since the CPI in 1983 was approximately 300 (base 1967 = 100) and since a new base is likely to be implemented in the mid-1980s, a substantial change in Colas is likely to take place over the next few years. The BLS has been using a 1977 = 100 base for many of its wholesale price indices, and it appears likely that this will be the new base for the CPI as well (*Monthly Labor Review,* September 1983). In 1977 the CPI averaged 181.5 (1967 = 100). Therefore, the change in base to 1977 will cause a given cents-per-point Cola formula to give substantially smaller raises (a 45 percent reduction). In other words, after the change in base, a one-cent-per-0.3 Cola would have to change to one cent per 0.165 points to give the same yield as before.

Tables 3-13 and 3-14 illustrate the average waiting time for a Cola to begin its payments (measured from the start of the contract). Colas in manufacturing begin paying off sooner than those in non-manufacturing by a 4.2-month margin. Among the former set of industries, Colas in the nondurable goods sector take longer to begin payments than those for durables. In nonmanufacturing, Colas in construction, retail trade, and services average a long waiting time for the initial payment. The trend over the 1970s and early 1980s has been toward a shorter payoff period, especially for manufacturing.

A final set of Cola characteristics we wish to pursue concerns the relationship between bargaining unit traits and the type of Cola. In particular, we focus on the single employer–multiemployer distinction and the number of workers covered by the agreement. Tables 3-15 and 3-16 illustrate this breakdown. For both manufacturing and nonmanufacturing, multifirm contracts are more likely to have caps than single-firm agreements. For nonmanufacturing, multiemployer Colas also are more likely than single-firm units to have minimum adjustments.

The relationship between bargaining structure and formula differs for the manufacturing and nonmanufacturing sectors. In manu-

Table 3–13.   Average Months before First Cola Payment by Industry.

Manufacturing

Industry

20	Food	8.0 months
21	Tobacco	7.0
22	Textiles	11.5
23	Apparel	13.7
24	Lumber	9.2
25	Furniture	10.1
26	Paper	12.1
27	Printing	10.6
28	Chemicals	7.7
29	Petroleum	0.0
30	Rubber	7.6
31	Leather	4.0
32	Stone, glass, clay, concrete	10.3
33	Primary metal	4.9
34	Fabricated metal	6.9
35	Machinery, except electrical	5.9
36	Electrical machinery	8.0
37	Transportation equipment	5.9
38	Measuring instruments	5.5
39	Miscellaneous manufacturing	8.6
	Total	6.8

Nonmanufacturing

1	Agriculture	5.5 months
10	Metal mining	5.2
11	Anthracite mining	12.3
12	Bituminous coal	2.0
15	General construction	16.4
16	Other construction	15.9
17	Special trade construction	11.6
19	Ordnance	7.0
41	Transit	4.1
42	Trucking	10.8
44	Water transport	18.0
45	Air transport	5.0

Table 3–13.   (Continued)

Nonmanufacturing (continued)

Industry

48	Communications	12.0 months
49	Electric, gas, and sanitary	9.0
50	Wholesale trade — durable	8.2
52	Retail trade — building materials	9.0
53	General merchandise	13.3
54	Food stores	12.2
55	Automotive dealers, service	24.0
58	Eating and drinking	5.5
59	Miscellaneous retail	13.7
62	Securities	12.0
63	Insurance	2.9
65	Real estate	11.9
73	Business services	12.8
76	Miscellaneous repair	6.0
78	Motion pictures	18.0
79	Amusement	12.3
80	Health services	12.2
89	Miscellaneous services	12.0
	Total	11.0

Source: Authors' data base.

facturing, single-firm agreements are more likely to have the relatively generous one-cent-per-0.3 formula than multifirm contracts; for nonmanufacturing, the opposite conclusion holds. In addition, single-firm Colas in manufacturing are less likely to preserve wage differentials than multifirm agreements. On the other hand, in nonmanufacturing, single-firm Colas are more likely than multifirm Colas to preserve wage differentials. This finding is due to the large percentage (28.6 percent) of single firm contracts that call for percentage increases in wages lower than the percentage increase in prices.

Bargaining unit size also bears different relationships to Cola type in the two overall sectors. In manufacturing, capped Colas arise more frequently in small contracts; this type is found in large contracts for the nonmanufacturing sector. In each sector, the relatively

Table 3-14.   Average Months before First Cola Payment by Year of Negotiation.

Year	Manufacturing	Nonmanufacturing	Total
1966	11.5 months	—	11.5 months
1967	9.6	—	9.6
1968	10.3	—	10.3
1969	10.7	12.0	10.7
1970	13.1	14.0	13.3
1971	11.1	13.1	11.4
1972	9.9	8.8	9.8
1973	6.9	11.3	7.7
1974	6.0	11.4	6.9
1975	7.7	11.8	8.3
1976	6.5	11.8	7.5
1977	4.6	10.6	5.9
1978	6.0	11.5	7.4
1979	5.0	8.0	5.9
1980	4.7	10.1	6.0
1981	6.4	9.5	7.0
Total	6.8	11.0	7.6

Source: Authors' data base.

Table 3-15.   Characteristics of Colas by Bargaining Structure, 1966-81.

	Manufacturing		Nonmanufacturing	
Cola Type	Multifirm	Single Firm	Multifirm	Single Firm
No minimum or maximum adjustment	52.3%	61.8%	60.3%	79.4%
Minimum adjustment	8.4	9.4	18.9	6.7
Maximum adjustment	39.3	29.8	34.7	18.8
1¢/0.3	24.7	30.0	28.4	21.1
1¢/0.4	30.9	38.5	23.5	26.5
1%/1%	9.3	2.1	15.7	4.9
$x\%/1\%$ $(x \neq 1)$	2.5	2.9	2.4	28.6

Note: Each entry gives the percentage of agreements with a given bargaining structure type having the relevant Cola characteristic. For example, the table shows that in manufacturing, 52.3 percent of multifirm Cola contracts had no minimum or maximum adjustment.

Source: Authors' data base.

Table 3-16.   Average Bargaining Unit Size by Type of Cola

Cola Type	Manufacturing	Nonmanufacturing
No minimum or maximum	4,191.9 workers	7,045.4 workers
Minimum	4,761.3	7,635.4
Maximum	2,287.5	8,430.4
1¢/0.3	4,715.4	7,976.7
1¢/0.4	2,969.1	5,410.8
1%/1%	1,159.7	7,296.1
x%/1% ($x \neq 1$)	3,246.7	12,475.8
Average size for indexed contracts	3,501.6	7,295.4

Source: Authors' data base.

generous one-cent-per-0.3 formula occurs in larger units. Finally, for manufacturing, bargaining units with wage-differential-preserving Colas have small average size; for nonmanufacturing these units have relatively large average size.

CONCLUSIONS

This chapter has presented a variety of descriptive statistics concerning our unique data base on Colas. The representativeness of the sample compared with published sources was confirmed. Average characteristics of indexed and nonindexed contracts were compared. The incidence of Colas was tabulated by year of negotiation, union, and industry. Finally, characteristics of Colas were compared across these and other dimensions.

Our data reveal the following major findings about Colas. First, over the 1966–81 period, there was a generally rising incidence of Colas, with some leveling off after 1976. This incidence is dominated by the three-year bargaining cycles of the UAW, USW, and Teamsters. Second, Colas are concentrated in several key industries such as metals, machinery, transportation equipment, and trucking. Third, indexed agreements on average: (1) cover larger bargaining units; (2) are located in more concentrated industrialization; (3) are more likely to cover workers outside the South or in metropolitan areas; (4) are more likely to be single-firm contracts; (5) have longer duration; and (6) have higher wage levels than unindexed contracts. Fourth, among contracts with Colas, there has been a falling incidence of caps. The dominant formulas as of 1981 were one cent per 0.3 points and one cent per 0.4 points, Colas in nonmanufacturing being more likely to return equal percentage (as opposed to equal cents) increases than those in manufacturing. Finally, multiemployer Colas are more likely to have caps than single-firm Colas.

The data in this chapter are presented as a method of illustrating the nature of our sample. The tables are not intended to test hypotheses about Colas, although several hypotheses might be advanced about any particular tabulation. In the following two chapters, economic theories about wage indexation will be surveyed in an attempt to generate hypotheses to be tested rigorously with our data base.

NOTES

1. We are indebted to the following research assistants, who aided in collecting and assembling these data: Debashish Bhattacherjee, Andrew Bruns, Daniel Burgard, Cynthia Gramm, Steven Merkin, Christopher Pawlowicz, Ronald Seeber, and Roger Wolters.
2. In computing our figures, we have taken the negotiation rather than the relationship as the unit of observation. In many cases, the same relationship appears several times. In addition, the size of the contract is measured as of 1975, even if the negotiation took place in another year. Unfortunately, problems of data availability prevent us from tabulating the number of workers covered in any other year.
3. Our figures for the timing of reviews change less than the BLS figures because we credit a Cola as having, say, quarterly reviews even if the reviews start in later years.
4. Recall the similarity in average size for major agreements in manufacturing and nonmanufacturing.

REFERENCES

Bureau of National Affairs. *Daily Labor Report* (various issues).
Card, David. 1983. "Cost-of-Living Escalators in Major Union Contracts." *Industrial and Labor Relations Review* 37, no. 1 (October 1983): 34–48.
Freeman, Richard B., and James L. Medoff. 1979. "New Estimates of Private Sector Unionism in the United States." *Industrial and Labor Relations Review* 32, no. 2 (January): 143–74.

U.S. Bureau of Labor Statistics. 1977. *Characteristics of Major Collective Bargaining Agreements, July 1, 1975*. Bulletin No. 1957. Washington, D.C.: U.S. Government Printing Office.

――――. *Current Wage Developments* (various issues).

――――. *Industry Wage Surveys* (various issues).

――――. 1983. *Monthly Labor Review* 106 (September).

――――. *Wage Chronologies* (various issues).

U.S. Department of Commerce. 1972. *1972 Census of Manufactures*. Washington, D.C.: U.S. Government Printing Office.

Wilton, David A. 1979. "An Analysis of Canadian Wage Contracts with Cost-of-Living Allowance Clauses." Discussion Paper No. 165. Ottawa: The Centre for the Study of Inflation and Productivity, Economic Council of Canada.

Chapter 4

Economic Effects of Wage Indexation: A Survey of Theories and Evidence

As noted in previous chapters, policymakers in the United States have often expressed concern about the link between Colas and the level of price inflation in the economy. Numerous formal and informal theories about the impact of Colas on macroeconomic stability have been proposed to investigate this relationship. The majority of this work has focused on the impact of economywide indexation, but these models can also provide significant insight into the U.S. experience with limited indexation.

On a more micro level, there appears to be a close link between contract length and Cola acceptance by management and the targeting of Colas for elimination by management in troubled industries. Each of these might cause a relationship between Colas and strike activity. We have also pointed out the narrowing effect of cents-per-hour Colas on wage differentials and the possible problems this narrowing might cause.

This chapter surveys formal and informal theories about the various economic effects of wage indexation. Conditions under which Colas can have stabilizing or destabilizing macroeconomic effects are discussed. The effect of Colas on industrial peace is explored, as is their impact on wage differentials. Available empirical evidence on these effects is also surveyed.

Equations 4-1 through 4-9, 4-11, and 4-12 are reproduced with the permission of North-Holland Publishing Company, Amsterdam.

COLAS AND MACROECONOMIC STABILITY

A large body of theoretical work has sought to determine whether wage indexation leads to more or less stable output, employment, or prices. In addition, several economists have been concerned over the question of whether the presence of wage indexation influences the role of monetary policy. For example, does wage indexation increase or decrease the ability of an announced monetary policy rule to affect output and employment? These are important issues, since one of the major functions of government policy is to increase macroeconomic stability. Economists have disagreed over the likely effects of wage indexation on macroeconomic stability. The causes of disagreement are rooted in differing assumptions about the sources of instability and about how workers and firms behave in an environment of uncertainty.

Early advocates of a general government policy of indexation emphasized the problem of unexpected price movements as justification for their position. For example, Friedman (1968, 1974) argued that, in the absence of wage indexation, mistakes by workers in perceiving the price inflation rate lead to fluctuations in output and employment. Specifically, suppose that the economy is in an initial state of equilibrium with given levels of employment and output and no price inflation.[1] Suppose, following Friedman (1968), that businesses are able to perceive correctly the rate of price inflation while workers do so with a lag. If the monetary authority disturbs this equilibrium by suddenly raising the money supply, prices will begin to rise, for example, by 6 percent per year. Firms will then try to expand and will begin to bid wages up. By assumption, workers do not yet perceive the new inflation rate. Thus, if wages begin to rise by 3 percent per year, workers will (incorrectly) perceive a 3 percent *rise* in real wages, while firms will (correctly) perceive a 3 percent *fall* in real wages. In this situation, workers' perceptions will lead them to increase the supply of labor (assuming that labor supply is a positive function of the real wage perceived by workers), and firms' perceptions will lead to a rise in the quantity of labor demanded. Employment will thus rise, as will output. However, when (if) workers' perceptions catch up with reality, labor supply and employment will fall to their original levels. The opposite outcome for employment holds for an initial, unexpected fall in the money supply.

This explanation for the short-run tradeoff between inflation and unemployment has been criticized for its assumption that workers' perceptions lag behind those of businesses (Lucas 1972). However, the same results can be obtained by assuming that wages are set (either in union contracts or by nonunion employers) at less frequent intervals than those at which prices are adjusted. This wage-setting behavior might be the result of long-term contracting where it is more costly to adjust wages than prices. In this case, once wages are set, an unexpected rise in prices lowers real wages, and an unexpected fall in prices raises real wages. If current employment responds to current real wages, then the assumption of fixed nominal wages in the presence of unexpected price changes can also lead to output and employment fluctuations.[2]

How does wage indexation affect the economy's response to changes in the money supply? Friedman (1974) noted that if wages were completely indexed to the price level, then unanticipated (or anticipated) shocks to the money supply would have no effect on real wages. If real wages are held constant, then there is no incentive for firms to change the quantity of labor demanded or for workers to change the quantity of labor supplied. Therefore, employment and output would be unaffected by changes in the money supply.[3] Workers' living standards and society's real GNP would be insured. According to Friedman (1974), indexation is especially helpful when a contractionary monetary policy is used in an attempt to reduce inflation. Without indexation, a reduced money supply lowers inflation and raises real wages under either the expectations model or the long-term contracting model. This rise in real wages will cause unemployment if businesses are free to adjust the quantity of labor hired in response to real wage changes. Indexation, by keeping real wages constant, makes this unemployment unnecessary and thus reduces the pain associated with a contractionary monetary policy. In fact, full indexation of wages removes any effect of monetary policy (announced or unannounced) on employment and output, as long as prices are flexible. In such a world, the only role for monetary policy would be to stabilize prices, and the monetary authority would not be tempted to try to affect output or employment.

Indexation of long-term contracts other than labor agreements has also been advocated for the same reasons that favor wage indexation. For example, indexing long-term bonds would eliminate the real capital gain or loss that lenders or borrowers would experience during an unanticipated inflation (Bach and Musgrave 1941; Giersch 1974; Friedman 1974). By reducing this risk, indexed bonds or loans could raise both the supply of and demand for loanable funds and thus improve the workings of the capital market. If the government were forced to issue indexed (rather than conventional) bonds and to index the income tax brackets, then a powerful incentive for inflationary finance would be removed (Friedman 1974). Without indexation of its bonds, the federal government can lower the real burden of its current debt by raising the money supply. Indexation of bonds raises nominal interest and principal payments under inflationary finance. With progressive taxes and no indexation, inflation raises taxes faster than it raises incomes. Thus, by raising the money supply, government can raise the share of GNP it controls. By indexing tax brackets, the government's share of GNP would be less affected by inflation than without indexing. A further advantage of complete indexation would be to reduce the income redistribution among firms, consumers, and workers (as well as between private and public sectors, as just discussed) that accompanies unanticipated inflation. That is, with indexation, there would be fewer "gainers" and "lowers" under inflation than if there were no indexation. Thus, political conflicts that accompany inflation might well be reduced (Goldstein 1975; Braun 1976).

This optimistic picture of indexation in general and wage indexation in particular has been challenged on a number of grounds. First, it has been pointed out that changes in the money supply are not the only factor that leads to macroeconomic instability. Changes in productivity or input supplies (termed "real shocks") can also affect the economy, and wage indexation has a different impact under these real shocks than under changes in the money supply ("monetary shocks").[4] Second, advocates of indexation assume that employment, and therefore output, is determined by employers at all times. However, the effects of indexation depend crucially on the determinants of employment in an uncertain environment.[5] Third, advocates of indexation assume that the economy is competitive. The effects of indexation are likely to be different for economies characterized by monopoly power (in either the product markets or in labor markets). Fourth, several authors have argued that wage indexation exacerbates price fluctuations and makes inflation more difficult to control.[6] In addition, by reducing the political costs of inflation, indexation might reduce the government's will to fight inflation (Giersch 1974). These objections to wage indexation are now discussed in turn.

Real versus Monetary Shocks

Gray, Fischer, and others[7] have constructed macroeconomic models of the effects of wage indexation under various kinds of shocks to the economy. A basic result of these early models (Gray 1976; Fischer 1977c) was that wage indexation stabilized output and production under monetary shocks but destabilized these outcomes under real shocks. Although these results have been challenged in more elaborate models (Barro 1977; Cukierman 1980), the finding that wage indexation could exacerbate economic instability has immediate policy implications. Specifically, it is possible that an appropriate government policy regarding indexation would be to encourage less-than-full indexation of wages to prices. To understand the reasons indexation might have adverse effects, it is helpful to sketch out the logic behind these models that challenge the idea of complete indexation.

The following model of the effects of indexation is due to Gray (1976). Fischer's (1977c) model is also similar. Both models assume a one-sector economy with one variable factor of production: labor. Suppose that output is related to labor input by the following production function:

$$y_t = a_t f(l_t), \quad a_t = 1 + e_{1t}, \tag{4-1}$$

where for each period t

$y_t = $ output

e_{1t} is a random error term with $E(e_{1t}) = 0$

$l_t = $ quantity of labor hired

$f(-)$ is a production function such that $f' > 0$, $f'' < 0$.

Suppose further that money is supplied according to

$$m_t^s = b_t \bar{m} \quad \text{and} \quad b_t = 1 + e_{2t}, \tag{4-2}$$

where $m_t^s = $ money supply

e_{2t} is a random variable with $E(e_{2t}) = 0$

$\bar{m}$ is a constant.

Third, assume a quantity theory of demand for money,

$$m_t^d = P_t y_t, \tag{4-3}$$

where $m_t^d = $ demand for money

$P_t = $ price level.

Fourth, assume that in each period the price level adjusts to equate the supply of and demand for money. Finally, assume that labor is supplied according to

$$l_t^s = g(w_t), \quad g' > 0, \tag{4-4}$$

where $l_t^s =$ labor supply

$w_t =$ real wage.

This simple model, with a few additional assumptions stated below, allows investigation of the macroeconomic effects of wage indexation, although the model abstracts from such problems as investment, interest rates, and relative price fluctuations. Equations 4–1 and 4–2 embody the concepts of real and monetary shocks, respectively. A real shock is conceptualized here as a change (e_{1t}) in the productivity of labor. In more complicated models, a real shock could be related to changes in materials supplies or international redistribution of wealth. Even these more complex kinds of real shocks would influence domestically consumed output per worker; thus, Equation 4–1 may be more general than it appears. A monetary shock is pictured as a change (e_{2t}) in the money supply. This characterization accords with our earlier discussion of indexation and monetary disturbances. In Equation 4–3, a unitary velocity of money is assumed for convenience.

To assess the effects of wage indexation, some assumptions about wages and employment must be made. First, following Gray (1976) and Fischer (1977c), assume that a base nominal wage W^* must be set before the values of the real and monetary shocks become known. If there is no indexation, W^* is fixed for the entire period; with indexation the wage will change as the price level changes. Assume that W^* is set to equate the supply of and demand for labor when there are no shocks to the economy. Second, assume that, whenever demand and supply of labor are not equal (due to the wage-setting assumption), employment is determined by the firms' demand for labor, not the workers' supply. These two assumptions accord well with long-term contracting in U.S. unions.[8] Wages (or the wage schedule) are set, and the employer then has the freedom to determine the quantity of labor hired (Ulman 1974). The consequences of relaxing these assumptions are discussed below.

To assess the effects of indexation, note that, due to the production function (Equation 4–1), the profit-maximizing employer's demand for labor can be expressed as

$$l_t^d = h\left(\frac{w_t}{a_t}\right) \quad \text{where } h' < 0. \text{ (Gray, 1976)} \tag{4-5}$$

Consider two polar cases: monetary shocks only and real shocks only. In an economy experiencing monetary shocks only, e_{1t} would be set equal to 0. Therefore,

$$y_t = f(l_t) \quad \text{and} \tag{4-6}$$

$$l_t = l_t^d = h(w_t). \tag{4-7}$$

By letting W_t be the resulting nominal wage ($W_t = W^*$ with no indexation, and W_t varies with P under indexation),

$$m_t^s = (1 + e_{2t})\bar{m} = m_t^d = P_t y_t = \left(\frac{W_t}{w_t}\right) f(h(w_t)) \tag{4-8}$$

With no indexation, W is constant at W^*. As e_{2t} rises, w_t (the real wage) falls while l_t^d and y_t rise. With complete indexation, W_t rises exactly as fast as P_t, so w_t remains constant. Therefore l_t^d and y_t also remain constant. Full indexation thus reduces the effects of monetary shocks on output and employment to 0. This is the result discussed by the earlier advocates of indexation.[9]

In an economy subject to real shocks only, $e_{2t} = 0$. In this case,

$$m_t^s = \bar{m} = m_t^d = \left(\frac{W_t}{w_t}\right)(1 + e_{1t}) f\left(h\left(\frac{w_t}{1 + e_{1t}}\right)\right) \tag{4-9}$$

A rise in e_{1t}, all else equal, raises the demand for labor and thus the supply of output. Therefore, to maintain money market equilibrium (see Equation 4-9), W_t/w_t must fall or w_t must rise (or both). With no indexation, W_t is fixed, so w_t must rise. The only way this can occur is for the price level to fall. The rise in real wages helps offset some of the positive effect of the real shock on l^d and thus y. With complete indexation, w_t is constant, so W_t must fall. With indexation, the real wage does not rise; thus, with complete indexation, there is no offset to the initial real shock. There are greater fluctuations in output and employment under real shocks with complete wage indexation than without indexation.

A related example of a real shock is the increase in foreign oil prices in 1973–74 or 1979–80. These increases can be viewed as a transfer of wealth from oil-consuming countries to oil-producing countries. In the absence of any offsetting productivity increases (or, controlling for productivity changes), the new equilibrium, market-clearing real wage must be lower as a result of OPEC's "tax" on the output of U.S. workers. Wage indexation, by keeping the real wage (deflated by the CPI) constant, would lead to a larger fall in employment and output than with no indexation. While the average U.S.

worker's real (CPI-deflated) wage fell during these periods, workers with generous Colas had real wage protection. This real wage protection, especially in 1979–80, accelerated the decline of employment in autos and steel (see Chapter 2).

Although the discussion of models with only monetary shocks or only real shocks is useful, both kinds of shocks are likely to be present. Suppose the objective of government in forming a policy toward wage indexation is the minimization of output fluctuations. In this case, Gray (1976) shows that the optimal degree of indexation lies between 0 and 1 and is a weighted average of the variance of monetary and real shocks.[10] The greater the shifts in the money supply relative to productivity shifts, the closer we should come to full indexation. Friedman (1974) anticipated this result by pointing out that, in the United States, swings in the money supply are generally far greater than changes in productivity. On the other hand, in an economy with a stable money supply and severe productivity shocks, indexation should be close to 0. An implication of a partial degree of indexation (i.e., less than 1) is that changes in the money supply will affect real wages and thus output. In this case, the monetary authority might well be tempted to use monetary policy to affect employment as well as prices.

It should be pointed out that in an economy with real and monetary shocks and long-term labor contracts, there exist wage-setting schemes that lead to smaller output fluctuations than simple indexation to the CPI. Specifically, Karni (1983) argues that indexing wages to unanticipated output changes as well as to price changes can lead to an end-period wage that would clear the labor market given the real and monetary shocks to the system. The allocation of resources that would obtain if wages adjusted instantaneously can therefore be duplicated. However, such contracts are not observed. Contingent wage contracts in the United States almost exclusively use some measure of prices as the basis for wage adjustment. It is likely that problems of negotiation cost and moral hazard prevent the existence of wage adjustment contractually based on unanticipated movements in output (Karni 1983). In addition, Fischer (1977a) has argued that complicated indexing schemes can be set up where future wages are set in accordance with at present unformed *expectations* rather than realization of inflation. For example, under such arrangements, at the beginning of a two-year contract, the parties would set wages for the next year based on current inflationary expectations. However, the contract would defer the setting of the wage level for the second year until expectations of inflation for that year have been formed. These contracts can then duplicate spot market wage-setting arrangements. However, Fischer (1977a) notes that this type of indexation is also unseen in practice.

The Determination of Employment

The basic result of the models of Gray (1976) and Fischer (1977c) was that indexation stabilizes output and employment under monetary shocks and destabilizes them under real shocks. This finding was based on an assumption that in disequilibrium situations, employment was demand determined. This assumption, and the predictions that follow from it, have been questioned by Cukierman (1980) and Barro (1977). Cukierman argues that in disequilibrium, employment is as likely to be supply determined as demand determined. Barro argues that labor and management should be able to arrive at an optimal contractual employment level that indexation would not influence. Each of these assumptions about employment influences predictions about the impact of indexation. However, the empirical relevance of both of these alternatives to the Fischer (1977c) and Gray (1976) approaches may be questionable.

To assess the impact of supply-determined employment (i.e., Cukierman's (1980) model), return to the model in Equations 4-1 through 4-9.[11] However, now assume that in disequilibrium, the quantity of labor hired equals labor supply,

$$l_t = l_t^s = g(w_t). \qquad (4\text{-}10)$$

Suppose initially that there are only monetary shocks. Then $e_{1t} = 0$. Equilibrium in the money market requires

$$m_t^s = (1 + e_{2t})\bar{m} = m_t^d = \frac{W_t}{w_t} f(g(w_t)). \qquad (4\text{-}11)$$

With no indexation, a rise in the money supply will raise P_t and lower the real wage and thus output. With indexation, the real wage is constant, so employment and output are unchanged. Thus, under monetary shocks, indexation reduces the variability of output and employment, even when employment is supply determined. However, the model has the empirically implausible result that without indexation a rise in the money supply raises prices and lowers output.

In the face of real shocks only,

$$m_t^s = \bar{m} = m_t^d = \frac{W_t}{w_t}(1+e_{1t})f(g(w_t)). \qquad (4\text{-}12)$$

Without indexation, a rise in productivity must lower prices, raise the real wage, and thus increase employment and output. With indexation, the real wage remains constant, so employment is constant and output rises by less than if the real wage had risen. In this case, indexation stabilizes output and employment in the face of real shocks as well as monetary shocks. Note that with real shocks, indexation also reduces price fluctuations by reducing the rise (fall) in output that accompanies a rise (fall) in productivity. This finding is due to the assumption of a fixed money supply: Price and output changes must be offsetting.

Cukierman's (1980) results suggest an especially helpful role for indexation when there are real shocks and employment is supply determined. In this case, indexation reduces swings in output, employment, *and* prices. However, as implied earlier, employment in U.S. collective bargaining is not determined by labor supply but is, rather, employer determined. Thus, this advantage of indexation is unlikely to be realized.

Barro (1977) argues that labor and management can design contracts that lead to higher joint utility than in regimes where employment is demand or supply determined. Specifically, he hypothesizes that they should set employment at the level that would clear the labor market in the absence of real or monetary shocks. In such a world, indexation could have no effect on output and employment since these would not vary. Again, we do not typically observe such fixed-employment contracts in U.S. collective bargaining, and Barro's predictions are subject to empirical questioning (Fisher 1977a).

Although the type of contract suggested by Barro is not generally observed, the concept of optimal contracting complicates the analysis of the effects of indexation. Specifically, as discussed in Chapter 5, indexing can be seen as real wage insurance (Azariadis 1978). If workers do not currently have indexation, then its imposition by the government will not necessarily leave the market-clearing base wage (W^*) unchanged. If workers are more risk averse than firms, a government policy of forcing wage indexation might lower this market-clearing wage or change other aspects of the employment contract.

An analogy is the case where a rise in the minimum wage leads to a fall in fringe benefits. In any event, the models considered so far assume that the presence or absence of indexation has no effect on wages and employment levels that we would observe in the absence of shocks. The response of labor contracts to the imposition or prohibition of indexation is an area of inquiry that could lead to results counter to those of the early models. This response is explored in Chapter 5.

Imperfect Competition

An important element in the predictions of Friedman (1974), Gray (1976), and Fischer (1977c) is the assumption that firms will hire more labor only if the real wage falls, all else equal. Though this assumption holds in competitive markets, Phelps and Winter (1970) show that it does not necessarily hold where firms have some (albeit temporary) monopoly power. These authors postulate a model in which individual firms charge a price based on what they perceive the industry average to be. This price discretion by firms leads to more sluggish price movements than wage movements (which are, in this model, determined in competitive labor markets). According to Phelps and Winter, firms' monopoly power permits them to expand while paying higher real wages. If indexation is introduced into such an economy, output and employment would become less stable even in the face of monetary shocks. This result would occur since indexation would limit the rise (fall) in marginal costs during an expansion (contraction). In the face of real shocks, indexation would again have destabilizing effects for the same reasons as under monetary shocks. It is difficult to evaluate Phelps and Winter's model, since the available evidence on the short-run relationship between output and real wages is mixed.[12] However, the prediction of a slower price than wage adjustment goes counter to intuition. Rees (1970), for example, argues that, other than house rents, wages are the stickiest prices in the economy.

A related theme is found in the "bargaining power" view of wage determination. In this view, low unemployment raises unions' ability to raise real wages. If this model were valid, indexation would lead to less stable employment and output under any kind of shock than with no indexation. This result occurs for the same reason it does under the Phelps–Winter model. In fact, wage indexation has been praised in Australia as a method of restraining unions' ability to make real wage gains in excess of productivity gains (Braun 1976). However, in a situation with very powerful unions, the imposition of wage indexation would probably lead to other changes in collective bargaining contracts that might undo the effects of the wage policy.

Dynamic Stability of the Economy

The models discussed so far give "equilibrium" predictions about the short-run effects of wage indexation. The stability of these equilibria or actual adjustment paths taken to stable equilibria are not modeled. Several authors have constructed dynamic models in which indexing exerts a destabilizing force.[13] The intuitive notion behind such models is that in the presence of wage indexation, a temporary shock to prices (e.g., a crop failure) is transmitted throughout the economy, causing further inflation. Without indexation, the temporary shock might not have any appreciable macroeconomic effects. Cukierman and Razin (1977) have constructed a dynamic model where markets do not clear instantaneously but rather adjust with lags. Their theoretical results depend, clearly, on the values of the adjustment parameters. However, they do support the simple, intuitive notion stated above: Stability of the indexed economy implies stability of the nonindexed economy, but there is a range of adjustment parameter values for which the nonindexed economy is stable while the indexed economy is not. Under monetary shocks, the fact that indexing reduces output fluctuations takes away the stabilizing response of higher output to higher prices when the money supply rises. However, although not mentioned by Cukierman and Razin, the possibility of real shocks (and demand-determined employment) also implies more monetary instability as output movements are accentuated.[14] Peel (1977) comes to a similar conclusion about price stability. The model of Butterfield and Kubursi (1981) does not confront this issue directly.

In contrast to these models, Gultekin and Santomero (1979) find that by restoring equilibrium in the labor market, wage indexation raises economic stability. Although not mentioned by these authors, such a result could only obtain under monetary shocks. What accounts for the difference in predictions about the effects of indexation on stability under monetary shocks? In Gultekin and Santomero's model, the demand for money is a function of wage income and profit income (i.e., workers and capitalists might have different velocities of money). It is possible that a change in income distribution changes the demand for money. Suppose that without indexation the money supply rises and this lowers the real wage. If the demand for money falls, an unstable state exists. Indexation prevents this instability from happening by keeping income distribution constant. In Cukierman and Razin, demand for money depends only on prices and income. The difference between these models can only be resolved empirically. However, there is some possibility that indexation will destabilize prices. None of these models admits the possibility of markup pricing, under which indexation would lead to less stable price behavior.

Empirical Evidence

The most empirically plausible models imply that indexation stabilizes output and employment under monetary shocks and destabilizes them under real shocks. Under markup pricing or in situations where the demand for money is insensitive to income distribution, indexation destabilizes the money market; otherwise, it can have a stabilizing effect on money markets. As noted in Chapter 2, the U.S. government has on several occasions acted as if indexation would produce such instability.

Empirical evidence on the effects of indexation is limited due to the severe problems of causality detection and of finding the appropriate control group. This literature consists of macroeconometric comparisons of countries with and without indexation (Cukierman 1977), case studies (Page and Trollope 1974; Plowman 1981), and time series studies of individual economies (Kahn 1981; Vroman 1982).

Although the purpose of this book is to present a study of wage indexation in the United States, it is useful to consider at least briefly the experience of other countries. For example, wage indexation in Israel has been nearly universal since 1952 (Cukierman 1977), while it covers a minority of the U.S. work force.[15] Cukierman uses this difference between the two countries to test the effects of indexation on the inflation-employment tradeoff. By including the Cola factor in an Israeli aggregate wage equation and by assuming the other parameters would be unaffected by reducing or eliminating the Cola, he is able to test the effects of indexation on the Israeli economy. He then estimates a model for the United States and attributes some of the difference between the inflation-unemployment tradeoffs to indexation in Israel. Indexation in the United States is ignored in his analysis. Cukierman finds that the long-run inflation-unemployment relationship is steeper for Israel than for the United States and that some of this difference is due to inclusion of the Cola factor in Israeli wage expectations. This evidence does suggest that wage indexation would accentuate price swings and reduce output swings. At least for Israel, then, the monetary shocks, demand-determined employment model seems appropriate.

Other countries besides Israel and the United States have had some experience with wage indexation. Since 1920, in addition to these two, all of the following nations have had some form of wage indexation at some time: Australia, Belgium, Brazil, Canada, Chile, Denmark, Finland, France, Ireland, Italy, the Netherlands, Norway, and the United Kingdom (Page and Trollope 1974). Page and Trollope noted the behavior of inflation, real wages, and other macroeconomic indicators before, during, and after indexation in each of these countries.[16] For several countries (Brazil, Finland, Australia, and the Netherlands), it was found that indexation had adverse inflationary effects because of rising import prices. These higher prices were reflected in wages and sometimes pensions and were transmitted throughout the price structure. A particular problem arises when a country devalues its currency, automatically raising import prices. The presence of indexation can contribute to a spiral of devaluations. It is possible that a country with more dependence on foreign trade is more subject to real shocks than a more isolated economy. If this is true, then if employment is demand determined, indexation is more likely to destabilize output and prices in the country with more trade.[17]

Indexation appears to have had little average effect on real wages in the countries that have adopted indexation (Page and Trollope 1974). Real wage growth has accelerated during indexation, compared to the preindexation period, in about as many cases as it has decelerated. Although the indexation scheme varies across countries, this finding would be expected if economic agents' anticipations of inflation were on average realized, that is, under rational expectations. If price expectations are on average unbiased, then a wage-setting policy based on expected inflation (i.e., without indexing) should yield the same average result as one based on actual inflation (i.e., with indexing).

Wage indexation covers slightly more than half of U.S. union workers and a much smaller percentage of nonunion workers.[18] Since less than one-quarter of U.S. workers are unionized (see Table 2-3) and since workers with Colas get less-than-full inflation protection (see Table 2-10), the macroeconomic effects of wage indexation must be limited. Using data on the extent of Cola coverage for union and nonunion workers and estimates of the generosity of the Cola provision, Wayne Vroman (1982) estimated the aggregate effects of Colas in the United States for 1980. He found that only about 9.4 percent of inflation is automatically reflected in the aggregate wage level. That is, if prices rise by 1 percent, U.S. Colas will raise the average wage level automatically by only 0.094 percent, a very small response. This result is in great contrast to a country such as Israel, where the wage response is roughly 0.86 percent for a 1 percent price rise (Razin and Lusky 1979). Vroman's result might be an underestimate because he ignored the possibility of spillovers within the union sector or from union to nonunion wages. Specifically, Cola increases could cause other wages to change. Kahn (1981) computed a range for the effects of union Colas on total wage inflation based on a variety of estimates for these spillovers.[19] The response computed by Kahn for the years 1957–75 ranged from 0.05 percent to 0.31 percent. Even the top of this range (computed using maximum parameter values for the spillovers) indicates a small degree of indexation in the United States.

To summarize, the empirical evidence on the macroeconomic effects of wage indexation suggest that these effects are important in highly indexed countries such as Brazil and Israel. However, in the United States, the aggregate effects appear to be small but, according to Vroman (1982), they have grown over the 1974–80 period of high and uncertain inflation. (A 1975 study by Douty for the 1974 period estimated a 0.05 percent effect of Colas.) The possibility of a more indexed U.S. economy looms if we experience further bouts of unanticipated inflation.

MICROECONOMIC EFFECTS OF INDEXATION: STRIKES AND WAGE DIFFERENTIALS

In addition to overall effects on output, employment, and the price level, wage indexation is likely to have some effect on resource allocation. This effect depends on the actual characteristics of the wage-price link used in a given situation. Two microeconomic impacts hypothesized for Colas are strike reductions and various effects on wage differentials. To the extent that Colas have these effects, a government policy of encouraging Colas will indirectly reduce the incidence of strikes but influence the wage structure, perhaps introducing rigidities. This latter impact would contribute to a higher "full employment" unemployment rate compared to the case where relative wages are allowed to adjust in response to relative excess demand for labor across markets.

Colas and Strikes

The presence of Colas could reduce the incidence and severity of strikes through two mechanisms. First, by making long-term contracts more attractive, Colas can reduce the number of opportunities (i.e., contract negotiations) for a strike. Second, Colas could reduce the probability that any given negotiation will result in a strike. There are ample theoretical justification for and evidence on the positive relationship between Colas and contract length (see Chapters 5 and 6). However, the theory and evidence on the effect of Colas on the probability that a given negotiation will result in a strike are less clear.

A theory of strikes is needed to make theoretical predictions about the effect of Colas on strikes. Economists have typically viewed strikes as the result of imperfect information of differing perceptions between labor and management (Hicks 1963; Reder and Neumann 1980). If the parties could foresee the outcome of a strike, they could come to that agreement without incurring the costs of the strike. In the context of Colas and strikes, the uncertainty is over price inflation, and labor and management might have differing price expectations (Kaufman 1981; Mauro 1982). Mauro claims that a Cola can remove the real wage (or limit it) as a bargaining issue, thus increasing the likelihood of a settlement without a strike. On the other hand, he argues, a Cola might raise the firm's uncertainty about nominal wages or wages deflated by the firm's own price. Thus, a Cola could either raise or lower strike incidence. Kaufman (1981) emphasizes divergent inflation expectations between labor and management as a cause of strikes. Thus, by reducing the effects of unanticipated inflation or deflation, Colas reduce the cyclical variability of strikes but do not necessarily affect their average level. The evidence on the effects of Colas on strikes suggests insignificant (usually negative) effects on the level (Mauro 1982) and a smaller influence of inflation on strikes in bargaining units with Colas than in those without Colas (Kaufman 1981). Combined with Mauro's findings on the effect of Colas on the probability that a negotiation will lead to a strike, the positive association between Colas and contract duration implies an overall negative effect of indexation on strikes in any year.

The research of Mauro and Kaufman examines the effects of existing Colas on the incidence of strikes. However, the dynamic questions of removing, modifying, or adding a Cola can also be related to strike incidence. In particular, the Cola concept may be an issue that is difficult to compromise and might thus be associated with difficult negotiations. The workers' desires for real wage insurance might come into conflict with employers' wishes for predictable money wages. For example, in concession bargaining workers have often insisted on an eventual return to unlimited Colas. Companies appear equally insistent on limiting the costs that Colas can impose.

Colas and Wage Differentials

Wage indexation can affect the wage structure in a variety of ways. Colas can influence general wage dispersion as well as union–nonunion, interindustry, and skill differentials. These effects have implications for the level and structure of employment.

Hamermesh (1983) has argued that there is a negative relationship between reliance on unexpected inflation (either through Colas or through reopeners) and industry or local labor market conditions in setting wages. This relationship arises as risk-averse workers weigh the costs and benefits of local or industry labor market disequilibrium and loss due to unanticipated inflation. As unanticipated inflation rises, workers have an increasing incentive to tie their wage increases to the CPI rather than to particular supply and demand conditions (Hamermesh 1983). When this model is tested empirically, Hamermesh finds that rising inflation uncertainty lowers the variance of wages across industries. He argues that this finding is due to greater incentives for formal or informal wage indexation as inflation becomes more uncertain. However, the presence of Colas per se accounted for only a small portion of the relationship between inflation uncertainty and wage dispersion. An inference from Hamermesh's study is that widespread indexation would reduce the ability of relative wages to adjust and would therefore raise unemployment.

In contrast to Hamermesh's results, Kaufman and Stephan (1981) found a major impact of Colas on interindustry wage differentials. These authors found a rising differential across industries over the 1970s, a significant portion of which was due to Colas in high-wage industries. Kaufman and Stephan's findings on Colas can in part be explained by the fact that, on average, inflation was underpredicted in the 1970s (see Table 2-7). Since in the 1970s high-wage workers were more likely to get Colas (Tables 3-6, 3-7, and 3-8), if nonindexed wages were based on expected inflation, then Kaufman and Stephan's results would be anticipated for this period. Hamermesh's data covered 1955-81 or 1965-81 (depending on the sample used), periods in which inflation was less uniformly underpredicted than the 1970s. This difference in sample period might account for Hamermesh's weaker results. Although wages can be revised in future negotiations to take account of unrealized expectations, Kaufman and Stephan's findings indicate that such revisions, if they took place, might not have been sufficient to prevent a widening of interindustry wage differentials. Similarly, Moore and Raisian (1980) find a widening union–nonunion differential, *ceteris paribus,* over the 1970s. Some of this widening was presumably due to Colas.

An implication of these studies of the 1970s is that Colas might have added to the decline of many high-paying, unionized industries such as autos, steel, trucking, and railroads. Documentation for several specific industries is clear (see Chapter 2), and the findings of Kaufman and Stephan as well as Moore and Raisian show that these effects were important for the economy as a whole in the 1970s.

A final impact of wage indexation on the wage structure is a reduction of skill differentials. This decrease takes place because most Colas provide for equal cents-per-hour increases. Using Canadian 1968-75 data, Wilton (1979) compared the degree of inflation protection provided by Colas for workers earning the base wage and for workers earning average wages. For this period, he found that the lowest paid workers with indexation received 58 percent inflation protection through Colas, and the average worker received 49 percent protection.[20] Thus, in the absence of compensating wage increases, the 60 percent inflation that took place in Canada over the 1968-75 period (Wilton 1979: 5) would have diminished the skill differential (between average- and low-paid workers) by about 5.4 percentage points. Our own data (to be analyzed in Chapter 6) will also shed light on this issue. Colas, in their predominant form, place continual downward pressure on skill differentials and can induce responses by labor and management to reestablish differentials or to substitute skilled for unskilled labor.

CONCLUSIONS

This chapter has summarized the theoretical and empirical evidence on the macro- and microeconomic effects of wage indexation. Theoretical models have been devised implying that under some conditions, Colas could stabilize output, employment, and prices, while under other conditions, Colas could have a destabilizing effect. Empirical evidence on these conditions as well as on the effects of Colas themselves suggests a stabilizing effect on output and employment and a destabilizing effect on prices. Microeconomic effects include a reduced strike incidence (through long-term agreements), reduced sensitivity of strikes to inflation, increased rigidity of the wage structure, widening union–nonunion and interindustry wage differentials during unanticipated inflation, and reduced skill differentials.

A purpose for investigating the effects of wage indexation is to provide some guide as to the likely impact of various government policies toward indexation. Such guidance can only be given if the parties' response to these policies is known. Part of this response, ignored in the literature cited in this chapter, could be to change other aspects of the labor contract in response to government directives about indexing. To account for such changes, an understanding of how labor and management form contracts under various kinds of constraints is necessary. The next chapter attempts to aid this understanding by surveying existing theories and evidence regarding the demand for wage indexation.

NOTES

1. The assumption of no price inflation is made purely for convenience and is not necessary to the analysis that follows.
2. The direction of the response of employment to real wages is discussed in some detail below.

3. · Similar arguments have been made by Friedman's predecessors. See Fisher (1922) or Jevons (1896).
4. See Braun (1976), Gray (1976, 1978), Fisher (1977c), and Cukierman (1980).
5. See Cukierman (1980) and Barro (1977).
6. See Douty (1975), Cukierman and Razin (1977), Gultekin and Santomero (1979), Butterfield and Kubursi (1981), Peel (1977), and Braun (1976) for discussion of this issue.
7. See note 4.
8. Deferred wage increases, a prevalent feature of U.S. union contracts, are omitted from this model for convenience only.
9. See note 3.
10. Danziger (1981) shows that under different functional forms for disturbances, the optimal degree of indexation need not lie between 0 and 1. The key point is that optimal indexation is not necessarily full indexation (i.e., equal to 1).
11. Cukierman's (1980) model has the additional complications associated with interest rates, investment, and demand shocks. Further, he considers the general case where employment is a weighted average of supply and demand. However, the main results emerge from the simple model considered in the text.
12. See Neftci (1978), Otani (1978), Kahn (1980), and Geary and Kennan (1982).
13. See Cukierman and Razin (1977) and Peel (1977).
14. Recall that under real shocks and supply-determined employment, indexation stabilizes prices and quantities (Cukierman 1980).
15. Razin and Lusky (1979) find that the effective degree of indexation (i.e., the wage response to unanticipated inflation) is 86 percent, a far higher figure than in the United States (see Chapter 6).
16. The other indicators included savings, investment, growth, and interest rates (Page and Trollope 1974).
17. Several economists have considered the role of wage indexation in an open economy under various exchange rate schemes (Marston 1982; Flood and Marion 1982; Turnovsky 1983). A number of complications arise in this work compared to the analysis of a closed economy (Gray 1976; Fischer 1977c). First, the choice of a particular index on which to base wage increases must be made. Should the index include import prices or not? If it does, then a country's exchange rate policy directly affects wage payments. Second, can wage indexation insulate the economy from foreign disturbances in the same way that it can for domestic disturbances? The answer to this question depends on the type of exchange rate policy used. Under fixed exchange rates, a small country is insulated from these shocks; under flexible rates, it is not, when indexation is "optimal" in the sense of minimizing output fluc-

tuations (Flood and Marion 1982). However, insulation from foreign shocks is not an end in itself. If society desires to minimize output fluctuations around potential GNP, then flexible exchange rates are better than fixed rates (Flood and Marion 1982). Third, can the government of a small, open economy coordinate indexation and exchange rate policies? Turnovsky (1983) shows that in general these policies are substitutes: If wages are fully indexed, then exchange rate policy becomes ineffective. On the other hand, if exchange rate policy is aimed to exactly accommodate the demand for money, then indexation becomes ineffective. These issues are not pursued in great detail here because of the relative insulation of the U.S. economy compared to those of Europe.

18. Recall the finding in Table 2–14 that in the 1974–75 period, only 4 to 11 percent of nonunion workers were getting increases called Colas; further, it is likely that many of these increases were discretionary, that is, not automatically tied to the CPI.

19. The studies on spillovers cited were: Mehra (1976), Johnson (1977), Flanagan (1976), Mitchell (1980), and Susan Vroman (1980).

20. Although base wages were included in Wilton's (1979) contract file, average wages had to be proxied from government sources.

REFERENCES

Azariadis, Costas. 1978. "Escalator Clauses and the Allocation of Cyclical Risks." *Journal of Economic Theory* 18, no. 1 (June): 119–55.

Bach, G.L., and R.A. Musgrave. 1941. "A Stable Purchasing Power Bond." *American Economic Review* 31, no. 4 (December): 823–25.

Barro, R.J. 1977. "Long-Term Contracting, Sticky Prices, and Monetary Policy." *Journal of Monetary Economics* 3, no. 3 (July): 305–16.

Braun, Anne Romanis. 1976. "Indexation of Wages and Salaries in Developed Economies." *International Monetary Fund Staff Papers* 26, no. 1 (March): 226–71.

Butterfield, David W., and Atif A. Kubursi. 1981. "Wage Indexation and the Unemployment–Inflation Tradeoff." *Journal of Macroeconomics* 3, no. 2 (Spring): 227–45.

Cukierman, Alex. 1977. "General Wage Escalator Clauses and the Inflation Unemployment Tradeoff." *Economic Inquiry* 15, no. 1 (January): 67–84.

———. 1980. "The Effects of Wage Indexation on Macroeconomic Fluctuations: A Generalization." *Journal of Monetary Economics* 6, no. 2 (April): 147–70.

Cukierman, Alex, and Assaf Razin. 1977. "The Effects of Indexation of Wage Contracts on Macro-Economic Stability." *European Economic Review* 9, no. 1 (April): 83–96.

Danziger, Leif. 1981. "On Optimal Wage Indexation When Shocks Are Real." *Economics Letters* 7, no. 1: 51–53.

Douty, H.M. 1975. "Cost-of-Living Escalator Clauses and Inflation." Prepared for the Council on Wage and Price Stability. Washington, D.C.: U.S. Government Printing Office.

Fischer, Stanley. 1977a. "'Long-Term Contracting, Sticky Prices, and Monetary Policy': A Comment." *Journal of Monetary Economics* 3, no. 3 (July): 317–23.

———. 1977b. "Long-Term Contracts, Rational Expectations, and the Optimal Money Supply Rule." *Journal of Political Economy* 85, no. 1 (February): 191–206.

———. 1977c. "Wage Indexation and Macroeconomic Stability." In *Stabilization of the Domestic and International Economy* (Carnegie–Rochester Series on Public Policy, vol. 5), edited by K. Brunner and A. Meltzer, pp. 107–47. Amsterdam: North-Holland.

Fisher, Irving. 1922. *The Purchasing Power of Money.* New York: Macmillan.

Flanagan, Robert. 1976. "Wage Interdependence in Unionized Labor Markets." *Brookings Papers on Economic Activity,* No. 3: 635–73.

Flood, Robert P., and Nancy P. Marion. 1982. "The Transmission of Disturbances Under Alternative Exchange-Rate Regimes with Optimal Indexing." *Quarterly Journal of Economics* 97, no. 1 (February): 43–66.

Friedman, Milton. 1968. "The Role of Monetary Policy." *American Economic Review* 58, no. 1 (March): 1–17.

———. 1974. "Monetary Correction." In *Essays on Inflation and Indexation,* edited by H. Giersch, pp. 25–61. Washington, D.C.: American Enterprise Institute.

Geary, Patrick T., and John Kennan. 1982. "The Employment–Real Wage Relationship: An International Study." *Journal of Political Economy* 90, no. 4 (August): 854–71.

Giersch, Herbert. 1975. "Index Clauses and the Fight Against Inflation." In *Essays on Inflation and Indexation,* edited by H. Giersch, pp. 1–23. Washington, D.C.: American Enterprise Institute.

Goldstein, Morris. 1975. "Wage Indexation, Inflation, and the Labor Market." *International Monetary Fund Staff Papers* 25, no. 3 (November): 680–713.

Gray, Jo Anna. 1976. "Wage Indexation: A Macroeconomic Approach." *Journal of Monetary Economics* 2, no. 2 (April): 221–35.

———. 1978. "On Indexation and Contract Length." *Journal of Political Economy* 86, no. 1 (February): 1–18.

Gultekin, Bulent, and Anthony Santomero. 1979. "Indexation, Expectations, and Stability." *Journal of Money, Credit and Banking* 11, no. 1 (February): 1–21.

Hamermesh, Daniel. 1983. "Inflation and Labor-Market Adjustment." Unpublished paper, Michigan State University.

Hicks, John R. 1963. *The Theory of Wages,* 2nd ed. New York: St. Martin's Press.

Jevons, W. S. 1896. *Money and the Mechanism of Exchange.* New York: D. Appleton.

Johnson, George E. 1977. "The Determination of Wages in the Union and Non-Union Sectors." *British Journal of Industrial Relations* 15, no. 2 (July): 211–25.

Kahn, Lawrence M. 1980. "Bargaining Power, Search Theory and the Phillips Curve." *Cambridge Journal of Economics* 4, no. 3 (September): 233–44.

———. 1981. "Wage Indexation and Wage Inflation in the U.S.." Unpublished paper, University of Illinois.

Karni, Edi. 1983. "On Optimal Wage Indexation." *Journal of Political Economy* 91, no. 2 (April): 282–92.

Kaufman, Bruce. 1981. "Bargaining Theory, Inflation, and Cyclical Strike Activity." *Industrial and Labor Relations Review* 34, no. 3 (April): 333–55.

Kaufman, Bruce, and Paula Stephan. 1981. "The Determinants of Inter-industry Wage Changes: 1970–1979." Unpublished paper, Georgia State University.

Lucas, R.E., Jr. 1972. "Expectations and the Neutrality of Money." *Journal of Economic Theory* 4 (April): 103–24.

Marston, R.C. 1982. "Wages, Relative Prices and the Choice Between Fixed and Flexible Exchange Rates." *Canadian Journal of Economics* 15, no. 1 (February): 87–103.

Mauro, Martin. 1982. "Strikes as a Result of Imperfect Information." *Industrial and Labor Relations Review* 35, no. 4 (July): 522–38.

Mehra, Y.P. 1976. "Spillovers in Wage Determination in U.S. Manufacturing Industries." *The Review of Economics and Statistics* 58, no. 3 (August): 300–312.

Mitchell, Daniel J.B. 1980. "Union/Nonunion Wage Spillovers: A Note." *British Journal of Industrial Relations* 18, no. 3 (November): 372–76.

Moore, William, and John Raisian. 1980. "Cyclical Sensitivity of Union/ Nonunion Relative Wage Effects." *Journal of Labor Research* 1, no. 2 (Spring): 115–32.

Neftci, Salih N. 1978. "A Time-Series Analysis of the Real-Wages Employment Relationship." *Journal of Political Economy* 86, no. 2 (April pt. 1): 281–91.

Otani, I. 1978. "Real Wages and Business Cycles Revisited." *The Review of Economics and Statistics* 60, no. 2 (May): 301–4.

Page, S.A.B., and Sandra Trollope. 1974. "An International Survey of Indexing and its Effects." *National Institute Economic Review,* no. 70 (November): 46–59.

Peel, D.A. 1977. "On the Case for Indexation of Wages and Salaries." *Kyklos* 30, no. 2: 259–70.

Phelps, Edmund S., and Sidney G. Winter, Jr. 1970. "Optimal Price Policy under Atomistic Competition." In *Microeconomic Foundations of Employment and Inflation Theory,* edited by Edmund S. Phelps, pp. 309–37. New York: Norton.

Plowman, David H. 1981. *Wage Indexation.* Sydney: Allen and Irwin.

Razin, Assaf, and Judith Lusky. 1979. "Partial Wage Indexation: An Empirical Test." *International Economic Review* 20, no. 2 (June): 485–94.

Reder, Melvin, and George Neumann. 1980. "Conflict and Contract: The Case of Strikes." *Journal of Political Economy* 88, no. 5 (October): 867–87.

Rees, Albert. 1970. "The Phillips Curve as a Menu for Policy Choice." *Economica* 37, no. 187 (August): 227–38.

Turnovsky, Stephen J. 1983. "Wage Indexation and Exchange Market Intervention in a Small Open Economy." *Canadian Journal of Economics* 16, no. 4 (November): 574–92.

Ulman, Lloyd. 1974. "Connective Bargaining and Competitive Bargaining." *Scottish Journal of Political Economy* 21, no. 2 (June): 97–109.

Vroman, Susan. 1980. "Research Note: Union/Non-Union Spillovers." *British Journal of Industrial Relations* 18, no. 3 (November): 369–71.

Vroman, Wayne. 1982. "Escalator Clauses and Price-Wage Feedback in the U.S. Economy." Unpublished Paper, The Urban Institute.

Wilton, David A. 1979. "An Analysis of Canadian Wage Contracts with Cost-of-Living Allowance Clauses." Discussion Paper No. 165. Ottawa: The Centre for the Study of Inflation and Productivity, Economic Council of Canada.

Chapter 5

Theories about the Demand for Wage Indexation

The previous chapter surveyed theories and evidence suggesting that wage indexation influences macroeconomic outcomes. Government policies such as wage guidelines which directly or indirectly influence Cola formulation can therefore indirectly influence inflation, GNP growth, and so on. To evaluate the impact of these indirect government policies, the determinants of wage indexation must be known.

Study of the determinants of Colas can also provide insight into the behavior of workers and firms under conditions of uncertainty. The concept of uncertainty has achieved much importance in both micro- and macroeconomic theory (Varian 1978; Barro 1977), and Colas may be seen as an attempt to insure real wages against an uncertain price level. In addition, Colas can be a way of facilitating long-term agreements that save on negotiating costs. Finally, the determinants of the demand for indexation have considerable practical importance for labor and management. Bargaining representatives need to know what workers and managers are willing to trade in order to achieve various levels of indexation.

The task of theories about wage indexation is to provide an understanding of the patterns of Cola incidence and strength that are observed. In particular, the following features of U.S. indexation must be explained by any useful theory of the demand for indexation.

Equations 5-1, 5-2, 5-4, and 5-7 are reproduced with permission of the University of Chicago Press, Chicago.

First, formal indexation exists almost exclusively in union contracts in the United States, but it is much more widespread in countries such as Brazil and Israel. Second, among union workers in major agreements, only 55 to 60 percent have Colas, and those with Colas tend to be in large bargaining units and strong unions. Third, Colas by most measures give only partial protection against inflation, and this degree of protection varies widely across bargaining units and industries. Fourth, the incidence and strength of wage indexation change substantially over time. Fifth, most Colas provide equal cents-per-hour raises for each worker in a given bargaining unit, thus narrowing wage differentials. Sixth, Cola plans have a variety of idiosyncracies, including caps, delays in payments, and corridors. Finally, beginning with the 1948 General Motors (GM)–United Auto Workers (UAW) agreement, there has been a strong positive association between indexation and contract duration.

The theories surveyed in this chapter shed light on these features of U.S. wage indexation. Elements common to these theories include decisionmaking under uncertainty, attitudes toward risk, and efficient bargaining — that is, an arrangement where for any outcome of bargaining it is impossible to design another contract making one party better off without making the other party worse off (Hall and Lilien 1979).

THE DEMAND FOR INDEXATION: RISK SHARING AND UNCERTAINTY

A basic feature of all theories about indexation is that setting wages at the firm level is a costly process. Some of these costs for nonunion firms involve wage surveys as well as the administrative changes necessary when pay rates change. These costs and those associated with collective bargaining, such as the negotiators' time and the potential cost of a strike, are also present for union firms. They imply that a firm can save money by adjusting (or negotiating) wages at periodic intervals (e.g., one year or three years) instead of continuously in response to economic events. Indexation can be useful in such circumstances because it allows wages to adjust automatically in response to these events (e.g., inflation) without costly renegotiation. To implement an indexation scheme, the parties must agree on what constitutes an "economic event" and on how to measure the event.

Wage indexation in practice is based almost exclusively on the CPI, reflecting in part workers' concern with inflation. In addition, the CPI is used because it is widely available and cannot be manipulated by either party (Hall and Lilien 1979).

Models of the demand for indexation attempt to characterize the types of uncertainty that face labor and management during the life of an agreement (or, for nonunion firms, the interval between wage adjustments). For example, Shavell (1976) has constructed a general two-party model where one party must make a deferred payment to the other. It is analogous to a union contract with a Cola where the parties cannot foresee the price level that will prevail when the deferred payment is made. Shavell assumes that in this situation, the parties will come to a "Pareto optimal" or efficient contract. As noted, such a contract can be defined by the condition that for any efficient contract, there exists no other contract that leaves one party better off without making the other party worse off. The relative risk aversion of labor and management, the (possibly different) expectations of labor and management about future inflation, and the correlation of workers' other income and firms' revenue with inflation are all crucial elements in this model.

In this model, Pareto optimal contracts maximize the worker's expected utility (which depends on real income of the representative worker) with management's expected utility (which depends on real profits) held constant.[1] Under such an optimization, it is impossible to make either party better off without making the other worse off. The optimal indexing agreement gives a schedule of wage payments that correspond to each inflation rate. A necessary and sufficient condition for Pareto optimality, if neither party prefers risk, is (Shavell 1976: 162)

$$d_e(s)V'[(e(s)-x(s)] = kd_u(s)U'(u(s)+x(s)),   \text{(5-1)}$$

where $d_e(s)$ and $d_u(s)$ are, respectively, the employer's and worker's subjective density functions over CPI levels, s; $V(-)$ and $U(-)$ are, respectively, the employer's and worker's utility functions; k is a positive constant; $e(-) = $ real revenue; $x(-) = $ real wage; and $u(-) = $ worker's real nonlabor income. Equation 5-1 is a well-known result from the economics of insurance (Arrow 1963). It implies that if both parties have the same expectations — that is, $d_e(-) = d_u(-)$ — then their marginal utilities will be proportional in all states.

By differentiating 5-1 with respect to the CPI(s), the slope of the

optimal real wage schedule with respect to inflation can be obtained
— that is, $x'(s)$. This yields the following expression for the optimal
degree of indexation:

$$x'(s) = \frac{e'(s)p_e(s) - u'(s)p_u(s) + \left[\dfrac{d_u'(s)}{d_u(s)} - \dfrac{d_e'(s)}{d_e(s)}\right]}{p_e(s) + p_u(s)}, \quad (5\text{-}2)$$

where $p_e(s)$ and $p_u(s)$ are, respectively, the employer's and worker's absolute risk aversion, written as functions of s (Shavell 1976:
163). Equation 5-2 has a number of implications for the degree of
indexation.

First, the degree of real wage indexation — that is, $x'(s)$ — is a positive function of the growth in the worker's subjective probability of
higher inflation minus that of the firm. This is intuitive since higher
indexation would be expected the more the firm discounts the likelihood of high inflation rates compared to the worker. Second, if both
parties are risk averse and have the same expectations and if real
revenue and real nonlabor income are constant, then the optimal
contract keeps the real wage constant. That is, wages are 100 percent
indexed to the CPI. This result is logical since 100 percent indexation
guarantees that real profits and workers' real incomes are constant.
Third, if the firm (worker) is risk neutral and the worker (firm) is risk
averse, then the contract will leave the worker's (firm's) real income
constant. However, if both parties are risk neutral, they are indif-
ferent among degrees of indexation even under risk neutrality (see
below).

Fourth, Shavell's analysis becomes slightly more complicated when
the firm's real revenue and the worker's real nonlabor income are
differently affected by inflation. For example, if inflation raises real
revenue and lowers real nonlabor income, then $x'(s) > 0$. In this case,
nominal wages are more than 100 percent indexed to offset simultaneously the changes in the firm's and worker's real incomes. On the other
hand, if revenue and nonlabor income move similarly with inflation,
then the less risk averse party insures the more risk averse. Since firms
are usually considered the less risk averse (Azariadis 1975; Blinder
1977), this implies that the real wage would move in the opposite
direction of real nonlabor income. If workers' nominal income from
savings moves more slowly than inflation (as Blinder argues is likely),
then $x'(s) > 0$ — more than 100 percent indexation. In this sense,
Blinder argues that wage and bond indexation are substitutes.

Given rates of return on savings, $u'(s)$ is higher in *absolute value* as savings grow since interest is compounded on a larger base. Blinder notes that in this framework, if $u'(s) < 0$, then the optimal degree of indexation is higher the larger is the worker's stock of wealth. Further, Cousineau, Lacroix, and Bilodeau (1983) state without proof that in this model a higher expected rate of inflation raises the degree of indexation. However, it is not clear that such a prediction is valid, even in the presence of nonlabor income. To see this, suppose the CPI starts at 1, the worker has fixed nominal nonlabor income b and a base money wage of w_0. Let $\epsilon(c)$ be the nominal percentage degree of indexation, where c is the expected price level in the next period. To keep real income y_r constant,

$$y_r = \frac{b + w_0(1 + \epsilon(c)(c-1))}{c} = b + w_0. \qquad (5\text{-}3)$$

Solving for $\epsilon(c)$,

$$\epsilon(c) = \frac{b + w_0}{w_0}. \qquad (5\text{-}4)$$

Thus, the degree of indexation is independent of the expected price level. Of course, if b or w_0 depend on the expected future price level, then so might the degree of indexation. More generally, if the firm's revenue or the worker's nonlabor income is a nonlinear function of the CPI, then the degree of indexation might not be constant over the life of the contract. This is also a result of Azariadis's (1978) model (see below).

A final implication of Shavell's analysis is that competition in the labor market and heterogeneous tastes among workers generate a market tradeoff between expected real wages and the degree of indexation. More risk averse workers will seek lower wage, more indexed contracts; less risk averse workers will seek higher wage, less indexed agreements.

Shavell's model is consistent with several of the features of indexation in U.S. collective bargaining discussed earlier. First, the degree of indexation varies across bargaining units. Any of the elements of Shavell's model could explain this — for example, difference in beliefs, tastes, or the sensitivity of real revenue or nonlabor income to inflation. Second, the degree of indexation is usually less than 1 ($x'(s) < 0$). This is likely to occur under a variety of circumstances. One set of conditions leading to this result occurs when the worker has no nonlabor income, the firm's revenue moves more slowly than inflation, and both parties are risk averse. However, the observation that indexation is almost nonexistent outside union contracts (an observation not noted by Shavell) is difficult to reconcile with Shavell's approach. He does point out that low quitting costs reduce the likelihood of reaching a binding agreement. Since union workers are less likely to quit than nonunion workers (Freeman 1980), quit propensities might explain the absence of indexation in the nonunion sector. However, we do not observe indexation even in low turnover nonunion settings. On the other hand, Shavell's model makes no allowance for the costs imposed on the employer by a union's strike threat. As discussed below, consideration of these costs helps provide a plausible explanation of the concentration of Colas in the union sector.

It should be pointed out that in Shavell's view, bargaining power influences only the height of the payment schedule, not its slope. The $x(s)$ function is determined solely by a comparison of marginal utilities. Any bargaining considerations can be taken into account by appropriate side payments (i.e., the height of the payment schedule). In models where side payments are ruled out, bargaining power can enter into the determination of the optimal degree of indexation (Card 1982; Ehrenberg, Danziger, and San 1983).[2]

Since Shavell's model of indexation as the pooling of risks, several more elaborate models based on a similar foundation have appeared. These models have added new factors that influence indexation. For example, Azariadis (1978) has constructed a general equilibrium model of indexation as the optimal sharing of risks due to inflation — a similar theme to Shavell's. Azariadis adds the following elements to the simple analysis in Shavell's paper. First, the parties design a wage-employment contract rather than merely setting the degree of indexation. Second, Azariadis includes savings in a two-period model. Third, he explicitly introduces money supply and demand with real and nominal shocks to the system. Finally, he proposes specific production and utility functions to produce a general equilibrium contracting solution. On the other hand, Azariadis makes the simplifying assumption that workers do not have sufficient access to capital markets to purchase indexed bonds as a hedge against inflation. This assumption is made on the grounds that only 5 percent of a typical American's income is from property (Azariadis 1978: 121). Thus, wage indexation is the only method for hedging.

Azariadis finds that the optimal degree of indexation lies between 0 and 1. This follows in part from his one-commodity model with no nonlabor income for workers (see Equation 5-2 for the contrasting results in Shavell). Indexation is perfect when shocks are purely nominal (in his terminology, permanent) and is a negative function of the contribution of real shocks to overall price variance. These findings are similar to Gray's (1976, 1978), which were not based on a risk-pooling model. Instead, her "optimal" degree of indexation was based on minimizing output fluctuations (see Chapter 4). Evidently, her result holds up even under Azariadis's more explicit model of labor–management interaction. Further, Azariadis's model indicates that the degree of indexation is not independent of the price level, since the optimal labor and capital income shares depend on the price level. However, the actual dependence of the indexation parameter on prices cannot be determined a priori.

Finally, Azariadis offers some observations about the impact of a government policy of imposing a different degree of indexation (possibly a 0 degree) from one that would be optimal. In particular, he notes that aggregate well-being would fall if government forces the parties away from the optimum degree of indexation. This fall in real "income" would presumably result in decreased effective demand for output and associated macroeconomic changes. If firms are much less risk averse than workers, a government policy outlawing wage indexation would probably raise wage levels (but lower workers' utility) due to labor supply effects (Shavell 1976), just as interest rate ceilings might lead to increased "service charges" for getting a loan.

While the Azariadis model puts indexation in a general equilibrium context, its aggregate nature yields no predictions about cross-sectional differences in indexation. As noted, Shavell's model suggests that these differences are likely to be affected by differences in the sensitivity of revenue or nonlabor income to inflation as well as differences in beliefs or risk aversion. In addition, neither of these models poses any role for bargaining power because of the possibility of side payments (see above).

The issues of cross-sectional differences in wage indexation and bargaining power are given explicit treatment by Card (1982) and Ehrenberg, Danziger, and San (1983). Each of these models has the following form: Let $U(-)$ and $V(-)$ be the worker's and employer's utility functions (assumed to depend on income only). The two parties choose an indexation function $w(p)$ to maximize

$$E(U(w/p)+hV(\pi/p)),\qquad\qquad(5\text{-}5)$$

where w is the money wage, p is the price level, π is nominal profits, and h is a parameter reflecting the employer's relative bargaining power. Expresson 5-5 assumes that the worker is employed at wage w. Both Card and Ehrenberg, Danziger, and San also consider the case where the worker faces some probability of unemployment. In this case, the worker's expected utility is

$$E(qu(w/p)+(1-q)u(a)),\qquad\qquad(5\text{-}6)$$

where q is the probability of employment and a is the worker's income opportunity when not employed (either unemployment insurance or another job).

A key difference between these bargaining power models and the earlier work on indexing and risk sharing concerns the implications of a value of h less than $1/N$, where N is total union membership. When $h < 1/N$ in Equation 5-4, a unit of employer's utility is "worth" less than a unit of worker's utility. In this case, the "optimal" contract will not maximize the total well-being; instead, worker preferences get more weight than employer preferences. The models of Azariadis and Shavell implicitly assumed that $h = 1/N$, so that total welfare was being maximized. Any bargaining considerations could be handled through lump sum transfers (e.g., bonuses or severance pay). Maximizing of Equation 5-4 with $h < 1/N$ assumes that these transfers do not take place, presumably because of the high cost of their negotiation (Card 1982). The models of Card and Ehrenberg, Danziger, and San are compromises between "pure" efficient bargaining as in Shavell or Azariadis and the noncooperative views in Gray (1976, 1978) or Fischer (1977c).

In addition to their parameterization of bargaining power, the recent indexation models consider the impact of uncertainty about the firm's product demand, prices of nonlabor inputs, productivity, and the workers' opportunities when laid off. The first three types of uncertainty reflect in a specific way Shavell's concept of the firm's revenue uncertainty; the fourth effect brings in a union's wage-employment tradeoff.[3]

To highlight the effects of the output demand, input prices, and risk aversion, Ehrenberg, Danziger, and San construct a model with fixed employment (an assumption they later relax). In this context, labor and management are assumed to maximize an expression such as 5-5. Profits are affected by product demand characteristics, nonlabor input prices, wages, and productivity. It is assumed that the output demand price and the nonlabor input price (1) move homogeneously with degree one with respect to expected inflation, (2) are influenced (perhaps differently) by unanticipated inflation, and (3) have some residual variance. The firm does not learn about these prices until after the contract is signed.

The first-order condition corresponding to maximization of 5-5 is

$$U' = hNEV', \tag{5-7}$$

where N is employment and the expectations operator (E) is taken with respect to the firm's uncertainty over product demand, input prices, and productivity (Ehrenberg, Danziger, and San 1983). Equation 5-7 is analogous to 5-1 with bargaining power added and differences in beliefs omitted. By differentiating 5-7 with respect to inflation, the optimal degree of indexation can be obtained as (Ehrenberg, Danziger, and San 1983: 222)

$$\epsilon = \frac{dw}{dp} \cdot \frac{p}{w} = 1 - \frac{EV''A\left(\dfrac{\pi + wN}{p}\right)}{SEV' - \dfrac{wN}{p}EV''}, \tag{5-8}$$

where $A =$ inflation elasticity of the firm's real value added; $\pi =$ profits; $w =$ wage rate; $p =$ price level; and $S =$ worker's level of relative risk aversion.

Several predictions emerge from Equation 5-8. First, when the firm is risk neutral and the worker is risk averse, wages are perfectly indexed. This is the same finding as in earlier models. Second, $\epsilon \gtrless 1$ as $A \gtrless 0$ if firms are risk averse ($V'' < 0$). Firms for which real value added rises (falls) with inflation (due either to product demand or input prices) will desire $\epsilon > 1$ ($\epsilon < 1$). Again, this is Shavell's result without labor income. Thus, the elasticity of product demand with respect to unanticipated inflation raises, and the elasticity of other input prices lowers, the degree of indexation.[4] Third, an increase in employee risk aversion (S) moves ϵ toward 1 (i.e., raises ϵ when $A < 0$ and lowers ϵ when $A > 0$). Fourth, increased inflation uncertainty raises the probability of indexation (i.e., the probability that the net benefit of some level of indexing is positive) and moves ϵ toward 1 if the shocks to inflation, demand, and input price have some joint distribution. In this case, the more shocks there are to inflation, the less information is obtained from the correlations between these shocks and those to demand and input prices. On the other hand, if all of the real values in the model are unaffected by the distribution of p (i.e., are deterministically related to its realized value), then inflation uncertainty only raises the probability of indexing without affecting ϵ (Ehrenberg, Danziger, and San 1983: 224-25). Since shocks to overall inflation (e.g., money supply growth) also are likely to affect demand and input prices, it seems reasonable to assume some distribution for these shocks. In this case, rising inflation uncertainty would move ϵ toward 1. Fifth, an increase in overall uncertainty about productivity, demand, or input prices moves ϵ away from unity if workers are more risk averse than firms and toward unity if firms are more risk averse than workers. Since workers are probably more risk averse than firms, the effect is to move ϵ away from unity.

To assess the effect of this uncertainty or any other variable on the probability of indexation, the authors note that indexing probably involves costs (e.g., it makes relative wages rigid, a possibly undesirable outcome for the firm). The probability of observing an indexed contract, then, is the likelihood that the benefits of the optimal ϵ exceed the costs. Ehrenberg, Danziger, and San approximate this net benefit and show that it is a positive function of ϵ. Thus, for example, residual uncertainty about real value added raises the probability of indexing when $\epsilon > 1$ and lowers it when $\epsilon < 1$ if workers are more risk averse than firms. However, the authors show that when the parties are equally risk averse, residual uncertainty raises the net benefit of indexing.

A final consideration regarding Equation 5-8 is to note that bargaining power (h) does not appear there explicitly. However, other variables such as wages and profits, themselves functions of bargaining power, do appear in 5-8. To assess the effects of bargaining power (these are not discussed by Ehrenberg, Danziger, and San 1983), recast the basic model as follows. Assume labor and management bargain exclusively over ϵ to maximize

$$W(\epsilon) + hY(\epsilon), \qquad (5\text{-}9)$$

where $W(-)$ and $Y(-)$ are, respectively, the worker's and employer's indirect expected utilities expressed as functions of ϵ. To maximize 5-9, the first-order condition is

$$W'(\epsilon) + hy'(\epsilon) = 0, \qquad (5\text{-}10)$$

and (assuming an interior solution) the effect of employer bargaining power h on the degree of indexation can be computed using

$$W''(\epsilon)\frac{d\epsilon}{dh} + Y'(\epsilon)hY''(\epsilon)\frac{d\epsilon}{dh} = 0. \qquad (5\text{-}11)$$

Thus (in the absence of bargaining over expected wage levels),

$$\frac{d\epsilon}{dh} = \frac{-Y'(\epsilon)}{W''(\epsilon) + hY''(\epsilon)}. \qquad (5\text{-}12)$$

Employer bargaining power raises (lowers) the degree of indexation whenever a rise (fall) in ϵ raises employer expected utility. Returning to the Ehrenberg, Danziger, and San model, condition 5-12 can be applied to their result for ϵ. Whenever the optimal ϵ exceeds 1, it must be true that $Y'(\epsilon) > 0$, since $W'(\epsilon) < 0$ when wages are already over-indexed. In addition, similar reasoning implies that if $\epsilon < 1$, $Y'(\epsilon) < 0$. If $W'(\epsilon)$ and $Y'(\epsilon)$ were both positive or both negative for same ϵ, then this ϵ could not be optimal. Therefore, a rise in employer bargaining power moves the optimal degree of indexation away from 1, since the second-order condition for maximization of 5-9 is

$$W''(\epsilon) + hY''(\epsilon) < 0. \qquad (5\text{-}13)$$

In other words, when $\epsilon > 1$ and thus $Y'(\epsilon) > 0$, an increase in h will raise ϵ since employer utility now has more weight; when $\epsilon < 1$ and thus $Y'(\epsilon) < 0$, higher h means a lower ϵ, again because employer utility now has more weight than before.

To assess the effect of bargaining power on the probability of indexation, recall that the benefit of a Cola is a positive function of the optimal degree of indexation. Thus, since higher union bargaining power moves ϵ toward 1, higher union bargaining power raises the incidence of indexation when $\epsilon < 1$ (countercyclical real value added) and lowers incidence when $\epsilon > 1$ (procyclical real value added). Since worker bargaining power is at its weakest with no unions, we should observe Colas with indexation greater than 1 in nonunion firms with procyclical real value added, as well as the highest degree of indexation in this setting. Since we rarely observe Colas in the nonunion sector, this theory of indexation is incomplete. As discussed below, a key to understanding Cola incidence for nonunion and union workers concerns contract duration and the bargaining costs imposed by a credible strike threat.

Although the Ehrenberg, Danziger, and San simplified model considers the effects of uncertainty about productivity, input prices, and output demand, it makes no allowance for unemployment or workers' opportunities outside the firm. The authors consider these issues at length and thereby arrive at a model similar in spirit to that of Card, whose 1982 paper explicitly considers workers' outside opportunities and the possibility of unemployment. In addition, Card's framework implies a role for indexation even when both parties are risk neutral — a role denied in all of the work considered so far in this chapter. In this instance, the worker's expected utility is given by 5-6 above. Employer profits are assumed to depend on similar factors as in Ehrenberg, Danziger, and San, except that productivity is nonstochastic. In bargaining, there may be incentives for workers to misrepresent a, their contract wage opportunities, and firms to misrepresent characteristics of input prices and output demand (Hall and Lilien 1979). Thus, in long-term contingent contracts, the parties need to rely on indicators, such as the CPI, that cannot be manipulated. In Card's view, the CPI may have informational content about these other factors if shocks to these variables are correlated. Thus, though the basic setup of Card's model is similar to that in 5-6 and 5-7 above, some novel conclusions result. For example, in the case of risk neutrality, there might still be some wage indexation due to movements in a. Specifically, the optimal degree of indexation in this case is

$$\epsilon = 1 + b_a, \tag{5-14}$$

where b_a is the regression coefficient for the shocks in the log of real alternative wages on shocks in inflation (Card 1982: 13). If alternative real wages respond positively (negatively) to unanticipated inflation, then indexation will be greater (less) than 1.[5] Card observes that b_a is likely to be negative, suggesting less-than-complete wage indexation. When risk aversion, employment contingent wages, or both are brought into the model, then ϵ depends not only on b_a, but also on b_m and b_d, respectively the regression coefficients of input prices and output demand shocks on inflation shocks.[6] The results for b_m and b_d are similar to those found in Ehrenberg, Danziger, and San.[7] Card argues that real raw materials prices move procyclically and real durable manufactured goods prices are countercyclical. He thus predicts that ϵ should be higher in nondurable manufacturing and services than in durable manufacturing. This result is not borne out in our data (see Chapter 6). As was the case in the other models surveyed so far, Card's has a hard time explaining why there is virtually no indexation outside the union sector. Although differences in b_a for union and nonunion workers could explain this fact, it does not seem a plausible explanation. Alternative jobs for union and nonunion workers typically constitute some portion of the nonunion sector (due to queues in the union sector).[8] Thus, b_a is not likely to be very different for union or nonunion workers.

COLAS, CONTRACT LENGTH, AND UNION–NONUNION DIFFERENCES IN INDEXATION

As previously noted, models of efficient risk sharing have not been able to explain why indexation is limited to the union sector. Consideration of contract length and negotiation costs can help provide this explanation.

Labor history and current data show a strong positive association between wage indexation and contract length in the union sector.[9] Gray (1978) has constructed a model of indexation demand that predicts this association.[10] In her model there is no risk aversion. Instead, the parties are concerned with fluctuations in output and the costs of contract negotiations. A key assumption is that uncertainty about inflation increases with the length of the parties' required forecasts. Thus, frequent renegotiation of an agreement implies smaller deviations of actual real wages from expected wages. Output and employment can reach their desired levels more quickly with more frequent negotiations.[11] However, with contracting costs, the parties must weigh the costs of frequent negotiations with the costs of fluctuations in output from its desired level (Gray 1978: 7). The implied optimization process requires that increased monetary and real (i.e., productivity) uncertainty decrease contract length and that rises in contracting costs increase contract length.

Gray also presents a model that includes costs of indexation. As noted, some of these costs might include the undesirability of relative wage rigidity on the part of firms or "administrative costs" associated with Colas. In this context, she shows that Colas will appear only in longer contracts. The gains from indexing are greater with longer contract duration.

The connections between gains from indexation and contract duration and between contract duration and negotiation costs help explain union–nonunion differences in indexation. A rise in negotiation costs lowers the frequency of negotiation. With longer contract length, there is a greater chance that the gains from indexation outweigh the costs. Thus, the likelihood of wage indexation rises. A crucial difference between the union and nonunion sectors is the strike threat posed by unions. This threat is a major component of the cost of negotiating a contract. In fact, as was noted in Chapter 2, union employers such as GM initially sought long-term agreements to reduce the chances for a union to strike. Thus, the strike threat raises the likelihood of indexation by making a long-term agreement more attractive. Colas are often viewed by management as the price that must be paid in order to gain labor peace through a long-term contract (see Chapter 2). This connection between bargaining costs, duration, and Colas is underscored by the fact that indexation is virtually nonexistent among union contracts with one-year duration (Sheifer 1979). Colas yield smaller gains to both parties in bargaining units where the union's strike threat is weak enough to permit annual negotiations. Since nonunion wages are also set about every year (Flanagan 1976), there appears to be a similarity between wage-setting practices for union workers with one-year contracts and those for nonunion workers, neither of which typically include indexation.

Strikes and bargaining costs help explain why union workers are more likely to have Colas than nonunion workers. However, they do not explain why Colas are virtually nonexistent outside the union sector. For the typical nonunion firm and worker, the gains to indexing in our relatively noninflationary environment must be less than the costs associated with using a formula to set wages (see above). If our economy were subject to significantly greater inflation uncertainty (such as Israel's or Brazil's), then real wage insurance in the form of Colas would become more valuable for workers and, possibly, firms as well.

Consideration of the union strike threat as a cost of negotiation suggests an increase in the likelihood of observing indexation with more credible threats. This conclusion holds whether the optimal degree of indexation is greater or less than 1, provided that longer duration in nonindexed agreements raises losses due to unanticipated inflation, product demand changes, et cetera. However, bargaining costs per se do not influence the degree of indexation once the decision to index has been made (Gray 1978). Thus, when consideration of the strike threat is combined with the risk-sharing impact of bargaining power, higher union bargaining power still moves the degree of indexation toward 1. Further, when $\epsilon < 1$, there are now two reasons for a positive effect of union bargaining on the probability of indexing: (1) a rise in ϵ, and (2) increased contracting costs. However, when $\epsilon > 1$, an unambiguous prediction about the effect of union bargaining power on the probability of a Cola cannot be made. Although ϵ falls (lowering this likelihood), contract costs rise (increasing this probability). Finally, as noted in Shavell's (1976) side payments model, union bargaining power does not affect the degree of indexation. However, if the strike threat raises negotiation costs, then even in his model, union bargaining power raises the incidence of wage indexation. [12]

SUMMARY AND CONCLUSIONS

This chapter has reviewed theories about the demand for wage indexation. A basic framework for these theories was provided by Shavell (1976). In his model, Colas can aid labor and management to share efficiently the risks of uncertain inflation. Employer and employee risk aversion, beliefs about inflation, and the effects of inflation on firm revenue and employee nonlabor income are all crucial determinants of the degree of indexation. This framework has been modified in several important ways. First, efficient bargaining models where both wages and employment are set have been devised. Second, various kinds of uncertainty, including output demand, input prices, productivity, money supply, and alternative job opportunities uncertainty, have been considered. Third, concepts of bargaining power, negotiation costs, and costs of indexing have been added to the basic framework.

Several predictions flow from this literature. For example, risk-averse workers and firms will ordinarily desire complete indexation of their total incomes. Efficient contracts balance out these desires, leading to some compromise in which neither firm nor worker income is necessarily completely indexed to the inflation rate. In addition, if workers have no nonlabor income, are fully tenured and risk averse, and firms are risk neutral, then the optimal degree of indexation, ϵ, is 1. Moreover, if firms and workers are both risk averse and workers can switch jobs, the following features move ϵ toward 1: an elasticity of real product demand, real nonlabor income, real alternative wages, or real input prices, with respect to inflation closer to 0; a rise in worker risk aversion; an increase in inflation uncertainty; a decrease in residual uncertainty about productivity, input prices, output demand, or alternative wages; and an increase in worker bargaining power (when labor and management cannot make lump sum transfers to each other). Further, anything that raises the optimal degree of indexation raises the probability of observing a Cola; higher contracting or lower indexation costs also raise this probability. Since a more credible union strike threat raises the expected costs of contract negotiations, union bargaining power raises the incidence of Colas as long as $\epsilon < 1$ and has theoretically ambiguous effects when $\epsilon > 1$.

The absence of a strike threat in the nonunion sector helps explain the lower Cola incidence in that sector. The virtual absence of formal indexation for nonunion workers is more difficult to explain. It is likely that high costs of indexation, low variance of unanticipated inflation, and low costs of annual wage setting help explain this absence. However, none of the theories described can explain why Colas generally give equal cents-per-hour raises and thus narrow wage differentials. A theory that includes bargaining among coalitions within a union as well as union–management bargaining might prove helpful to resolve this question.

Finally, the theories surveyed in this chapter indicate that if the government imposes wage indexation, companies will be able to offer lower levels of wages or benefits.[13] On the other hand, if Colas are outlawed, firms will have to raise wages or benefits. These compensating changes in labor costs suggest smaller long-run effects of such policies on economic welfare than otherwise.

NOTES

1. This formulation gives the same results as maximizing management's expected utility, holding the union expected utility constant.
2. The issue of bargaining power and wage indexation is discussed at greater length later in this chapter.
3. Card (1982) and Ehrenberg, Danziger, and San (1983) discuss these features. In addition, Blanchard (1979) has devised a model of optimal indexing with consideration of raw materials prices. His conclusions on the effects of these prices are similar to those of the other two papers (see below).
4. See Blanchard (1979) for this latter result.
5. Card (1982) notes that if the contract also makes wages contingent on employment, then ϵ also may depend on $b_m, b_d...$, the "effects" of inflation shocks on raw materials price shocks and output demand shocks. In these cases, the CPI is used to obtain information about the factors affecting demand for labor and should thus affect wages.

6. See note 5.
7. Ehrenberg, Danziger, and San (1983) extend their model to allow unemployment. The effects of unemployment insurance (UI) are then investigated. A rise in experience rating r of UI is found to move ϵ toward 1, while for low values of r a rise in UI benefits moves ϵ away from 1.
8. For evidence and modeling of the union queuing process, see Abowd and Farber (1982) and Blau and Kahn (1983).
9. See Chapters 2 and 3 as well as Sheifer (1979).
10. Ehrenberg, Danziger, and San's (1983) paper also considers contract length and obtains similar results as Gray (1978).
11. This result occurs because Gray (1978) assumes that the employer sets the quantity of labor hired on the basis of actual real wages.
12. If risk aversion declines with income or assets (Azariadis 1975), then risk aversion may be less in strong unions than in weak unions. However as long as real wage insurance is a normal good, rising union power moves ϵ toward 1.
13. As long as worker risk aversion is greater than risk aversion of company negotiators, this will be the case.

REFERENCES

Abowd, John, and Henry Farber. 1982. "Job Queues and the Union Status of Workers." *Industrial and Labor Relations Review* 35, no. 2 (April): 359–67.

Arrow, Kenneth J. 1963. "Uncertainty and the Welfare Economics of Medical Care." *American Economic Review* 53, no. 5 (December): 941–73.

Azariadis, Costas. 1975. "Implicit Contracts and Underemployment Equilibria." *Journal of Political Economy* 83, no. 6 (December): 1183–1202.

———. 1978. "Escalator Clauses and the Allocation of Cyclical Risks." *Journal of Economic Theory* 18, no. 1 (June): 119–55.

Barro, Robert. 1977. "Long-Term Contracting, Sticky Prices, and Monetary Policy." *Journal of Monetary Economics* 3, no. 3 (July): 305–16.

Blanchard, Olivier. 1979. "Wage Indexing Rules and the Behavior of the Economy." *Journal of Political Economy* 87, no. 4 (August): 798–815.

Blau, Francine D., and Lawrence M. Kahn. 1983. "Job Search and Unionized Employment." *Economic Inquiry* 21, no. 3 (July): 412–30.

Blinder, Alan. 1977. "Indexing the Economy Through Financial Intermediation." In *Stabilization of the Domestic and International Economy* (Carnegie-Rochester Series on Public Policy, vol. 5), edited by K. Brunner and A. Meltzer, pp. 69–105. Amsterdam: North-Holland.

Card, David. 1982. "Indexation in Long Term Labor Contracts: A Theoretical and Empirical Analysis." Unpublished paper, University of Chicago.

Cousineau, Jean-Michel; Robert Lacroix; and Danielle Bilodeau. 1983. "The Determinants of Escalation Clauses in Collective Agreements." *The Review of Economics and Statistics,* 65, no. 2 (May): 196–202.

Ehrenberg, Ronald; Leif Danziger; and Gee San. 1983. "Cost-of-Living Adjustment Clauses in Union Contracts: A Summary of Results." *Journal of Labor Economics* 1, no. 3 (July): 215–45.

Fischer, Stanley. 1977. "Wage Indexation and Macroeconomic Stability." In *Stabilization of the Domestic and International Economy* (Carnegie-Rochester Series on Public Policy, vol. 5), edited by K. Brunner and A. Meltzer, pp. 107–47. Amsterdam: North-Holland.

Flanagan, Robert. 1976. "Wage Interdependence in Unionized Labor Markets." *Brookings Papers on Economic Activity,* No. 3: 635–73.

Freeman, Richard. 1980. "The Exit-Voice Tradeoff in the Labor Market: Unionism, Job Tenure, Quits and Separation." *Quarterly Journal of Economics* 94, no. 377 (June): 643–73.

Gray, Jo Anna. 1976. "Wage Indexation: A Macroeconomic Approach." *Journal of Monetary Economics* 2, no. 2 (April): 221–35.

————. 1978. "On Indexation and Contract Length." *Journal of Political Economy* 86, no. 1 (February): 1–18.

Hall, Robert, and David Lilien. 1979. "Efficient Wage Bargains under Uncertain Supply and Demand." *American Economic Review* 69, no. 5 (December): 868–79.

Shavell, Steven. 1976. "Sharing Risks of Deferred Payment." *Journal of Political Economy* 84, no. 1 (February): 161–68.

Sheifer, Victor J. 1979. "Cost-of-Living Adjustment: Keeping Up With Inflation?" *Monthly Labor Review* 102, no. 6 (June): 14–17.

Varian, Hal. 1978. *Microeconomic Analysis.* New York: Norton.

Chapter 6

Empirical Results: Cola Incidence and Strength of Indexation

The previous chapter provided a discussion of the economic determinants of the incidence of Cola clauses in union contracts as well as strength of indexation for those contracts that contain Colas. In this chapter these results are used to formulate empirical models to test hypotheses about Cola incidence and the degree of indexation using our data base of union contracts. Estimates of the degree of indexation found in the manufacturing sector of the U.S. economy are also provided. Finally, our results are compared to those found in other empirical studies.

As is true in most empirical studies, the translation of a theoretical model to an empirical model often is not straightforward. This chapter therefore begins with a discussion of measuring the degree of indexation in union contracts.

MEASURING THE STRENGTH OF COLAS

In the simplest, one-period model of Cola formulation, characterization of the Cola is straightforward. The contract is either indexed or not. If it is indexed, the degree of indexation can be summarized by the elasticity of the wage rate with respect to the aggregate price level,

$$\epsilon = \frac{dw}{dp}\frac{p}{w} \qquad (6\text{-}1)$$

153

although ϵ need not be constant over a contract. This elasticity provides a natural bridge to the models discussed in Chapters 4 and 5. As noted in Chapter 5, a number of economic variables influence the optimal level of this elasticity for any given bargaining unit.

As we move to a multiperiod context, however, the picture becomes considerably more clouded. Unless both parties agree that no changes in demand and supply conditions will occur over the life of the contract, some mechanism for changing wages over the contract must be bargained. Suppose, for example, that both parties agree that a certain positive level of inflation $\dot{p}$ will occur with certainty over the contract life. This inflation rate will erode the real wage throughout the contract. The problem faced by the bargainers is to design a nominal wage rate schedule that will yield the optimal level of real wages. This problem has been investigated by Christofides (1982), and his line of reasoning is followed here.

The standard answer to this question is simply to adjust the nominal wage w to rise instantaneously according to $w(1+\dot{p})$. However, it is quite costly to change wages constantly. An alternative is to design a nominal wage schedule that yields the optimal real wage bill over the life of the contract, even though the actual real hourly wage at a given point might deviate from the optimal path for the optimal real wage. One possibility is to "front-load" the contract so that the real hourly wage is above the optimal wage at the beginning and below the optimal wage at the end. A second alternative is to build in noncontingent wage increases to be paid at future times during the contract. This would allow the nominal wage to move as a step function and reduce the difference between optimal and actual real hourly wages during the contract. A third alternative is to agree to pay a "catch-up" wage increase at the end of the current contract or the beginning of the next contract.

These three alternatives are examples of possible methods of approximating the optimal real wage path using discrete, noncontingent wage increases. If the inflation rate is known with certainty, the parties can mimic a pure indexation scheme that makes wage changes contingent upon actual inflation rates. However, the inflation rate is never known with certainty. Thus, as noted in Chapters 4 and 5, indexation provides the additional benefit of acting as real wage insurance against unanticipated changes in prices.

As Card (1983) notes, most multiperiod, indexed contracts provide a combination of noncontingent and contingent wage increases. The noncontingent portion of the wage increase might simply reflect anticipated increases in productivity that are not associated with price changes. In this case, the second period wage w_2 can be written as (Card 1983)

$$\log w_2 = \log w_2^N + \epsilon^* \log p, \qquad (6\text{-}2)$$

where w_2^N is the noncontingent wage reflecting productivity increases and ϵ^* is the optimal degree of indexation bargained between the parties. Suppose that some fraction f of the optimal wage change associated with expected price changes, $\epsilon^* E[\log p]$, is incorporated in the noncontingent wage increase. Then the second period wage can be rewritten as

$$\log w_2 = \log w_2^N + \epsilon^*(\log p - fE[\log p]) + \epsilon^* fE[\log p]$$
$$= \log w_2^{N^*} + \epsilon^*(\log p - fE[\log p]), \qquad (6\text{-}3)$$

where $w_2^{N^*}$ now combines both wage changes due to anticipated price changes and due to changes in productivity. This formulation gives a natural interpretation of Cola provisions such as triggers and delays before the beginning of indexation which were discussed in Chapter 3.

This presentation shows that empirical measurement of the optimal degree of indexation ϵ^* might not be as straightforward as is suggested in a one-period model, due to the presence of deferred, scheduled wage increases. The standard method of measuring this elasticity is to use the *ex post* realization of price changes and contingent wage changes. This will tend to underestimate the true elasticity to the extent that some of the optimal change in wages associated with price changes is given in the form of noncontingent wage increases. Alternatively, the sum of contingent and noncontingent *ex post* wage increases might be used. This will tend to overestimate the elasticity to the extent that productivity changes were built into the noncontingent wage changes.

Another possibility, suggested by Card (1982, 1983) is to estimate the desired degree of indexation by the *ex ante* formula as measured at the start of escalation. If Equation 6-3 is reasonably representative of the wage bargain, the "marginal" elasticity given by the indexation formula will be a better measure of the desired elasticity than either elasticity measure that involved using *ex post* realizations of contingent wage increases. This approach has the further advantage that no data on price changes or expected price changes are required. We simply need to know the escalation formula and the wage level.

The major problem with the *ex ante* approach is that it ignores facets of escalation formulas that limit the degree of indexation at points after the start of escalation. Corridors and maximums on Cola payments are obvious examples. Thus, use of only the *ex ante* formula will tend to overestimate the desired degree of indexation to the extent that these payment limits were anticipated *ex ante* by the parties. These contract provisions occur with fair regularity (see Chapter 2) and are not random occurrences in contracts. Corridors and maximums may be a way of designing a nonlinear indexation function.

The missing ingredient in these *ex post* and *ex ante* measures of elasticities is information on price expectations. If the price expectations of the parties can be measured, then the contingent changes in wages due to *unanticipated* inflation can be inferred from the formulas, where all aspects of the Cola are taken into account. This measure of the desired degree of indexation will be purged of the problems due to noncontingent increases that are associated with *ex post* measures and will not require assumptions about Cola limits that are implicit in the *ex ante* measures of marginal elasticities.

Since most Cola formulas are given in cents-per-unit change in the CPI, measurement of ϵ will depend on the time frame used as well as the wage level benchmark, even if one has solved the *ex ante-ex post* problem. Consider the following example: Suppose that the Cola formula gives one cent per c points change in CPI. Define the degree of indexation at time t,

$$\epsilon_t = \left(\frac{d \ln w}{d \ln P} \right)_t = \left(\frac{dw}{dP} \Big/ \frac{P}{w} \right)_t. \tag{6-4}$$

We begin with wage level w_0 and CPI level P_0. By the Cola formula, the wage at time t is

$$w_t = w_0 + \frac{P_t - P_0}{c}. \tag{6-5}$$

The degree of indexation at time t is therefore

$$\epsilon_t = \frac{dw}{dP} \cdot \frac{P_t}{w_t} = \frac{1}{c} \cdot \frac{P_t}{w_0 + \dfrac{P_t - P_0}{c}} = \frac{P_t}{cw_0 + P_t - P_0}. \tag{6-6}$$

Suppose further that there is some positive level of inflation throughout the time period. Differentiating the degree of indexation at time t with respect to the price at time t yields

$$\frac{d\epsilon_t}{dP_t} = \frac{cw_0 + P_t - P_0 - P_t}{(cw_0 + P_t - P_0)^2} = \frac{cw_0 - P_0}{(cw_0 + P_t - P_0)^2}. \qquad (6\text{-}7)$$

Since the denominator of 6-7 is always nonnegative, change in the degree of indexation will depend on the starting conditions. If the original formula was unit elastic ($cw_0 = P_0$), the degree of indexation will not change. If the formula was greater than unit elastic ($cw_0 < P_0$), the degree of indexation will fall. Finally, if the formula had an elasticity less than 1, the degree of indexation will rise through time.

Further, the speed of adjustment (downward or upward) of the degree of indexation through time depends on how much higher or lower the original indexation was from unit elasticity. To see this result, we differentiate the log of the degree of indexation at time t with respect to the price to yield

$$\frac{d(\log \epsilon_t)}{dP_t} = \frac{cw_0 - P_0}{(cw_0 - P_0)P_t + P_t^2} = Y. \qquad (6\text{-}8)$$

We then differentiate 6-8 with respect to the initial condition $cw_0 - P_0$

$$\frac{dY}{d(cw_0 - P_0)} = \frac{P_t^2}{[(cw_0 - P_0)P_t + P_t^2]^2} > 0. \qquad (6\text{-}9)$$

Thus, the speed of adjustment depends on the original level of indexation. This result is shown in Figure 6-1.

Although this stylized representation of the degree of indexation ignores many possible Cola attributes (maximums, corridors, triggers, etc.), it does point out some measurement issues that are germane in the analysis and representation of Cola strength when formulas are primarily given in cents per point change in the CPI. First, measured values for wage elasticities at the beginning of indexation will be biased in a very particular way even if no maximums or other provisions exist. Elasticities greater than 1 will be overestimates; elasticities less than 1 will be underestimates. Second, elasticities measured for low-wage workers will typically be larger than elasticities for high-wage and average-wage workers. However, with no Cola maximums these elasticities will tend to come closer together over the contract.

In the *ex post* measures of elasticities that are estimated in this chapter, contract length is used as our unit of observation. Thus, even when these *ex post* measures are treated properly, they will typically be lower than beginning elasticities if the beginning elasticities

Figure 6-1. Degree of Indexation and Time.

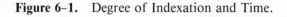

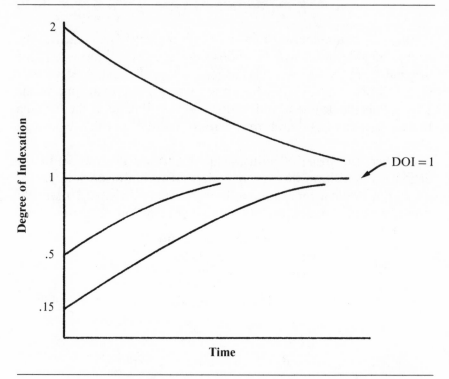

were greater than unit elastic and less than the beginning elasticities when the beginning elasticities were less than 1.

In summary, there are several candidates for measuring *the* degree of indexation of wages. Each approach has its advantages and disadvantages. In fact, Ehrenberg, Danziger, and San (1983) argue that it might be impossible to summarize Cola information in a single number. Their approach is to analyze each component of the Cola formula separately (e.g., frequency of review, presence of a minimum or maximum payment, type of formula (cents/CPI change), etc.).[1] They hoped that the impact of their explanatory variables would be consistent across the results for their vector of independent variables. Unfortunately, the results are very mixed, and no clear pattern emerges. This is not unexpected since there are a large number of combinations of these provisions that can yield the same desired wage-price function. There is no a priori reason for believing that good (i.e., more lucrative) provisions are highly correlated with each other or are related to the explanatory variables in the same way.

Our approach is to provide several measures of the degree of indexation of contracts. The first is an *ex post* measure of the proportion of the total wage increase that is contingent on price changes. *Controlling for the level of inflation,* we argue that higher values of this index indicate larger utility associated with risk sharing. The remainder of our measures involve estimation of standard wage elasticities for a subset of our data base. An "actual" elasticity that is purely *ex post* and suffers from the criticisms given above is estimated. We also estimate an "expected" elasticity—that is, an elasticity contingent upon expectations when the contract was signed. This is an *ex ante* measure, but it still has some of the problems associated with the "actual" elasticity since there is no way to separate the proportion of the noncontingent wage increase that might have been due to expected inflation. Finally, the elasticity of wages with respect to *unanticipated* inflation is estimated. This measure provides further information about the "optimal" degree of indexation discussed in Chapter 5.

EMPIRICAL PROCEDURES: COLA INCIDENCE

Unlike the degree of indexation of a contract, the presence or absence of a Cola in a contract is fairly straightforward and therefore subject to fewer measurement problems. In our analysis the presence of a Cola is defined as any situation in which future wage increases are tied to price changes. Noncontingent wage increases (i.e., flat cents/hour or percentages) which are called Colas in contract language are therefore assumed to be unindexed, but all Colas that have maximums or corridors are included in the indexed category.[2]

Although, in principle, the total (weighted) utility to the parties of having a Cola (and associated degree of indexation) is a continuous variable, in this initial analysis, we only observe whether or not the contract contains a Cola. Suppose that the (net) utility of a Cola can be expressed as

$$L = B'x + v \qquad (6-10)$$

where x is a vector of the determinants of this utility, B is a vector of coefficients, and v is a random error term. Assume that

$$COLA = 1 \quad \text{if } L > 0$$

$$= 0 \quad \text{otherwise,} \qquad (6-11)$$

where COLA is the empirical observation that a Cola is present in the contract.

This formulation is captured in the following probit function for the probability an agreement has a Cola clause:

$$P(COLA = 1) = F(B'x), \qquad (6\text{-}12)$$

where $COLA$ equals 1 if the agreement has a Cola clause and 0 if otherwise; $F(\cdot)$ is the cumulative distribution function for a standard normal random variable; B is a column vector of probit coefficients; and x is a column vector of explanatory variables.

From our discussion in the previous chapter, the vector x should include variables that empirically capture the following theoretical constructs:

- relative risk aversion of the parties;
- impact of inflation on the worth of the firm and workers' incomes and alternatives;
- costs of indexation and bargaining;
- uncertainty about future prices;
- bargaining power of the parties; and
- information content of the price measure used in the formula.

Unfortunately, there rarely exist perfect empirical counterparts to these constructs. A listing of the variables that we have used and their explanations is given in Table 6-1. A discussion of our interpretation of these variables follows.

Explanatory variables that measure industry and labor market structure could be proxies for bargaining power, the cost of indexation or bargaining, or relative risk aversion. Workers in large bargaining units ($SIZE$) and in highly organized industries (UN) might have less nonunion competition than otherwise and thus more bargaining power. As noted in Chapter 5, some models that are based on efficient bargaining and that posit a constant level of risk aversion for workers imply that higher union bargaining power moves the optimal degree of indexation toward 1. If the optimal degree of indexation is less than 1, increases in union bargaining power will increase the probability of indexation. Since indexation only rarely exists in nonunion situations, it seems safe to argue that employers do not want indexation in the absence of union demands. Even if the efficient-bargaining model is denied, greater union strength means a greater ability to impose costs on the employer if disagreement on an issue

Table 6–1. Variables Included in Estimating Equations for the Probability that a Contract Contains a Cola.

Name	Explanation [a]	Exclusions for Nonmanufacturing [b]
SIZE	number of workers covered by the agreement	
UN	percentage of the particular industry's workers covered by collective bargaining (in percentage points)	
CR8	eight-firm concentration ratio for the industry (percentage of the value of shipments in percentage points)	*
CRAFT	fraction of the industry's unionized workers who were craftsmen	
OPER	fraction of the industry's unionized workers who were operatives	
LGSMSA	fraction of the industry's unionized workers who lived in the thirty-four largest standard metropolitan statistical areas (SMSAs)	
MAR	fraction of the industry's unionized workers who were married with spouse present	
MALE	fraction of the industry's unionized workers who were male	
WHITE	fraction of the industry's unionized workers who were white	
ED	average grades of school completed for the industry's unionized workers	
EXP	average potential experience (age-ED-5) of the industry's unionized workers	
EXP^2	average of (age-ED-5)^2 for the industry's unionized workers	
CHILD	average number of dependent children of the industry's unionized workers	
SOUTH	1 if the contract covers workers only in the South (census definition) and 0 otherwise	

Table 6–1.   (Continued)

Name	Explanation	Exclusions for Nonmanufacturing
MULTI	1 if the agreement is a multifirm contract and 0 if a single-firm contract	
CONSOL	percentage of unionized workers in the industry organized by the largest union (in percentage points) in that industry	
COEFF	respectively, the coefficient on log (consumer price index) and the	*
SIGMA	standard error of the regression from a regression of the log of the industry's wholesale price index on the log of the consumer price index, using monthly data from 1971 to 1977	*
VARINFL	variance of twelve-month forecasts of consumer price inflation, as of the time of the signing of a particular agreement [c]	
TIME	time trend referring to the date of the signing of the contract	

[a] Full explanations of the data and data sources are given in Appendix 6A.

[b] Worker characteristics were for the industry rather than for just union workers. Variables with * were not included in the nonmanufacturing analysis due to lack of data.

[c] These forecasts are taken from the Livingston data (see Appendix 6A); since these data were collected every six months, interpolation was used to compute the variance for each month.

occurs. A strong union, for example, imposes high negotiation costs in the form of a more credible strike threat. This phenomenon implies that stronger unions will have contracts that are of longer duration and are more likely to contain a Cola clause than the contracts of weaker unions. Indeed, in the United States, wage indexation is almost exclusively a union phenomenon, and among one-year contracts there are virtually no Colas (see Chapter 5).

Some observers believe, however, that relative risk aversion is not constant but declines with income or assets (Azariadis 1975). Thus, the risk aversion of members of strong unions might be less than that for members of weak unions. However, as long as real wage insurance is not an inferior good, rising union power may still move ϵ toward 1. As long as $\epsilon < 1$ — a likely outcome — rising union bargaining power would raise the probability of observing a Cola.

Firms in concentrated industries ($CR8$) are better able to pass on wage increases to customers as price increases, reducing risks associated with indexation. Nonconstant risk aversion would also suggest that these firms would be less inclined to resist indexation. On the other hand, oligopolistic firms have more resources with which to fight unions. Studies of the effect of concentration on union wages have yielded mixed results.[3] Thus, $CR8$ has theoretically ambiguous effects on $P(COLA) = 1$.

The two variables measuring the degree of centralization of labor market bargaining ($CONSOL$ and $MULTI$) might also be related to bargaining power, although these relationships are theoretically ambiguous. Multifirm contracts ($MULTI$) might take wages out of competition and reduce the effective elasticity of demand for labor (compared to that under single-firm agreements), thus raising union power. On the other hand, multifirm contracts reduce unions' ability to whipsaw employers. The empirical evidence on these effects is mixed (Hendricks 1975; Feuille, Hendricks, and Kahn 1981; Hendricks and Kahn 1984). $CONSOL$ may be positively related to union power, since a higher value for $CONSOL$ implies a greater union ability to present a unified front to the employer. However, union rivalry might force union leaders to bargain more aggressively to impress their constituencies. Feuille, Hendricks, and Kahn (1981) found an insignificant wage effect for this variable.

Wage indexation introduces rigidities into the wage-setting process since the same formula would be applied under a possibly wide variety of circumstances. Thus, the informational content of the price index would decrease in a multifirm situation, and the costs of indexation might increase. A large number of unions in the industry ($CONSOL$) could also signal a wide variety of indexation plans. This would tend to increase the costs of indexation. Under both these interpretations, lower values of $CONSOL$ and values of 1 for $MULTI$ would be associated with a lower probability of a Cola.

The demographic variables ($CRAFT, OPER, MALE, WHITE, ED, EXP, EXP^2, MAR, CHILD$) represent the effects of individual productivity characteristics and discrimination on bargaining power as well as differences in relative risk aversion. Under the bargaining power interpretation, they might be expected to have the same effect on $P(COLA = 1)$ as they have on wage levels. In this case, all (except EXP^2) would be positively associated with Cola incidence. However, these variables can also be associated with lower relative risk aversion for reasons discussed earlier. The strongest candidates for this interpretation are probably the family variables (MAR, $CHILD$). Since more experienced workers are typically older, and older workers exhibit higher risk aversion in other areas (e.g., auto insurance rates), we anticipate an unambiguous positive impact of experience on Cola incidence. Finally, the costs of wage rigidity under Colas might be especially high for educated workers.

The location variables ($SOUTH$ and $LGSMSA$) are also associated with bargaining power, since unions are generally stronger in larger cities and in areas other than the South.[4] Moreover, the informational content of the CPI is considerably less outside SMSAs, further suggesting a positive effect for $LGSMSA$.

The variables $COEFF$ and $SIGMA$ are included in analysis of the manufacturing sample to attempt to proxy the relationship between industry prices and inflation. $COEFF$ is a measure of the responsiveness of the industry's price to the CPI; a higher value for this variable might indicate that inflation increases (or at least does not decrease) the firm's net worth. Unfortunately, increasing industry prices don't necessarily guarantee increasing profits for an individual firm. $SIGMA$ is a proxy for the unanticipated volatility of the industry's price and therefore is an inverse measure of the informational content of a CPI-based formula. On this ground, a high value should reduce the incidence of Cola clauses.[5]

$VARINFL$ is intended to capture uncertainty about future prices and is expected to increase the incidence of Cola clauses. The final variable is the time trend, $TIME$, which can pick up secular changes in the incidence of Colas as well as changes in the accuracy of Bureau of Labor Statistics (BLS) sampling of nonmajor agreements in the manufacturing sample. Because of the possible biases induced by inaccurate sampling of the small agreements in manufacturing, we reestimated Equation 6-12 by restricting the manufacturing sample to major agreements. The nonmanufacturing sample contains only major agreements. The results for this reestimation did not differ from the earlier results, suggesting that this sampling bias is small.

The analysis includes no measure of the expected rate of inflation or of contract duration. Theoretical models pose no role for the expected rate of inflation, except to say that ϵ need not be constant. As noted below, inclusion of such a variable yielded insignificant results and did not affect the other coefficients. The theory of Cola formulation suggests that indexation and contract length are chosen jointly (Gray 1978). Equation 6–12 represents a reduced form version of this choice and thus should not include contract duration. The inclusion of contract duration in this equation produced the expected significant positive coefficient for this variable but did not affect the other results.

EMPIRICAL RESULTS: INCIDENCE OF INDEXATION

The probit results for the probability that an agreement had a Cola are reported in Table 6–2. The variables *SIZE*, *UN*, and *CR8* (manufacturing only) each have significant, positive coefficients. These results are consistent with their interpretation as proxies for union bargaining power. The *SIZE* result is consistent with the comparison of Cola coverage among major agreements and among our sample of all contracts in manufacturing which was presented in Chapter 3. In addition, single-firm bargaining and union concentration raise the probability of Cola coverage (*MULTI* has a negative coefficient), as predicted, although the nonmanufacturing union concentration coefficient is insignificant. These results might reflect the difficulties that employer associations and groups of unions have in agreeing to a Cola package acceptable to all.

The occupational and personal characteristics coefficients differ more dramatically between the manufacturing and nonmanufacturing samples. Operatives, whites, and experienced workers (with up to twenty years of experience) in both manufacturing and nonmanufacturing are more likely than other workers to have Colas. More highly educated workers are less likely to be covered by indexation in both sectors. However, the coefficients for marital status, percentage male, and percentage craftsmen have opposite results in the two samples. The positive coefficients for *CRAFT* and *MALE* in the manufacturing sample would logically be interpreted as bargaining power proxies. However, in the nonmanufacturing sample the industries with few Colas and large sample sizes (construction – 1,446 contracts;

Table 6-2. Probit Results for the Probability that Contract Has a Cola Clause (asymptotic standard errors in parentheses).

Explanatory Variables	Manufacturing	Nonmanufacturing
CONSTANT	−5.4292[a]	−10.141[a]
	(.9379)	(1.739)
SIZE	.00004[a]	.00002[a]
	(.000008)	(.000003)
UN	.0065[a]	.0073[b]
	(.0014)	(.0033)
CR8	.0105[a]	−
	(.0010)	
CONSOL	.0008[a]	.0032
	(.0001)	(.0022)
CRAFT	3.5522[a]	−2.4039[a]
	(.2710)	(.3261)
OPER	3.4452[a]	1.4472[a]
	(.2622)	(.3528)
LGSMSA	2.5971[a]	1.8974[a]
	(.1823)	(.4253)
MAR	−5.5336[a]	.6840
	(.5792)	(.9921)
MALE	2.6565[a]	−1.6087[a]
	(.2145)	(.3702)
WHITE	2.4587[a]	8.3519[a]
	(.4248)	(.9013)
ED	−.4739[a]	−.2476[a]
	(.0727)	(.0907)
EXP	.4011[a]	.5326[a]
	(.0596)	(.1147)
EXP^2	−.0102[a]	−.0125[a]
	(.0013)	(.0024)
CHILD	.1937	.3875
	(.1620)	(.2965)
COEFF	−.0196[a]	−
	(.0039)	
SIGMA	1.0033	−
	(.6498)	
SOUTH	−.4133[a]	−.1567
	(.0485)	(.0966)
MULTI	−.1768[b]	−.2977[a]
	(.0737)	(.0742)

Table 6-2.   (Continued)

Explanatory Variables	Manufacturing	Nonmanufacturing
VARINFL	.4366[a]	.3129[a]
	(.0530)	(.0939)
TIME	.0364[a]	.0111
	(.0066)	(.0125)
Sample Size	6,065	3,270
(−2)×(Log-likelihood ratio)	1655.99	1172.4
degrees of freedom	20	17

[a] Coefficient is significantly different from 0 at 1 percent level (two-tailed test).

[b] Coefficient is significantly different from 0 at 5 percent level (two-tailed test).

electric, gas, and sanitary – 329 contracts) have many craftsmen and are largely male. Conversely, trucking (168 contracts) and food stores (324 contracts), which are often organized by the Teamsters, have a high percentage of contracts with Colas and few craftsmen. Food stores and communications (213 contracts) also have a low percentage of male workers even though their percentage of contracts with Colas is high. Thus, the bargaining power interpretation of these variables does not seem to carry over to the nonmanufacturing sample.

The two family variables (*MAR, CHILD*) were interpreted as possible measures of risk aversion. *CHILD* has the anticipated positive coefficient for both samples, but the coefficient is not significantly different from 0. The coefficient for *MAR* is also insignificantly positive for nonmanufacturing. However, it is negative and significant in the manufacturing sample. Since we control for the number of children in the estimation (*CHILD*), a smaller fraction of workers married with spouse present might indicate greater risk aversion (due to lack of a spouse's income) and thus greater Cola coverage.

The two locational variables (*LGSMSA* and *SOUTH*) have the anticipated signs for both samples. Colas are more likely to occur in industries located in metropolitan areas and outside the southern region of the country. This probably reflects both bargaining power and differences in the informational content of the national CPI.

Inflation uncertainty (*VARINFL*) has a significantly positive effect in both sectors, as predicted. The expected inflation rate was excluded from the analysis, since anticipated inflation can always be built directly into scheduled wage increases. Our positive result for *VARINFL*, however, might reflect a positive correlation between expected inflation and inflation uncertainty. To test for this, Equation 6-12 was reestimated by including the twelve-month CPI inflation forecast as of the start of the agreement. The expected inflation coefficient was positive and insignificant, and the *VARINFL* coefficient remained positive and significant (the other results were unchanged), reinforcing our conclusion about inflation uncertainty.

Finally, the two industry price measures (*COEFF* and *SIGMA*) performed poorly in the manufacturing equation. Both have signs that are opposite to our predictions and the *COEFF* result is significant. It should be noted that the variables are the result of supply and demand effects, making their interpretation problematic. These results are also not robust with respect to the chosen sample, the choice of time period to estimate *COEFF* and *SIGMA*, or the choice of other variables to be included in the model. Previously, we had estimated the same model with 495 fewer observations and had used a shorter time period to estimate *COEFF* and *SIGMA* (Hendricks and Kahn 1983). In that case, the coefficient for *SIGMA* was negative and significant and the *COEFF* coefficient was negative and insignificant. Estenson (1981) found the anticipated signs for both coefficients using only 140 contracts and no other explanatory variables. We also estimated Estenson's specification for our sample and were able to replicate his results. Obviously, intercorrelations between the price variables themselves (they are strongly negatively related to each other) and with other variables in the model make any conclusions questionable.

To our knowledge, there are three other empirical studies that analyze the incidence of Colas in union contracts using contract data. As mentioned above, Estenson analyzed 140 contracts using only *SIGMA* and *COEFF* as explanatory variables. Ehrenberg, Danziger, and San (1983) analyzed major contracts (1,036 contracts) from the BLS that were on file in 1981. Cousineau, Lacroix, and Bilodeau (1983) analyzed Canadian contract data (2,704 contracts) covering the 1967–78 period. Both of these later studies used a pooled sample of manufacturing and nonmanufacturing data.

Explanatory variables included in the analysis of the Canadian data were contract duration, expected inflation, the variance of inflation expectations, size of the unit, the real base wage level, a proxy for the sensitivity of the firm's net income to inflation (inflation rate times vacancy rate), and industry and controls period dummies. All the nondummy variables were found to be significantly positively related to Cola incidence. The real wage level is probably a good proxy for bargaining power, although the authors suggest a nonlabor income interpretation. Given the small percentage of total income of workers from capital (Azariadis 1978), the bargaining power interpretation probably makes more sense. Thus, with the exception of a significant effect of price expectations (measured by the current price level), the Canadian results are in accord with our U.S. results.

Ehrenberg, Danziger, and San (hereafter EDS) used a long list of explanatory variables, many of which were essentially the same as those used in this study. Their results for bargaining power-type variables measured by industry structure characteristics (*SIZE, UN, CR8*) were similar to ours although their coefficients were not significantly different from 0. Their location variables (*SOUTH, SMSA*) yielded results similar to ours as well. They also found no significant effect for price expectations (like our study and unlike the Canadian study) and the variance of these expectations (unlike both our study and the Canadian study). These time series variable results are not surprising given the limited variance available when contracts are gathered at a single point in time, as was the case in EDS.

The personal characteristics variables used in their study yielded some strange results. Percentage married was positively related to Cola incidence; all other variables (*AGE, WHITE, MALE, ED, CRAFT, CHILD*) were negatively related (although only *WHITE* and *AGE* were significant). The *ED* finding is similar to our results, but the other results are directly opposite to our manufacturing results and in some cases (*CHILD, AGE, WHITE*) to both our manufacturing and nonmanufacturing results. Some of their results might be explained by the mixture of different effects in the manufacturing and nonmanufacturing sectors. They could also have resulted from the inclusion of other variables not included in our study.

EDS also included measures of the relationship of industry prices and inflation. They used quarterly data on producer price indices. Their coefficients for the variables corresponding to *COEFF* and *SIGMA* in our study were insignificant although they did achieve the anticipated signs — *COEFF* as positive and *SIGMA* as negative.

The only variable included in the EDS study that yielded a significant coefficient and that was not proxied in our study was the import/sales ratio. They found that increases in imports as a percentage of sales reduced the probability of a Cola. This finding could reflect both the decreased informational content of the national CPI and the different impact of inflation on the worth of the firm in industries with high levels of imports; on the other hand, unions might be weakened by imports and thus be less likely to win Colas.

Although the results from these incidence studies are mixed, they generally support the theoretical predictions made in Chapter 5. Since our study has considerably more contracts, much more time series variation in time-related variables and a wider variety of contracts (since it includes both key and nonkey contracts in manufacturing), we believe that the EDS results are less likely to represent the actual relationships existing in the economy.

EMPIRICAL PROCEDURES: COLA STRENGTH

As our empirical results on Cola incidence have shown, a number of economic variables are associated with the presence of Colas in contracts in both the manufacturing and nonmanufacturing sectors of the economy. However, there is considerable variety in the type of indexation among contracts with Colas (see Chapter 3). In this section the strength of Colas within the manufacturing sector is investigated. Unfortunately, the same analysis for the nonmanufacturing data cannot be attempted since data on wage levels or wage changes were not available.

In general, as discussed in Chapter 5, the same constructs that influence the incidence of indexation will also influence the degree of indexation for contracts with Colas. This degree is analyzed in two stages. First, the determinants of D, the share of cost-of-living payments in total wage changes (including Cola) over the life of the contract, are analyzed. Second, Cola elasticities as discussed above are studied. A large value for either type of measure should indicate a high degree of indexation. Despite the fact that the D measure is *ex post* and suffers from the problems mentioned above, it has the distinct advantage that wage level information is not required. This is a large advantage since many contracts specify wage changes and Cola formulas but do not list wage levels. Thus, this measure of the degree of indexation allows us to use the largest possible sample size in testing hypotheses about Cola strength.

The vector of explanatory variables x (the same as in the analysis of Cola incidence) and $\dot{P}^a$ (the actual rate of price inflation over the life of the contract) are used when D is the dependent variable. This latter variable is added because although we are attempting to measure the *intended* degree of indexation, our proxy consists in part of the *realized* Cola payments. The latter can be affected by the parties' intentions (such as capping the Cola) as well as by actual inflation. By controlling for actual inflation, focus can be placed on the parties' intentions; each of the other explanatory variables in x is viewed as affecting the degree of indexation controlling for a given realized inflation rate. Two Colas can give different yields at the same realized inflation rate only if the Cola clauses themselves differ.

Although the same variables are used in our analysis of the degree of indexation (except the addition of $\dot{P}^a$) as in our analysis of Cola incidence, the discussion of Cola incidence above and the theoretical models in Chapter 5 suggest that these variables might have different impacts on Cola strength than on Cola incidence. Bargaining power proxies have a more ambiguous impact on the fraction of wage increases due to Colas since under nonconstant risk aversion, the proportion of the total wage package that is indexed might fall as power (and presumably income) increases. However, as noted, union bargaining power is expected to move ϵ toward 1. Constant risk aversion models predict that the impact of bargaining power and employee risk aversion is dependent on the impact of inflation on the firm (Ehrenberg, Danziger, and San 1983). Increased employee risk aversion would also lead to attempts to smooth the path of real wages. This would lead to optimal degrees of indexation nearer unity. Thus, increased worker risk aversion is associated with increased levels of indexation only when $\epsilon < 1$ (Ehrenberg, Danziger, and San 1983).

The same qualitative predictions hold for variables measuring uncertainty about prices, the informational content of prices, and the impact of inflation on the worth of the firm. That is, there will be a tendency for the optimal degree of indexation to move toward unity when inflation is more uncertain or contains less information and when inflation has no effect on the real net worth of the firm. Finally, there is no clear connection between the cost of indexation and the degree of indexation, since its impact will depend on who bears this cost.

In sum, the connection between the optimal degree of indexation and our variables is considerably more complicated than their connection with the probability of indexation. Most predictions still hold when indexation is less than unity. However, this is an empirical question.

EMPIRICAL RESULTS: PROPORTION OF COLA IN TOTAL WAGE INCREASE

The regression results for the degree of indexation among contracts with Colas, as measured by the share of cost-of-living payments in the total wage increase, are presented in Table 6-3. With the exception of the percentage married variable (*MAR*), all variables that have significant coefficients in this regression had significant coefficients with the same signs in the incidence analysis (see Table 6-2). Marital status has a significant positive influence on the degree of indexation among indexed contracts but was associated with a reduction in the probability of indexation in the manufacturing sector. An overall conclusion about its effect on Colas is thus difficult to make.

Three variables — size of the bargaining unit (*SIZE*), product market concentration (*CR8*), and percentage white (*WHITE*) — are not significant in this analysis although they were significant in the incidence analysis. Each appears to increase the probability of indexation but does not have any significant impact on the degree of indexation.

Actual inflation has a strong, significantly positive effect on the degree of indexation, as would be true almost by definition since an *ex post* measure is used in this analysis. The variance of expected inflation also has a strong, positive effect. This finding provides further support for the proposition that the optimal wage-price elasticity is less than 1. In models where aggregate price shocks are jointly distributed with shocks to the firm's input and output prices, a higher variance in expected inflation reduces the informational content of the aggregate CPI and drives the optimal indexation toward 1 (Ehrenberg, Danziger, and San 1983). Since higher variance is estimated to increase the degree of indexation, the optimal value must on average be below unity.

EMPIRICAL RESULTS: WAGE ELASTICITIES

Wage elasticities as a measure of the degree of indexation provide a connection with the theoretical models given in Chapter 5 and also

Table 6–3. OLS Regression Results for the Degree of
Indexation among Contracts with Colas (standard errors
in parentheses).

Explanatory Variables	Coefficients
CONSTANT	−1.9653 [a]
	(.3052)
SIZE ($\div 10^3$)	−.0008
	(.0018)
UN	.0017 [a]
	(.0004)
CR8	−.0005
	(.0026)
CONSOL ($\div 10$)	.0010 [a]
	(.0003)
CRAFT	.5213 [a]
	(.0780)
OPER	.3853 [a]
	(.0778)
LGSMSA	.1082 [b]
	(.0520)
MAR	.4535 [a]
	(.1790)
MALE	.2090 [a]
	(.0632)
WHITE	−.0870
	(.1144)
ED	−.0135
	(.0294)
EXP	.0453 [a]
	(.0164)
EXP^2	−.0011 [a]
	(.0004)
CHILD	.0568
	(.0468)
COEFF	−.0164 [c]
	(.0084)
SIGMA	.0149
	(.1319)
SOUTH	−.0287 [b]
	(.0145)
MULTI	−.1241 [a]
	(.0225)

Table 6–3.   (Continued)

Explanatory Variables	Coefficients
VARINFL	.0387[a]
	(.0050)
$\dot{p}^a$	.9553[a]
	(.0971)
TIME	.0115[a]
	(.0026)
Sample Size	1,765
R^2	.3317

Note: The dependent variable is $COL/(COL + SWC)$ where COL = cost of living payment and SWC = straight time wage increase. The unit of observation is the life-time of the agreement. The sample covers manufacturing only.

[a] Significant at 0.01 level, two-tailed test.

[b] Significant at 0.05 level, two-tailed test.

[c] Significant at 0.10 level, two-tailed test.

are comparible to calculations made by other authors. In this section information on three wage elasticities is provided. First, the actual elasticity of wages with respect to price change over the lifetime of the contract is computed. Second, the expected elasticity of wages with respect to price changes is estimated. This is computed using an estimate of the expected price change over the contract at the time the contract was signed. This elasticity therefore reflects an estimate of the wage-price change relationship that was anticipated by the parties at the time of the signing of the contract. Third, the elasticity of wages with respect to unanticipated inflation is estimated. This elasticity is called the unexpected elasticity. It is estimated by computing the change in wages associated with deviations from the expected inflation rate. That is, the wage change associated with the expected inflation rate is estimated first. The expected inflation is then altered and the wage change is recomputed. The difference between the new inflation rate and the expected rate and the difference between the new wage change and the expected wage change serve as the basis for computing the unexpected elaticity. Formally, the unexpected elasticity is

$$\epsilon_{UE} = \frac{\Delta W^{UE}/W}{\Delta P^{UE}/P}$$

$$= \frac{(\Delta W - \Delta W^E)/W}{(\Delta P - \Delta P^E)/P} , \qquad (6\text{-}13)$$

where ΔW^{UE} and ΔP^{UE} are unexpected wage and price changes, ΔW^E and ΔP^E are expected wage and price changes, and ΔW and ΔP are the price and wage changes that occur. Since this unexpected elasticity is a nonlinear function of price shocks, several alternative measurements (using different values for ΔP) are provided which it is hoped bracket the optimal degree of indexation.

To compute the actual elasticity, information is needed on actual price and wage changes and wage levels. To compute expected and unexpected elasticities, price expectations must be estimated, and full information on the Cola formula is required to evaluate the formula under different inflation scenarios. The Livingston forecasts of inflation were used to estimate price expectations. Our methods are described in Appendix 6A. Evaluation of Colas under different price scenarios is a formidable task for any large number of contracts. A computer program was therefore written that uses price information and Cola characteristics to compute wage changes. However, some formulas simply defy any reasonable parameterization. Contracts with extremely complicated formulas and contracts with formulas calling for percentage changes in wages rather than cents-per-hour changes (a small percentage in manufacturing) were therefore excluded from the analysis.

The wage level used to compute these elasticities is the wage for janitor or laborer in the contract. Since cents-per-hour Colas are used in combination with wage levels at the low end of the wage distribution, our estimates of elasticities will tend to be high.

The combination of the required wage level information, price expectations, and Cola formula information reduced the number of contracts that could be fully analyzed from 1,975 to 1,259.[6] To ensure compatibility, each of the wage elasticities is computed on this same sample. The bias in the selection of this sample from our total sample of indexed contracts is unknown. However, the average wage level in this subsample is higher than wage levels in the full sample. This might indicate a higher degree of indexation in the subsample to the extent that the degree of indexation is positively related to bargaining power (and wage levels).

Table 6-4.   Wage Elasticities for Janitor/Laborer Wages.

Year Negotiated (N)[a]		Expected Elasticity			Actual Elasticity		
		F^b	M^c	C^d	F	M	C
1970	(7)	.71	.49	–	.57	.39	–
1971	(115)	.75	.44	.48	.78	.33	.53
1972	(14)	.78	.25	.47	.87	.17	.53
1973	(63)	.91	.34	.59	.90	.31	.64
1974	(289)	1.15	.56	1.06	1.09	.50	1.07
1975	(100)	1.00	.53	–	.93	.46	–
1976	(183)	.86	.42	.59	.81	.32	.58
1977	(322)	.89	.42	.86	.88	.31	.87
1978	(81)	.81	.38	.69	.83	.32	.66
1979	(77)	1.01	.29	.87	1.03	.26	.87
1980	(8)	1.02	1.63	–	1.04	1.72	–
Average	(1,259)	.937	.462	.716	.920	.385	.720
Overall Mean			.814			.782	

[a] (N) = sample size.
[b] F = no maximum or corridor.
[c] M = maximum.
[d] C = corridor; no maximum.

Results of our computation of actual and expected elasticities are given in Table 6-4. These elasticities are tabulated both by year in which the contract was negotiated and by type of Cola formula. The actual elasticities in contracts with no maximum or corridor range from 0.57 in 1970 to 1.09 in 1974 with a mean over the 1970–80 period of 0.92. Thus, over this period, janitors/laborers in bargaining units with "free" Colas were compensated for each 1 percent increase in prices by a 0.92 percent increase in wages — slightly lower than perfect indexation. The corresponding expected elasticities range from 0.71 to 1.15 with a mean of 0.937. Thus, the expected and actual elasticities are quite close to one another in the long run.

As anticipated, large differences occur between contracts with and without maximum clauses. Both actual and expected elasticities are much smaller, averaging 0.385 and 0.462 respectively. The overall mean elasticities for all Cola types were 0.814 expected and 0.782 actual.

These elasticities measure the direct return from the Cola formula. They suggest that the lowest paid workers in bargaining units are fully compensated for inflation through the Cola clause only when free Colas are established. On average, Cola clauses only return 80 percent of inflation even for the lowest paid workers.

These elasticities reflect the portion of anticipated inflation covered by the Cola (the expected elasticity) as well as the response to unanticipated inflation (the actual elasticity). The unexpected elasticity reflects the return of the Cola formula beyond (or below) any return expected by the parties. It is therefore a cleaner representation of the degree of indexation to unexpected price shocks.

Our estimates of the unexpected elasticities for janitors/laborers are given in Table 6-5. These elasticities are again tabulated by Cola type and year negotiated. Three alternative measures are given. First, the response of Colas to actual unexpected inflation over the contract is given. Second, the Cola return if price change was two standard deviations above the expected price change is computed and used to compute the elasticity. Finally, an unexpected elasticity when prices were two standard deviations below expectations is provided.

The unexpected elasticities for free Colas are again found to be around 1 for most of our time period. The unexpected elasticities measured at +2 and −2 standard deviations average 1.09 and 0.955 respectively. The unexpected elasticity measured on the basis of actual unexpected inflation averaged 0.98. Contracts with Cola corridors yield similar results.

When unexpected inflation is quite high, contracts with maximums provide almost no inflation insurance. However, the estimated elasticities are not 0. For the actual level of unexpected inflation, the elasticity averaged 0.22 over the period; an inflation rate two standard deviations above expected would have yielded an elasticity of 0.198. Not surprisingly, the figure for inflation below expectations was much higher, averaging 0.319 over the period.

It should be emphasized that these unexpected elasticities are measured using contract length as the time unit of analysis. Elasticities estimated at points within the contract might vary. This is especially true when the unexpected elasticity is measured using actual CPI changes. For example, our forecasts of inflation for contracts negotiated in 1979 were typically below the actual values. Workers

Table 6-5.   Unexpected Elasticities for Janitor/Laborer Wages.

Year Negotiated (N)[a]		Based on Actual Inflation Minus Expected			Based on Inflation Two Standard Deviations above Expected			Based on Inflation Two Standard Deviations below Expected		
		F^b	M^c	C^d	F	M	C	F	M	C
1970	(7)	.69	.09	–	.31	.09	–	.61	.20	–
1971	(115)	–.07	.17	–.33	.70	.17	.43	–.08	.19	.31
1972	(14)	1.11	.04	1.04	1.36	.02	1.02	1.06	.07	1.00
1973	(63)	.94	.16	1.13	1.00	.20	1.19	.90	.22	1.10
1974	(289)	1.32	.33	1.43	1.13	.34	1.37	1.27	.45	1.40
1975	(100)	.97	.13	–	.89	.20	–	.94	.24	–
1976	(183)	1.05	.18	1.07	.93	.13	.80	1.02	.30	1.09
1977	(322)	1.10	.25	1.26	1.20	.14	1.22	1.08	.37	1.24
1978	(81)	.91	.16	1.10	1.14	.16	1.03	.87	.24	1.21
1979	(77)	1.18	.06	1.03	1.33	.03	1.05	1.14	.05	1.00
1980	(8)	1.06	–	–	1.19	–	–	1.01	–	–
Mean	(1,259)	.98	.22	1.06	1.09	.20	1.00	.96	.32	1.06
Overall Mean			.800			.850			.800	

[a] (N) = sample size.

[b] F = no maximum or corridor.

[c] M = maximum.

[d] C = corridor; no maximum.

were therefore paid considerably higher Cola payments than they could have expected over the contract. However, for three-year contracts negotiated in the later part of 1979, actual inflation and expected inflation were quite similar at the end of the contracts. This occurred because inflation turned down in the later months of 1982. Thus, there was little difference between expected and actual inflation over the contracts but a sizable difference in Cola payments. This resulted in very high estimated values for the unexpected elasticities for these contracts.

The reverse phenomena occurred for contracts negotiated in 1971. Most of these contracts had Colas that began in 1972 and were computed using a future base period CPI. Our forecasts tend to predict

Table 6-6. Wage/Cola Elasticities Estimated for "Average Union Worker."[a]

	Expected	Actual	Unexpected[b]
Mean	.656	.613	.660
Free	.756	.742	.820
Maximum	.373	.310	.290
Corridor	.577	.581	.660

[a] Assumes a ratio of Janitor-laborer/average wages of 1.24. See Appendix 6A.

[b] Based on unexpected elasticity computed from actual inflation rates in Table 6-4.

higher inflation over the first year than succeeding years during this time period. As a consequence, the difference between the expected base CPI forecasted and the actual one was greater than the difference between forecasted and actual ending CPIs. This resulted in estimates of negative elasticities for two of the three unexpected elasticities in 1971.

Although these averages provide good information for elasticities for janitor/laborer wages, a translation to elasticities for the average union worker covered by indexation would be beneficial. Unfortunately, no measure of average wages for each contract was available. To provide an approximation to this elasticity, we have attempted to estimate the ratio of janitor/laborer wages in our sample to the average union worker wage. Details of our approximation are given in Appendix 6A.

Based on our data and work by others on union coverage and union wage premiums, the average union worker is estimated to have made 24 percent higher wages than janitors/laborers in our sample. Our elasticity estimates are therefore divided by 1.24 to predict elasticities for the average-paid worker. These estimates are presented in Table 6-6. An average estimate of unexpected elasticity from Table 6-4 was used for this calculation. These estimates indicate that the typical indexed contract in our subsample returned about 61 percent of inflation through Cola payments while 66 percent of unanticipated inflation was covered. The estimated elasticity for unanticipated inflation in free Cola contracts was 0.82. The estimate for contracts with maximums is quite low (0.290) although some insurance value is evident.

The elasticity estimates made in this chapter are labeled "direct" estimates since they are computed directly from wage and price

180 WAGE INDEXATION IN THE UNITED STATES

Table 6-7. Actual Elasticities for U.S. and Canadian Data.

	All Colas		Free Colas		Maximum Colas	
	W^a	H-K^b	W	H-K	W	H-K
Base wage rate						
(Janitor/laborer rate)	.58	.78	.85	.92	–	.39
Average wage	.49	.61	.73	.74	.32	.31

[a] W = Wilton (see below).

[b] H-K = authors' calculations from Tables 6-4 and 6-6.

Sources: The "All Colas" estimates were taken directly from Wilton 1979: Table 6, p. 17. The "Free Cola" estimate is a combination of Wilton's unconstrained Colas and Cola contracts that cover only a portion of the contract period. The "Maximum Cola" estimate is a combination of all contracts with caps among Wilton's categories in Table 5, p. 16.

information. Wage elasticities have also been imputed from regression analysis of wage change and price change data. We label these as "indirect" estimates. Discussion of these indirect estimates will be taken up in Chapter 7.

There have been very few direct estimates of wage elasticities in the United States. Douty (1975) estimated that the typical indexed contract in the United States returned 49 percent of inflation for the 1968-74 period. Sheifer (1979) estimated this value to be 57 percent for 1977. These estimates correspond to our actual elasticity estimate for average union workers for 1969-81 of 61 percent. Thus, our estimate is slightly higher. This might reflect the different time periods used in the studies or the different samples of contracts.

Much more elaborate estimates of direct elasticities have been made from Canadian data by Wilton (1979) and Card (1982, 1983) using the same data set. This data set included all contracts covering more than 500 workers and covered the 1968-75 period. Of the total 1,405 settlements, 358 included a Cola clause.

Wilton (1979) computed actual *ex post* elasticities. The average elasticity over all contracts was 0.49 (see Table 6-7), the same estimate made by Douty (1975) for the United States. He also computed separate elasticities for unconstrained (free) Colas and for constrained (maximum) Colas and for base wage rates and average rates. The Canadian data yielded an approximate difference of 10 to 15

Table 6-8.   Canadian and U.S. Estimates of *Ex Ante* Wage Elasticities.

	Base Wage		Average Wage	
	C^a	$H-K^b$	C	$H-K$
Industry				
All manufacturing	.90	.98	.82	.82
Food products	.83	.92	.78	.74
Automotive	.90	.99	.82	.80
Iron and steel	.80	.95	.70	.77
Electrical equipment	.97	1.07	.85	.86
Nonmanufacturing	.98	–	.88	–
Union				
UAW	.90	1.09	.81	.88
USW	.86	.99	.76	.80
Non-UAW/USW	.95	–	.87	–

[a] C = Card 1983: Table 4, p. 46. Estimates for beginning of contract elasticities.

[b] H-K = authors' estimates based on Tables 6-5, 6-6, 6-9, and 6-10 for unexpected elasticity for contracts with free Colas.

percent between the base and average wage rates. A comparison of our estimated elasticities with Wilton's is given in Table 6-7. Our base rate (janitor/laborer) elasticities are higher than Wilton's. This might reflect the larger estimated differential between base and average rates in the United States.

Card (1983) used a subset of 281 of the 358 contracts used by Wilton (1979). He was primarily concerned with measuring the *ex ante* as opposed to the *ex post* wage elasticity. He accomplished this by measuring the marginal elasticity of wages with respect to price at both the start of the contract and the start of indexation. These elasticities ignore any corridors or limits that could change the elasticity over the contract by a great deal. They probably correspond most closely to our estimates of the unexpected elasticity for contracts with free Colas. Card also presents averages for selected unions and industries, and for base-wage, high-wage, and average-wage workers. For purposes of comparison, we will use his elasticity at the start of the contract since his elasticity measures varied only slightly.

A comparison of our results with Card's is presented in Table 6-8. The patterns of results across the industries and unions that Card

Table 6-9.   Elasticities by Industry for Janitor/Laborer Wages.

Industry	Actual Elasticity	Expected Elasticity	Unexpected Elasticity	Unexpected Elasticity for Contracts with Free Colas
Food and kindred products	.667	.713	.699	.921
Tobacco	.680	.724	.755	1.22
Textile mill products	.853	.874	.990	1.37
Lumber and wood	.400	.545	.184	.362
Furniture and fixtures	.445	.500	.404	.950
Paper	.451	.512	.495	.901
Printing	.974	1.04	1.08	1.08
Chemicals	.655	.743	.552	.794
Rubber	.835	.884	.892	1.08
Leather	.825	.833	1.05	1.05
Stone, glass, and clay	.677	.763	.560	.860
Primary metals	.902	1.02	.864	.947
Fabricated metals	.802	.869	.799	.953
Machinery	.771	.819	.850	1.087
Electrical machinery	.676	.734	.698	1.066
Transportation equipment	.779	.831	.854	.987
Measuring instruments	.355	.412	.275	1.035
Miscellaneous manufacturing	1.693	.675	.944	1.387

reports are quite similar. Our estimates of base-wage elasticities are higher than Card's; however, the mean wage elasticities are very similar, generally averaging around 0.8. It should be emphasized that these elasticities either ignore limits or are based on contracts without any limitations. To illustrate this point most dramatically, we have tabulated our actual, expected, and unexpected elasticities for free Colas in Table 6-9 by industry and in Table 6-10 by union.

Table 6–10.   Elasticities by Union for Janitor/Laborer Wages.

Union	Actual Elasticity	Expected Elasticity	Unexpected Elasticity	Unexpected Elasticity for Contracts with Free Colas
Allied Industrial Workers (AIW)	.729	.758	.803	.974
Boilermakers	.626	.643	.723	1.04
Carpenters	.638	.705	.648	.819
Brotherhood of Electrical Workers (IBEW)	.706	.772	.724	.945
Glass Bottle Blowers	.315	.387	.190	—
Meat Cutters (Retail Clerks)	.775	.813	.864	.929
Machinists (IAM)	.702	.756	.732	.957
Rubber Workers	.808	.864	.839	1.02
Steel Workers (USW)	.901	1.008	.890	.989
Electrical, Radio and Machine Workers (IUE)	.447	.500	.397	.942
Oil, Chemical and Atomic Workers (OCAW)	.700	.767	.667	1.09
Teamsters	.559	.641	.461	.803
Autoworkers (UAW)	.842	.889	.910	1.09

The unexpected janitor/laborer elasticities for contracts with free Colas are often over 0.9 and exceed 1 for many industries and several unions. However, there is a dramatic change in some of these elasticities when other contracts that have caps and corridors are included. For example, contracts in basic metal industries and in automotive equipment (USW and UAW) rarely have caps. Their measured elasticities therefore fall only slightly when capped contracts are included. However, in industries such as tobacco, measuring instruments, and electrical machinery there are sizable differences in the two estimates. The same result holds across unions. The International Union of

Electrical Workers (IUE), for example, has a free Cola estimate of 0.942; the estimate for all contracts is 0.397.

Thus, although our underlying data yield results similar to Card's elasticities when ignoring Cola limits, corridors, and triggers, our conclusions are quite different. When these Cola characteristics are taken into account, the degree of indexation to unexpected inflation is considerably below 1 for most contracts.

DETERMINANTS OF WAGE ELASTICITIES

The elasticities computed in the previous section can be analyzed in the same manner as our analysis of the proportion of Cola payments in total wage change. The same estimation equation is used, with the exception that expected price change is substituted for actual price change.[7]

Results for our estimate of expected elasticities and our three measures of unexpected elasticities are given in Table 6–11. On the whole, the results are disappointing. Only four variables (*UN, CRAFT, MULTI,* and *TIME*) are consistently significant. All have the same signs as they did in our analysis of the proportion of total wage changes that were indexed. The coefficients for the variance of expected inflation, the time trend, and expected inflation differ depending on the elasticity measure that is analyzed. *TIME* and *VARINFL* are significantly positively related to *UNEXP* and *UNEXP−2*; *VARINF* is insignificantly negatively related to *UNEXP+2* and *EXPECT*, and *TIME* is first positive and then negative for these latter two equations. The coefficient for $\dot{p}^e$ is significantly positive for *UNEXP+2* and *EXPECT* and insignificantly positive for the other two measures. All three of these time series have very high simple correlations over this sample period (approximately 0.8). These results might simply reflect the difficulty of isolating their independent impacts. They might also reflect the fact that $\dot{p}^e$ and *VARINFL* are used in the construction of the dependent variables, although this connection remains far from clear.

Two other studies have attempted to analyze differences in measured Cola elasticities. Ehrenberg, Danziger, and San (1983) attempted to proxy the elasticities using the Cola formula and average industry wages for a sample of major contracts. The variables that they used were described in the section on Cola incidence. They found that their measure of elasticity was significantly related to the quit

Table 6-11. OLS Regression Results for Various Wage Elasticities among Contracts with Colas (standard errors in parentheses).

Explanatory Variables	Dependent Variable			
	UNEXP[a]	UNEXP+2[b]	UNEXP-2[c]	EXPECT[d]
CONSTANT	-6.891[e]	-.9651	-6.3715[e]	2.9187[c]
	(1.579)	(1.2942)	(1.5418)	(.7903)
SIZE ($\div 10^3$)	.0009	.0001	.0009	-.0002
	(.0006)	(.0005)	(.0006)	(.0003)
UN	.0050[e]	.0049[e]	.0043[e]	.0010
	(.0019)	(.0016)	(.0019)	(.0010)
CR8	-.0005	-.0003	-.0007	-.0006
	(.0011)	(.0009)	(.0011)	(.0005)
CONSOL ($\div 10$)	.0197[g]	.0168[g]	.0132	.0185[c]
	(.0105)	(.0086)	(.0102)	(.0052)
CRAFT	1.6022[e]	1.4199[f]	1.5494[e]	.4868[c]
	(.3147)	(.2580)	(.3074)	(.1576)
OPER	.6651[f]	.1691	.6526[f]	-.1301
	(.3307)	(.2711)	(.3230)	(.1656)
LGSMSA	.0395	-.1094	.0434	-.1681
	(.2072)	(.1699)	(.2024)	(.1037)
MAR	1.1275	1.0831[g]	.6842	.4730
	(.7975)	(.6539)	(.7790)	(.3993)
MALE	-.2410	-.0730	-.2368	-.2233
	(.2930)	(.2403)	(.2862)	(.1467)
WHITE	.1564	.1933	.0684	-.0317
	(.4534)	(.3717)	(.4429)	(.2270)
ED	-.1269	-.1861[f]	-.1139	.0235
	(.0888)	(.0728)	(.0868)	(.0445)
EXP	.0152	.0196	.0171	.0193
	(.0676)	(.0554)	(.0660)	(.0339)
EXP^2	-.0004	-.0005	-.0004	-.0001
	(.0015)	(.0012)	(.0015)	(.0007)
CHILD	.1404	.2465	.1312	.3945[c]
	(.1996)	(.1636)	(.1949)	(.0999)
COEFF	-.0518	.0054	-.0461	.0149
	(.0382)	(.0313)	(.0373)	(.0191)
SIGMA	-.0043	-.2313	.1168	-.6046[f]
	(.5479)	(.4492)	(.5351)	(.2743)
SOUTH	-.0635	-.0381	-.0513	-.0492[g]
	(.0582)	(.0477)	(.0568)	(.0291)

Table 6-11. (Continued)

Explanatory Variables	Dependent Variable			
	UNEXP	UNEXP + 2	UNEXP − 2	EXPECT
MULTI	−.2896[e]	−.3108[e]	−.3067[e]	−.2700[e]
	(.0872)	(.0715)	(.0852)	(.0437)
VARINFL	.4619[e]	−.1341	.4447[e]	−.0404
	(.1084)	(.0888)	(.1059)	(.0543)
$\dot{p}^e$	.0157	.1224[e]	.0180	.1248[e]
	(.0417)	(.0342)	(.0407)	(.0209)
TIME	.0752[e]	.0148	.0733[e]	−.0556[e]
	(.0162)	(.0133)	(.0158)	(.0081)
Sample Size	1,091	1,091	1,091	1,091
R^2	.2170	.1932	.2084	.2761

[a] UNEXP = unexpected elasticity evaluated at actual level of unexpected inflation.

[b] UNEXP + 2 = unexpected elasticity evaluated at inflation two standard deviations above expectations.

[c] UNEXP − 2 = unexpected elasticity evaluated at inflation two standard deviations below expectations.

[d] EXPECT = expected elasticity.

[e] Significant at 0.01 level, two-tailed test.

[f] Significant at 0.05 level, two-tailed test.

[g] Significant at 0.10 level, two-tailed test.

rate, the number of unions in the industry, the variance of inflation, and a measure similar to our *SIGMA*. In all cases, a significant positive coefficient was found. The number of unions effect is the opposite to our finding for *CONSOL* earlier and is difficult to explain. The *SIGMA* result is also counterintuitive. However, the result for the variance of inflation supports our finding for two elasticity measures.

Card (1983) found significant industry and time fixed effects in his analysis of the Canadian data, although he did not attempt to test the effect of either specific industry attributes or business cycle phenomena. In a further analysis of the same data, Card (1982) compared empirical results based on a risk-averse model of Cola formulation and a risk-neutral version of the model. The risk-averse model performed better in this exercise. In this analysis he used industry estimates of labor and materials shares in total industry shipments, union mark-up over nonunion wages, the employment share of skilled and unskilled workers, and the correlations of selling prices and input prices with the CPI. The results suggested that the major portion of risk sharing occurred between skilled workers and firms and not for unskilled workers. Thus, characteristics of the input and output price shocks faced by the firm only influenced wage elasticities for contracts that were bargained in industries with a high proportion of skilled workers. This is an interesting result, although its explanation remains far from clear.

SUMMARY

Both the incidence of wage indexation and the strength of indexation among union contracts have been investigated in this chapter. Of the two concepts, it is clear that Cola incidence is much easier to measure than Cola strength. Our results seem to bear this out. Most of the explanatory variables in our incidence analysis have the anticipated signs and are highly significant. The same set of explanatory variables performs less well when we analyze the proportion of the total wage increase that is indexed and poorer still in analyzing various estimates of wage elasticities. However, several findings are consistent no matter which measure is used. First, the variance of inflation is almost always positively associated with both Cola incidence and strength, although the level of expected inflation is rarely significant. Second, bargaining power (as measured by several variables) is positively related to incidence and strength, suggesting that on average the optimal degree of indexation is less than 1.

Our estimates of the responsiveness of wages to unanticipated inflation further support the proposition that the optimal elasticity is less than 1 for most bargaining pairs. Although the elasticity with respect to janitor/laborer wages is approximately 0.8 to 0.9, the elasticity for the average worker seems to be nearer to 0.6. These estimates are based on direct measurement of the elasticities. Evidence on these elasticities based on indirect evidence through analysis of wage change data will be reviewed in the next chapter.

The data analyzed in this chapter represent a sizable step forward over previous studies. Typically, these studies had at best 300 to

400 indexed contracts to analyze; our analysis includes nearly 2,000 indexed contracts over an eleven-year period.

APPENDIX 6A
ESTIMATION OF EXPECTED INFLATION

The Livingston Surveys provide estimates for expected inflation based on a sample of predictions made by economists. The surveys were conducted every June and December beginning in 1946. Respondents were asked for their estimates of the level of the CPI six months later and twelve months later for each survey and, beginning in 1971, were also asked for their estimate eighteen months later for every other survey.

Most contracts last two years or longer. Thus, the Livingston forecasts will not necessarily represent inflation expectations over the life of the contract. One approach would be simply to use the one-year forecast as an approximation to expectations. This has the advantage of simplicity and is also subject to error only to the extent that the average expectation differs from true expectations and to the extent that one-year expectations differ from contract-length expectations. Another approach is to attempt to forecast contract-length expectations based on the Livingston data. This has the advantage of potentially being a more realistic index of expectations. It carries the disadvantage that errors in measurement of expectations in the Livingston data are compounded by errors introduced in constructing the new series.

In this chapter we have reported results based on our estimates of expectations constructed from the Livingston data. The analysis was also carried out using the one-year forecasts from the Livingston data. The results were quite similar to those that are reported. This section describes our method for imputing these forecasts from the Livingston data.

The data include a unique identification number for each respondent in the survey. Each respondent could therefore be matched with the response made on previous surveys. Suppose that we begin at time period t and label each succeeding survey as $t+1$, $t+2$, et cetera. At time t the respondent might be asked for the level of the CPI in six, twelve, and eighteen months. At time $t+1$ the same respondent might be asked for estimates of the level of the CPI six and twelve months later. Note that these estimates correspond to the twelve- and eighteen-month forecasts done at time t. If the respondents have no new information, assume that

$$\text{Forecast} + 12_t = \text{Forecast} + 6_{t+1} + \epsilon$$

$$\text{Forecast} + 18_t = \text{Forecast} + 12_{t+1} + \epsilon$$

where ϵ is a random error term.

Assume further that the only new information that the respondents have gathered is the change in the CPI between t and $t+1$. Then the change in the forecasts can be written as

$$(\text{Forecast} + 6_{t+1,i} - \text{Forecast} + 12_{t,i}) = \alpha + \beta(\text{CPI}_{t+1} - \text{CPI}_t) + \epsilon_i.$$

That is, the change in the forecast by individual i from t to $t+1$ is a linear function of the change in the CPI over this period. Note that the twelve-month forecast at $t+1$ could also be compared with the eighteen-month forecast at time t, or the six-month forecast at time $t+2$ could be compared with the eighteen-month forecast at time t. These comparisons lead to the following results:

$$\Delta\text{Forecast } 612 = -.137 + .266 \ \Delta\text{CPI} \quad N = 1{,}147 \quad (6A\text{-}1)$$
$$(.219) \ (.029)$$

$$\Delta\text{Forecast } 1218 = -.718 + .230 \ \Delta\text{CPI} \quad N = 439 \quad (6A\text{-}2)$$
$$(.464) \ (.060)$$

$$\Delta\text{Forecast } 618 = .523 + .100 \ \Delta\text{CPI} \quad N = 406 \quad (6A\text{-}3)$$
$$(.626) \ (.040)$$

The differences in forecasts could be used in a multitude of different ways to obtain forecasts for longer time periods. For example, consider a twenty-four-month forecast at time t. This would correspond to an eighteen-month forecast at time $t+1$ or a twelve-month forecast at time $t+2$. Suppose that the relationship given in 6A-1 is accepted. The twenty-four-month forecast at t could then be predicted as

$$\text{Forecast } 24_t = \text{Forecast } 18_{t+1} + .137 - .266 \, \Delta\text{CPI}_{t+1,t}. \qquad (6A\text{-}4)$$

Another possibility would be to use the relationship estimated in 6A-3 and predict

$$\text{Forecast } 24_t = \text{Forecast } 12_{t+1} - .523 - .100 \, \Delta\text{CPI}_{t+1,t}. \qquad (6A\text{-}5)$$

These, of course, do not exhaust all the possibilities. To make the problem tractable, we selected several alternate methods for estimating forecasts for twenty-four, thirty-six, and forty-eight months into the future for each survey point. These methods are given below.

twenty-four-month forecasts$_t$
a.   eighteen-month forecast$_{t+1}$ plus change in forecast predicted in 6A–1
b.   eighteen-month forecast$_{t+1}$ plus change in forecast predicted in 6A–2
c.   twelve-month forecast$_{t+1}$ plus change in forecast predicted in 6A–3
d.   twelve-month forecast$_{t+2}$ plus change in forecast predicted in 6A–1
e.   twelve-month forecast$_{t+2}$ plus change in forecast predicted in 6A–2
f.   six-month forecast$_{t+3}$ plus change in forecast predicted in 6A–1
g.   six-month forecast$_{t+3}$ plus change in forecast predicted in 6A–2

thirty-six-month forecasts$_t$
a.   eighteen-month forecast$_{t+3}$ plus change in forecast predicted in 6A–1
b.   eighteen-month forecast$_{t+3}$ plus change in forecast predicted in 6A–2
c.   twelve-month forecast$_{t+4}$ plus change in forecast predicted in 6A–1
d.   twelve-month forecast$_{t+4}$ plus change in forecast predicted in 6A–2
e.   twelve-month forecast$_{t+2}$ plus change in forecast predicted in 6A–3
f.   six-month forecast$_{t+5}$ plus change in forecast predicted in 6A–1
g.   six-month forecast$_{t+5}$ plus change in forecast predicted in 6A–2

forty-eight-month forecasts$_t$
a.   eighteen-month forecast$_{t+5}$ plus change in forecast predicted in 6A–1
b.   eighteen-month forecast$_{t+5}$ plus change in forecast predicted in 6A–2
c.   twelve-month forecast$_{t+6}$ plus change in forecast predicted in 6A–1
d.   twelve-month forecast$_{t+6}$ plus change in forecast predicted in 6A–2
e.   twelve-month forecast$_{t+6}$ plus change in forecast predicted in 6A–3
f.   six-month forecast$_{t+7}$ plus change in forecast predicted in 6A–1
g.   six-month forecast$_{t+7}$ plus change in forecast predicted in 6A–2

For example, Equation 6A–4 was used for the twenty-four-month forecast labeled a, and Equation 6A–5 was used for the twenty-four-month forecast labeled c. The twenty-four-month forecast labeled d was obtained from Equation 6A–1 using

$$\text{Forecast } 24_t = \text{Forecast } 12_{t+2} + .274 - .266\,\Delta\text{CPI}_{t+2,t}. \tag{6A–6}$$

That is, the difference in the forecasts is twice the constant term in 6A–1 plus the change in the CPI from t to $t+2$ multiplied by its coefficient. The other forecasts were computed in the same way.

Since we had no a priori expectations that any of our seven fore-casts were more acceptable than others, the seven were averaged to arrive at a single value for each forecast period. Thus, there were five forecasts available for half the Livingston survey dates (six and twelve from the surveys and twenty-four, thirty-six, and forty-eight by our estimations) and six forecasts for the other half (six, twelve, eighteen, twenty-four, thirty-six, forty-eight).

To evaluate Cola formulas and to predict expected inflation for each contract, expectations both between survey dates (December and June) and between predictions (e.g., between six and twelve months, twelve and eighteen, etc.) must be filled in. We took the simple approach that the expected inflation changed linearly between these points. This generated a series of expected CPI values for forty-eight months into the future for each month beginning in 1967 and ending in approximately 1979.[a]

Although actual inflation was less than expected inflation for some years during our time period, on average, expected inflation was below the inflation that actually occurred. The average differences between our twenty-four-, thirty-six- and forty-eight-month forecasts for expectations and actual inflation rates were 3.2 percent, 4.9 percent, and 6.5 percent. These all average to be approximately 1.6 percent per year.

Variances in expectations were computed based on the actual sample variance at a given point in time. These variances represent variation in sample predictions rather than estimates of forecast variances for any individual forecast. Thus, if all predictors estimated six-month inflation to be 6 percent with a confidence interval of plus or minus 3 percent, the estimated variance would be 0.

For the purpose of computing the unexpected elasticity, we needed some reasonable bounds on how far prices might deviate from expec-tations. Computation of the forecast error associated would be ex-tremely difficult. We chose the alternative of using the actual sample variances at the time the contract was signed and linearizing between points. Thus, estimates of unexpected inflation at plus or minus two standard deviations refer to plus or minus two standard deviations in the expected inflation rate based on the sample variance. These

[a] Since the forecasts use future values, contracts negotiated in 1980 with three-year durations could not be used since 1982 and 1983 expectations would be needed. We had the Livingston data only through 1981.

estimates probably underestimate the true variance associated with these forecasts.

Estimation of Wage Levels for "Average" Union Workers

To estimate wage-price elasticities for the average union worker, data were needed on wage levels for these workers. Unfortunately, no wage level data are available for union workers for this time period.

The Bureau of Labor Statistics (BLS) publishes data on average production worker wages in manufacturing. These averages can be expressed as follows:

$$\bar{W}_t = (1 - \alpha_t)\bar{W}_t^{Nu} + \alpha_t \bar{W}_t^u \qquad (6A\text{-}7)$$

where $\bar{W}_t$ is the average wage at time t, Nu and u superscripts refer to nonunion and union workers respectively, and α is the percentage unionized. Suppose γ_t is an estimate of the union–nonunion differential at time t. Then,

$$\bar{W}_t^{Nu} = \bar{W}_t^u / (1 + \gamma_t). \qquad (6A\text{-}8)$$

Combining 6A-7 and 6A-8 and rearranging,

$$\bar{W}_t^u = \bar{W}_t \left(\frac{1 + \gamma_t}{1 + \alpha_t \gamma_t} \right). \qquad (6A\text{-}9)$$

Thus, in addition to average production worker wages, estimates of union coverage and the union–nonunion differential are needed to estimate average union production worker wages. Estimates of the union–nonunion differential for 1970–77 were obtained from Moore and Raisian (1981). They ranged from 11 percent in 1970 to 20 percent in 1977. A value of 20 percent was used for 1978–80. Estimates of unionization in manufacturing were obtained from Current Population Survey (CPS) data on union numbers in manufacturing and total workers.

The combined estimates of the average union wage are presented in Table 6A-1. The ratio of average union wages to wage levels for janitors/labors in our sample ranges from 1.16 (1979) to 1.41 (1970) with a mean ratio of 1.24.

Wages in indexed contracts are higher than wages in nonindexed contracts. Thus, the typical worker covered by an indexed, union

Table 6A-1. Wage Level Comparisons: Our Sample versus Average Manufacturing.

Year	1 *Estimated Average Union* *Wage in Manufacturing*	2 *Average Wage For* *Janitor/Laborer in our Sample*	*Ratio* *1/2*
1970	$3.49	$2.47	1.41
1971	3.59	2.92	1.23
1972	3.91	3.00	1.30
1973	4.26	3.55	1.20
1974	4.67	3.81	1.23
1975	4.87	3.92	1.24
1976	5.38	4.25	1.27
1977	6.08	5.11	1.19
1978	6.51	5.29	1.23
1979	7.11	6.15	1.16
1980	7.69	6.48	1.19

Note: Wages are for year previous to negotiations.

Sources: Estimated from Average Production Worker Wages in Manufacturing USBLS, *Industry Wage Series* (various issues); union-nonunion differential estimates provided in Moore and Raisian 1981; estimated percentage unionization in manufacturing from the *Current Population Survey.*

contract probably has an average wage exceeding the 24 percent differential we have computed. In this case, our estimates of wage elasticities for the average union worker are probably high.

Data Sources

SIZE and *MULTI* were taken directly from the BLS contracts tape (see Chapter 3). *MULTI* is an aggregation of the two BLS categories "association" agreement and "industry/area" agreement, both of which describe multifirm contracts. *CONSOL* was calculated directly from the BLS tape. "Theoretical" industries for manufacturing were defined following Kaysen and Turner (1965) using the four-digit SIC codes assigned to each contract by the BLS. This variable is only an estimate since there are missing contracts in each industry. *SOUTH* was computed directly from the contract tape.

Concentration was taken from the U.S. Department of Commerce,

1972 Census of Manufactures. The unionization figures are a hybrid of data taken from Freeman and Medoff (1979) and from BLS estimates made in conjunction with its *Industry Wage Series.*

Occupational and demographic information (*CRAFT, OPER, MALE, MAR, WHITE, ED, EXP, EXP², CHILD, LGSMSA*) were provided by James L. Medoff from the 1973–75 *Current Population Survey* tapes for union workers in manufacturing. The same variables were gathered for nonmanufacturing from the 1979 *Current Population Survey.* However, they pertain to all workers, as opposed to just union members, due to small numbers of union workers in these industries.

Wholesale- and consumer-price data were taken from the BLS *Wholesale Prices and Price Indices* (1971 through 1977) and the *Monthly Labor Review,* various issues. The actual length of the time series available by industry varied due to BLS collection procedures and redefinitions of the standard industrial classification (SIC) of industries. In some cases, industry definitions changed slightly over the period. In these cases, we added a dummy variable for each time period after the change. The form of the regression equations that were computed for each industry was

$$\ln(\mathrm{CPI}_t) = \alpha + \beta_1 \ln(\mathrm{WPI}_t) + \beta_2 D_t + e_t, \qquad (6\mathrm{A}\text{--}10)$$

where D_t took on a value of 1 after any change in industry definition and 0 before any change and t refers to monthly data. A total of 193 industry regressions were run. Four-digit industries with no wholesale price information were matched with another industry in the same three-digit group when possible.

NOTES

1. They did not have access to all the characteristics of the Colas, so calculating *ex post* Cola yield was not possible in any event. *Ex ante* calculations were also not possible because they had no wage level information. Thus, this approach was literally forced upon the authors.
2. Contract reopeners that are contingent on price changes but have no specific formula are included in the nonindexed group.
3. See Feuille, Hendricks, and Kahn (1981) and Bloch and Kuskin (1978).
4. See Reynolds (1982: 319–41).
5. Estenson (1981) used 140 major manufacturing contracts to estimate the probability of a Cola clause. He used as explanatory variables the

equivalent of *COEFF* and *SIGMA* in 48 two-digit industry price regressions. In constructing these two variables, we have performed 193 four-digit industry price regressions.

6. Contracts negotiated in and beyond 1980 could not be used since price expectations after 1982 were not available at the time the calculations were made.

7. Note that a possible selectivity problem arises because the sample is limited to indexed agreements. However, identification problems are likely to limit the effectiveness of selectivity bias correction techniques.

REFERENCES

Azariadis, Costas. 1975. "Implicit Contracts and Underemployment Equilibria." *Journal of Political Economy* 83, no. 6 (December): 1183–1202.
———. 1978. "Escalator Clauses and the Allocation of Cyclical Risks." *Journal of Economic Theory* 18, no. 1 (June): 119–55.

Bloch, Farrell E., and Mark S. Kuskin. 1978. "Wage Determination in the Union and Nonunion Sectors." *Industrial and Labor Relations Review* 31, no. 2 (January): 183–92.

Card, David. 1982. "Indexation in Long Term Labor Agreemens: A Theoretical and Empirical Analysis." Unpublished paper, University of Chicago.
———. 1983. "Cost-of-Living Escalators in Major Union Contracts." *Industrial and Labor Relations Review* 37, no. 1 (October): 34–48.

Christofides, Louis N. 1982. "Nominal Wage Rate Revisions and Measured Compensation Against Anticipated Inflation." *Journal of Labor Research* 3, no. 3 (Summer): 359–65.

Cousineau, Jean-Michel; Robert Lacroix; and Danielle Bilodeau. 1983. "The Determinants of Escalation Clauses in Collective Agreements." *The Review of Economics and Statistics* 65, no. 2 (May): 196–202.

Douty, H.M. 1975. "Cost-of-Living Escalator Clauses and Inflation." Prepared for the Council on Wage and Price Stability. Washington, D.C.: U.S. Government Printing Office.

Ehrenberg, Ronald; Leif Danziger; and Gee San. 1983. "Cost-of-Living Adjustment Clauses in Union Contracts: A Summary of Results." *Journal of Labor Economics* 1, no. 3 (July): 215–45.

Estenson, David. 1981. "Relative Price Variability and Indexed Labor Agreements." *Industrial Relations* 20, no. 1 (Winter): 71–84.

Feuille, Peter; Wallace Hendricks; and Lawrence M. Kahn. 1981. "Wage and Nonwage Outcomes in Collective Bargaining: Determinants and Tradeoffs." *Journal of Labor Research* 2, no. 2 (Spring): 39–53.

Freeman, Richard B., and James Medoff. 1979. "New Estimates of Private Sector Unionism in the United States." *Industrial and Labor Relations Review* 32, no. 2 (January): 143–74.

Gray, Jo Anna. 1978. "On Indexation and Contract Length." *Journal of Political Economy* 86, no. 1 (February): 1–18.

Hendricks, Wallace. 1975. "Labor Market Structure and Union Wage Levels." *Economic Inquiry* 13, no. 3 (September): 401–16.

Hendricks, Wallace, and Lawrence M. Kahn. 1983. "Cost-of-Living Clauses in Union Contracts: Determinants and Effects." *Industrial and Labor Relations Review* 36, no. 4 (April): 447–60.

———. 1984. "The Demand for Labor Market Structure: An Economic Approach." *Journal of Labor Economics* 2, no. 3 (July): 412–38.

Kaysen, Carl, and Donald F. Turner. 1965. *Anti-Trust Policy*. Cambridge, Mass.: Harvard University Press.

Moore, William J., and John Raisian. 1981. "A Time Series Analysis of the Growth and Determinants of Union/Nonunion Relative Wage Effects, 1967–77." BLS Working Paper No. 115.

Reynolds, Lloyd G. 1982. *Labor Economics and Labor Relations,* 8th ed., Englewood Cliffs, N.J.: Prentice-Hall.

Sheifer, Victor J. 1979. "Cost-of-Living Adjustment: Keeping Up With Inflation?" *Monthly Labor Review* 102, no. 6 (June): 14–17.

U.S. Bureau of Labor Statistics. *Industry Wage Series* (various issues).

———. *Monthly Labor Review* (various issues).

———. *Wholesale Prices and Price Indexes,* 1971 through 1977 issues.

U.S. Department of Commerce. 1972. *1972 Census of Manufactures*. Washington, D.C.: U.S. Government Printing Office.

Wilton, David A. 1979. "An Analysis of Canadian Wage Contracts with Cost-of-Living Allowance Clauses." Discussion Paper No. 165. Ottawa: The Centre for the Study of Inflation and Productivity, Economic Council of Canada.

Chapter 7

Empirical Results: The Effects of Colas on Wage Inflation

One major focus of the previous chapter was an attempt to estimate the determinants of labor's and management's intentions regarding wage indexation. Of key interest were the factors that lead the parties to choose indexation and, among indexed contracts, to choose a Cola of given generosity. The ultimate effects of this choice on wage inflation over the 1968–83 period are analyzed in this chapter. As discussed in some detail in earlier chapters, a great deal of policy attention has been focused on Colas as a possible mechanism for transmitting inflation. Thus, it is important to know how much of the wage inflation in recent years can be attributed to Colas.

The results of the previous chapter suggest one answer to the policy question just raised. In particular, among contracts with uncapped Colas, the elasticity of janitor/laborer wages with respect to unanticipated inflation was 0.8 to 0.9 with a figure of about 0.6 for the average worker. Thus, about 60 percent of unanticipated inflation becomes transmitted to union wages in indexed contracts. Since less than 25 percent of workers are unionized, since 55 to 60 percent of union workers have Colas, and since 20 percent of Colas are capped, the overall effect of indexation in transmitting unexpected inflation should probably be small (Kahn 1981; Vroman 1982).

Knowledge about the effects of Cola formulas is important in evaluating wage indexation, but we must also be aware that the size of scheduled, noncontingent wage increases might be related to the presence of Colas. As was noted in Chapter 5, workers are probably willing to give up something in return for real wage insurance. If this price takes the form of lower overall raises or a lower effect of expected inflation on wages, then the overall impact of Colas might be even less inflationary than our modest estimates of Chapter 6 would suggest.

The overall effects of Colas on actual wage inflation are estimated in this chapter. Hypotheses are tested about four specific kinds of effects that the presence of a Cola can have on wage inflation. First, Colas can influence the response of wages to unexpected inflation. Second, the wage response to expected inflation can be affected by the presence of a Cola. Third, the overall level of wage increases can be affected by the existence of wage indexation. Finally, the degree to which current contracts compensate for past inflation can be affected by the presence of a Cola. Our results are compared to the small number of existing studies that attempt to estimate the effects of Colas on wage inflation.

Although Colas are the main focus, our data also allow examination of the effects of inflationary expectations on wages. In particular, as has been observed in the macroeconomics literature (Sachs 1980), if wage changes fully compensate for anticipated inflation, then unemployment can be lowered only if workers are "fooled." If expectations of inflation catch up to reality, then even an expansionary monetary policy will not permanently lower real wages and thus will not permanently lower unemployment (under demand-determined employment). This result, termed the natural rate hypothesis (NRH), implies a limited role for fiscal and monetary tools: These policies can, under the NRH, only work as long as expectations lag behind reality. As Table 2–7 shows for the 1970s, however, this state of affairs can persist for some time.

INITIAL RESULTS FOR THE EFFECTS OF COLAS

As noted earlier, many observers have held that Colas play an inflationary role in the United States. A simple test of this claim was performed by estimating the following regression:

$$\dot{W}_t = .0813 + .0049 \ MAX_t + .0318 \ FREE_t \qquad (7-1)$$
$$(.0007) \ (.0016) \qquad\qquad (.0012)$$

$n = 3,511$, $R^2 = .1707$, time period 1966–82; where

$\dot{W}_t$ is the annual average percentage wage increase (including Cola and scheduled wage increases) over the life of a contract signed at time t

$MAX_t = 1$ if the contract had a capped Cola
$\qquad = 0$ otherwise,
$FREE_t = 1$ if the contract had an uncapped Cola
$\qquad = 0$ otherwise.

In Equation 7-1, the contract is the unit of analysis. The results indicate that contracts with capped Colas had, on average, 0.49 percentage points higher annual wage increases than unindexed agreements. This effect was significantly different from 0 at better than the 1 percent level (two-tailed test). Further, contracts with uncapped Colas yielded 3.18 percentage points greater annual wage increases than unindexed agreements, another result statistically significant at better than the 1 percent level. The *FREE* effect of 3.18 percent is a sizable proportion of our sample average of 9.1 percent annual wage inflation. Finally, the *FREE* coefficient is significantly greater than the *MAX* coefficient at better than the 1 percent level, and the difference between the two effects is 2.69 percentage points. Thus, wage increases in capped Colas are closer to those in unindexed contracts than to those in uncapped Cola agreements. However, wage changes across any pair of the three types of contract are significantly different from each other.

The results from 7-1 appear to imply an inflationary role for Colas, especially those without ceilings. Our discussion from earlier chapters suggested that the effects of Colas depend on inflation. An indication of this dependence can be given by the results of estimating separate annual wage regressions,

$$WA_t = B'X_t + B_M MAX_t + B_F FREE_t + \epsilon_{72t}, \qquad (7-2)$$

where for each calendar year t and contract, $WA_t =$ annual rate of wage increase for that year including Cola and deferred increase; X_t is a vector of control variables including *CONSTANT, SIZE, UN, CR8, CONSOL, CRAFT, OPER, LGSMSA, MAR, MALE, WHITE, ED, EXP, EXP^2, CHILD, SOUTH,* and *MULTI* (all defined in Chapter 6); and ϵ_{72t} is an error term. The control variables are proxies for market and bargaining power effects in wage determination. The results of estimating 7-2 are given in Table 7-1.

The average effects for *MAX* and *FREE* in yearly wage equations are similar to those of Equation 7-1, which was based on the contract as unit of observation. *FREE* should have the largest effects during

Table 7-1. Wage Inflation Results for *MAX* and *FREE* in Annual Wage Regressions.[a]

Year	Average Wage Increase	MAX	FREE	Sample Size	Unexpected Inflation
1968-1969	7.17%	−.0253[d] (.0146)	−.0120 (.0192)	145	+3.2%
1969-1970	5.72%	.0173[d] (.0089)	.0334[b] (.0115)	302	+1.9%
1970-1971	6.68%	−.0002 (.0096)	−.0080 (.0096)	390	−0.4%
1971-1972	9.01%	.0126[d] (.0064)	.0337[b] (.0048)	498	+0.2%
1972-1973	6.55%	.0124[d] (.0067)	−.0072 (.0051)	597	+5.3%
1973-1974	7.16%	.0154[b] (.0030)	.0245[b] (.0028)	927	+6.8%
1974-1975	8.62%	.0108[b] (.0030)	.0346[b] (.0026)	1,339	−0.4%
1975-1976	9.32%	.0074[c] (.0032)	.0241[b] (.0028)	1,665	−1.2%
1976-1977	8.57%	.0014 (.0028)	.0057[c] (.0023)	1,704	+1.4%
1977-1978	8.53%	.0017 (.0032)	.0119[b] (.0026)	1,523	+2.7%
1978-1979	8.82%	.0074[d] (.0039)	.0173[b] (.0029)	1,163	+6.2%
1979-1980	9.50%	−.0084[c] (.0040)	.0265[b] (.0029)	922	+2.8%
1980-1981	9.25%	−.0046 (.0057)	.0234[b] (.0038)	687	−1.4%
1981-1982	9.27%	.0055 (.0055)	.0182[b] (.0037)	607	−3.3%
1982-1983	7.40%	.0055 (.0047)	−.0056 (.0035)	347	−1.3%
All years pooled	8.48%	.0070[b] (.0012)	.0199[b] (.0009)	12,816	−

[a]Unexpected inflation is the December–December difference between actual inflation and the Livingston forecast. See Table 2-7. For other variables included in the regressions, see text. The dependent variable is the percentage of wage change during the indicated year.

[b]Significant at 0.01 level, two-tailed test.

[c]Significant at 0.05 level, two-tailed test.

[d]Significant at 0.10 level, two-tailed test.

or following periods of high unanticipated inflation. This prediction generally holds true, as the *FREE* effect becomes large in 1969–70, 1973–75, and 1978–80. Further, the *FREE* effect falls during 1975–77 and 1980–83, periods of below-expected inflation. An interesting finding in Table 7–1 is that for 1983, the *FREE* effect was negative and nearly significant at 10 percent on a two-tailed test. Contracts with uncapped Colas did particularly badly either because of the negative unexpected inflation or the concession of scheduled wage increases in order to keep the Cola (see Chapter 2). The findings in Table 7–1 suggest that uncapped Colas have their largest effects during periods of unanticipated inflation. However, the table gives no guidance as to the magnitude or statistical significance of this relationship. To shed light on these two issues, more structure must be placed on the wage inflation equation. This is accomplished by using the augmented Phillips Curve approach.

AUGMENTED PHILLIPS CURVE ANALYSIS

The expectations-augmented Phillips Curve has been developed to analyze the determinants of aggregate wage inflation.[1] In this view, wage inflation for workers without Colas depends on labor market tightness and the degree of inflation expected over the duration of the contract. With wage indexation, wage inflation depends on these factors and on the degree of unexpected wage inflation.

This framework can be summarized by Equations 7–3, 7–4, and 7–5 (contract is the unit of analysis):

Contracts without Colas

$$\dot{W}_t = B_N{}'Z_t + z_N \cdot UMINV_t + a_N PE_t + \epsilon_{73t} \qquad (7\text{--}3)$$

Contracts with capped Colas

$$\dot{W}_t = B_C{}'Z_t + z_C \cdot UMINV_t + a_C PE_t + b_C(PA_t - PE_t) + \epsilon_{74t} \qquad (7\text{--}4)$$

Contracts with uncapped Colas

$$\dot{W}_t = B_F{}'Z_t + z_F \cdot UMINV_t + a_F PE_t + b_F(PA_t - PE_t) + \epsilon_{75t}, \qquad (7\text{--}5)$$

where for each contract signed at time t, Z_t is a vector including X_t and a time trend; $UMINV_t$ = reciprocal of the adult male unemployment rate as of the signing of the agreement; PE_t = annual rate of inflation expected as of the beginning of the contract; PA_t = actual annual rate of inflation over the life of the contract and ϵ_{73t}, ϵ_{74t}, and ϵ_{75t} are error terms.

In Equations 7-3 through 7-5, the Z variables serve as controls. For example, some industries or demographic groups might be experiencing changes in their relative wages. These changes would be reflected in relative wage increases or decreases. In addition, many of these variables may be related to bargaining power. The reciprocal of the adult male unemployment rate ($UMINV$) reflects labor market tightness; the other variables represent the effects of indexation, expected inflation, and unanticipated inflation. The adult male rate is used rather than the total unemployment rate because demographic changes in the labor force reduce the latter measure's usefulness as an indicator of labor market tightness. Separate regressions in 7-3 through 7-5 allow each of the three types of contract (no Cola, capped, and uncapped) to have a different response to each explanatory variable. In particular, the equations allow wage changes to differ across the three types of contracts even when inflation is 0 and fully anticipated. In addition, 7-3 through 7-5 estimate the effect of the two types of Cola interacted with unanticipated inflation $(PA_t - PE_t)$.

The results from estimation of 7-3 through 7-5 can yield information on several issues dealing with Colas and wage inflation. The most obvious is the overall effects of Colas on wage changes. These overall effects have been discussed above in the context of the price workers must pay in order to achieve indexation. A second related issue concerns the existence of a long-run tradeoff between inflation and unemployment. If the response of wages to expected inflation is less than full, then there might be such a tradeoff (Gordon 1976; Sachs 1980). This response is measured by the coefficients a_N, a_C, and a_F. To see this is the case, suppose that an announced rise in the money supply raises actual and anticipated inflation by the same amount. If a_N, a_C, and a_F were less than 1, then money wages would rise by less than the increase in prices, allowing actual and perceived real wages to fall. Thus, employment would rise if it were determined by demand (see Chapter 4). If, however, $a_N = a_C = a_F = 1$, then there is no long-run inflation-unemployment tradeoff. As noted, such an outcome has been called the NRH (Gordon 1976). Finally, in 7-3 through 7-5, b_C and b_F provide indirect estimates of unexpected inflation elasticities that can be compared to the direct elasticities computed in Chapter 6. However, the dependent variable in 7–1 is actual *total* wage change rather than wage change attributable to the Cola formula. If the price workers must pay in order to get a Cola is correlated with the amount of unanticipated inflation, then b_C and b_F will combine the effects of this price and the true Cola elasticities computed in Chapter 6. Thus, coefficients b_C and b_F measure the outcome of a slightly different experiment from the elasticities.

While 7–3 through 7–5 posit separate equations, pooling of the data on the three contract types can provide more efficient estimation of the parameters as well as the information necessary to compare coefficients across contract types. In the interests of parsimony, the coefficients on the control variables (B_N, B_C, B_F) and on the unemployment term (z_N, z_C, z_F) are restricted to be the same across contracts although the intercept term is allowed to vary. In addition, a version of the model is tested where each contract has the same response to expected inflation. Further, a version of the model is tested where the intercept terms of B_N, B_C, and B_F are constrained to be the same (as well as their other elements). In this last specification all contracts would yield the same wage inflation under a perfectly anticipated inflation rate of 0 (controlling for Z_t).

In this chapter, PE_t is the raw twelve-month Livingston forecast rather than our constructed forecast (see Appendix A). The model estimated using the latter forecast did not yield credible results. While a contract-lifetime inflation forecast is the theoretically appropriate expectation concept, our construct evidently is too "noisy" to use as an explanatory variable. In addition, the Cola-related variables in the chapter are treated as exogenous. Identification problems would be likely to make difficult any meaningful simultaneous equations analysis.

The results of the augmented Phillips Curve models are presented in Tables 7–2 and 7–3. The first column of Table 7–2 illustrates a very simple specification in which it is assumed that each type of contract has the same response to anticipated inflation. The PE_t coefficient is 0.9198 and is not significantly different from 1. The natural rate of unemployment hypothesis is therefore supported by this result: As long as expectations of inflation are unbiased or eventually catch up to reality, then price increases will be fully reflected in wages.

Within the specification of Table 7–2, column 1, the main effect of *MAX*, is virtually 0 and is insignificant, while that for *FREE* is 1.59

Table 7-2. Basic Augmented Phillips Curve Results, 1966–82 (asymptotic standard errors in parentheses).

Explanatory Variable	Coefficients	
	One PE_t Term for All Contracts	Different PE_t Terms by Cola Status
CONSTANT	.1940[a]	.1922[a]
	(.0380)	(.0387)
SIZE $(\div 10^3)$	.000005	.0000004
	(.00003)	(.00003)
UN	−.00003	−.00003
	(.00004)	(.00004)
CR8	−.00004	−.00004
	(.00003)	(.00003)
CONSOL	.00002	.00002
	(.00003)	(.00003)
CRAFT	.0010	−.00007
	(.0076)	(.0076)
OPER	−.0193[a]	−.0201[a]
	(.0073)	(.0073)
LGSMSA	−.0266[a]	−.0278[a]
	(.0051)	(.0051)
MAR	−.0057	−.0082
	(.0157)	(.0157)
MALE	−.0141[b]	−.0146[b]
	(.0060)	(.0060)
WHITE	−.0196[c]	−.0207[c]
	(.0117)	(.0117)
ED	.0080[a]	.0083[a]
	(.0020)	(.0020)
EXP	−.0056[a]	−.0059[a]
	(.0016)	(.0016)
EXP^2	.0001[a]	.0001[a]
	(.00003)	(.00003)
CHILD	.0090[c]	.0093[c]
	(.0047)	(.0047)
SOUTH	.0032[b]	.0032[b]
	(.0013)	(.0013)
MULTI	−.0089[a]	−.0088[a]
	(.0020)	(.0020)
TIME	−.0002[a]	−.0002[a]
	(.00004)	(.00004)

Table 7-2.   (Continued)

Explanatory Variable	Coefficients	
	One PE_t Term for All Contracts	*Different PE_t Terms by Cola Status*
UMINV	−.0642 [a]	−.0643 [a]
	(.0063)	(.0066)
MAX	−.0004	.0183 [a]
	(.0023)	(.0071)
FREE	.0159 [a]	.0162 [a]
	(.0019)	(.0058)
PE_t	.9198 [a]	−
	(.0790)	
PEU_t	−	.9491 [a]
		(.0806)
PEM_t	−	.6377 [a]
		(.1276)
PEF_t	−	.9399 [a]
		(.1096)
$(PA_t - PE_t)MAX_t$	.2073 [a]	.1404 [c]
	(.0771)	(.0807)
$(PA_t - PE_t)FREE_t$	.5289 [a]	.5333 [a]
	(.0582)	(.0619)
n	3,511	3,511
R^2	.3293	.3308

Note: Annual wage inflation over the contract life is the dependent variable. PEU_t, PEM_t, and PEF_t are respectively, PE_t interacted with a dummy variable for no Cola, MAX, and FREE.

[a] Significant at 0.01 level, two-tailed test.

[b] Significant at 0.05 level, two-tailed test.

[c] Significant at 0.10 level, two-tailed test.

percentage points and is highly significant. Thus, during a perfectly anticipated inflation (i.e., $PA_t = PE_t$), wages in contracts with capped Colas behave similarly to those in unindexed agreements, and those in contracts with uncapped Colas rise 1.59 percentage points faster than in the latter.

The significant MAX effect and about one-half of the FREE effect estimated in Equation 7-1 are therefore due to the interaction of unanticipated inflation or the other explanatory variables with these types of Cola. The interaction coefficients in Table 7–2, column 1 indicate that capped and uncapped Colas return 20.7 percent and 52.9 percent, respectively, of unanticipated inflation. These figures are smaller than the direct unexpected Cola elasticities we computed in Chapter 6. The positive *FREE* main effect suggests that this variable might be a proxy for union bargaining power: Even with a perfectly anticipated 0 inflation rate, wages rise faster in contracts with uncapped Colas than in other contracts, *ceteris paribus*. Of course, our earlier discussion implies that the *MAX* and *FREE* main effects might also include the price workers must pay in order to get indexation. The results of Table 7–2, column 1 indicate that the bargaining power effect cancels the price effect for *MAX* and more than outweighs the price effect for *FREE*.[2] These effects might also be reflected in wage *levels* rather than wage changes, as suggested by the positive correlation between wage levels and indexation (Chapter 3). However, the positive main *FREE* effect in Table 7–2's wage change results also suggests a bargaining power interpretation.

The results considered so far have assumed that all contracts have the same response to anticipated inflation. The second column of Table 7–2 relaxes this assumption by allowing each type of contract to have a different response. The hypothesis that all three had equal responses to anticipated inflation is easily rejected with an F-statistic of 3.95 with (2,3487) degrees of freedom. With PEU_t, PEM_t, and PEF_t included, *MAX* now has a significant main effect. This is canceled out by the smaller return to anticipated inflation in contracts with capped Colas than in other contracts. That is, during a perfectly anticipated inflation, contracts with capped Colas have greater (smaller) wage increases than those in unindexed contracts at inflation rates less (more) than 5.88 percent. Since the sample mean PE_t was 5.39 percent, on average, the *MAX* effect was very small when we set $PA_t = PE_t$. Specifically, at $PA_t = PE_t = 5.39$ percent, the effect of *MAX* (relative to no Cola) on wage inflation is 0.0015 (0.15 percentage points) with a standard error of 0.5954. The PEM_t effect in column 2 of Table 7–2 is significantly different (smaller) from those of PEF_t and PEU_t at better than, respectively, 5 percent and 1 percent levels on two-tailed tests. The PEM_t effect is significantly smaller than 1, the PEU_t and PEF_t effects are not. In capping a Cola, the parties appear to be planning a small response to anticipated (as well as unanticipated) inflation. However, at a 0 anticipated and realized inflation rate, capped Cola contracts do slightly (and insignificantly)

Table 7–3. Augmented Phillips Curve Results: No MAX or FREE Main Effects.

Explanatory Variable[a]	One PE_t Term for All Contracts	Different PE_t Terms by Cola Status
MAX	–	–
FREE	–	–
PE_t	1.1866[b] (.0689)	–
PEU_t	–	.9430[b] (.0806)
PEM_t	–	.9025[b] (.0757)
PEF_t	–	1.1660[b] (.0711)
$(PA_t - PE_t)MAX_t$	.1683[b] (.0522)	.2507[b] (.0696)
$(PA_t - PE_t)FREE_t$	.8980[b] (.0394)	.6264[b] (.1518)
n	3,511	3,511
R^2	.3140	.3284

[a] Other explanatory variables are the same as in Table 7–2.

[b] Significant at 0.01 level, two-tailed test.

better than uncapped Colas and significantly better than unindexed agreements. The responses to unanticipated inflation are similar in column 2 to those in column 1 of Table 7–2.

Earlier work to be discussed in more detail below (Vroman 1981; Mitchell 1980; Kaufman and Woglom 1984) on the effects of Colas did not use main effects for Cola or Cola type. We have therefore reestimated our model for comparison purposes without allowing for these main effects. The findings are shown in Table 7–3. The results indicate a stronger response to expected inflation than in Table 7–2. In fact, for column 1 of Table 7–3 and for the PEF_t term in column 2, the NRH is (just barely) rejected on the high side. In addition, for the response of uncapped Colas to unanticipated inflation, the results are closer to the elasticities of Chapter 6. However, the F-tests clearly reject the specification in Table 7–3. Main effects of MAX and FREE should be included in the regression. The F-statistics are 38.89 for column $1 - F(2,3489)$ — and 6.172 for column $2 - F(2.3487)$ — both significant at better than the 1 percent level.

Wage Inflation Results for Other Variables

Table 7-2 contains findings for all variables in the basic augmented Phillips Curve models. The results for the non-Cola or inflation-related variables were robust to alternative specifications. They indicate that, on average, over the 1966–82 period, operatives, workers in large SMSAs, men, whites, workers outside the South, and workers under multifirm agreements all received lower wage increases, *ceteris paribus,* than otherwise. Unions with more educated workers did better than those with less educated workers, *ceteris paribus.* This last result apparently contradicts a trend toward declining rewards to higher education (Freeman 1976). Perhaps the higher wage growth associated with higher education levels was unique to the union sector or was canceled out by employment effects.

Finally, the effect of the reciprocal of the male unemployment rate is consistently opposite to what one would have expected. *UMINV* has a negative, significant coefficient in each case. To test whether this finding was due to problems with the *UMINV* variable as an indicator of labor market pressure, the basic model was reestimated using the Conference Board's Help Wanted Index (HELP) instead of *UMINV*.[3] HELP has been used in previous work as a proxy for vacancies (Reid 1981; Kahn 1981). The results were similar to those using *UMINV*: High values of HELP were associated with low values of wage inflation, *ceteris paribus.* The other variables were unaffected.

The behavior of the economy in the 1970s might explain the negative relationship between labor market pressure and wage inflation. Most of our observations come from the 1973–81 period, which was characterized by two severe bouts of inflation brought on by oil crises. In each case, the economy was sent into a recession at the same time that inflation was high. Hence, we observe the negative association between labor market pressure and wage inflation.

Our results for the effects of Colas and unemployment on wage inflation can be compared to those of Mitchell (1980). He analyzed a sample of 172 contract negotiations over the 1954–76 period. He used

Bureau of Labor Statistics (BLS) data to impute rates of wage increase in the contracts since wage level data were not available. Estimated wage increases were then regressed on the previous year's inflation rate, the reciprocal of the overall unemployment rate, inflation over the life of the contract interacted with a Cola dummy variable, and an indicator of the industry's relative wage before the signing of the agreement. In addition, a specification with a profit-to-sales ratio for the company was estimated. The results on the Cola-inflation interaction term correspond to the actual degree of indexation, although he made no attempt to distinguish anticipated from unanticipated inflation.

Mitchell found an overall significant effect of 0.4 to 0.6 for the Cola variable—a somewhat smaller estimate than our result for $FREE(PA_t - PE_t)$. However, our base wage is for janitors and laborers; he used an estimate of average wages. Our results from Chapter 6 indicate that these findings for uncapped Colas are compatible with Mitchell's. Further, he estimated a degree of indexation of 0.84 for low-wage workers in long-term indexed agreements.[4] The specification that is closest to Mitchell's is in Table 7-3, column 1, where the $FREE(PA_t - PE_t)$ effect is 0.898—a similar result to Mitchell's. Note that he used previous inflation rather than a direct measure of price expectations. Finally, he found that unemployment generally had the expected effect on wage increases for 1954-76. Thus, the unemployment-wage relationship has changed in the 1970s.

CATCH-UP MODELS OF WAGE INFLATION

The augmented Phillips Curve model assumes that wage setting is an exclusively forward-looking process. The past has no influence on wages except through $UMINV_t$ or PE_t. However, it has been pointed out that labor and management might take into account past mistakes as well as anticipate future inflation (Christofides, Swidinsky, and Wilton 1980). Some anecdotal evidence for such a process was given in Chapter 2 in our description of the capping of the United Auto Workers' Cola in 1967. During those negotiations, it was explicitly stated that the future negotiation (i.e., for the 1970 agreements) would take account of any unintended effects of the 1967 caps.

The econometric problem posed by this backward-looking behavior is to translate it into a wage inflation equation. Two alternative specifications for these catch-up models have been suggested: catch-up based on previous *unanticipated* inflation (Vroman 1981) and catch-up based on previous *uncompensated* inflation (Christofides, Swidinsky, and Wilton 1980). The specifications are illustrated in Equations 7–6 and 7–7.

Catch-up for unanticipated inflation

$$\dot{W_t} = E'Z_t + e_1 UMINV_t + e_2 MAX_t + e_3 FREE_t + a_3 PEU_t + b_3 PEM_t$$
$$+ b_4 PEF_t + d_{cl}(PA_t - PE_t)MAX_t + e_{cl}(PA_t - PE_t)FREE_t$$
$$+ f_{13} \cdot (PA_{t-1} - PE_{t-1}) \cdot UNCOL_t + f_{23} \cdot (PA_{t-1} - PE_{t-1}) \cdot MAX_t$$
$$+ f_{33}(PA_{t-1} - PE_{t-1}) \cdot FREE_t + \epsilon_{76t} \qquad (7\text{--}6)$$

Catch-up for uncompensated inflation

$$\dot{W_t} = F'Z_t + f_1 UMINV_t + f_2 MAX_t + f_3 FREE_t + a_4 PEU_t$$
$$+ a_5 PEM_t + a_6 PEF_t + d_{cc}(PA_t - a_5 \cdot PE_t) \cdot MAX_t$$
$$+ e_{cc}(PA_t - a_6 \cdot PE_t) \cdot FREE_t + f_{14}(PA_t - a_4 PE_t) \cdot UNCOL_t$$
$$+ (1 - d_{cc}) f_{24}(PA_{t-1} - a_5 \cdot PE_{t-1}) \cdot MAX_t$$
$$+ (1 - e_{cc}) f_{34}(PA_{t-1} - a_6 \cdot PE_{t-1}) \cdot FREE_t + \epsilon_{77t}, \qquad (7\text{--}7)$$

where $t - 1$ refers to the previous contract
     $UNCOL_t = 1$ if the contract has no Cola
               $= 0$ otherwise, and
     ϵ_{76t} and ϵ_{77t} are error terms.

Equations 7–6 and 7–7 allow the return to PE_t and the catch-up to vary by Cola status. In 7–6, past unexpected inflation enters in as $(PE_{t-1} - PA_{t-1})$. Thus, for unindexed contracts, for example, future expected inflation affects current wage negotiations through coefficient a_3. If during the previous contract there was unanticipated inflation, it affects current wages through f_{13}. Indexed contracts, according to 7–6 allow for two "bites" at unanticipated inflation: once through d_{cl} and e_{cl} and once through f_{23} or f_{33}.

In contrast to 7–6, Equation 7–7 describes the catch-up as a response to uncompensated rather than unanticipated inflation. To see this, consider unindexed agreements. Future anticipated inflation affects current wages through a_4. Then the extent of actual inflation *not* reflected in wages over the life of the contract is $(PA_t - a_4 PE_t)$. This expression is thus termed uncompensated inflation. It equals unanticipated inflation if $a_4 = 1$. For indexed contracts, 7-7 allows indexation to future uncompensated inflation through d_{cc} and e_{cc} and catch-up to past uncompensated inflation through $(1 - d_{cc})f_{24}$ and $(1 - e_{cc})f_{34}$. Note that for indexed contracts the extent of past inflation not compensated for in the previous contract is $(1 - d_{cc})(PA_{t-1} - a_5 PE_{t-1})$ or $(1 - e_{cc})(PA_{t-1} - a_6 PE_{t-1})$.

An important implication of the catch-up model in 7-7 — uncompensated inflation — is that the return to expected inflation need not be 1 in order for the NRH to be true (Christofides, Swidinsky, and Wilton 1980). For example, for unindexed agreements, the long-run wage effect of a perfectly anticipated inflation is $a_4 + f_{14} - a_4 f_{14}$. If the NRH holds for unindexed agreements, $a_4 + f_{14} - a_4 f_{14} = 1$. On the other hand, in 7-6 for unindexed agreements, the effect of a perfectly anticipated inflation is a_3. For the NRH to hold in this case, $a_3 = 1$. Finally, note that 7-6 and 7-7 impose specific restrictions on the ways in which past inflation affects current bargaining. These models are tested against an unrestricted catch-up equation where past actual and expected inflation enter separately into the wage inflation regressions.

The results for the various catch-up models are reported in Tables 7-4, 7-5, and 7-6. In general, the results for expected inflation and the response of Colas to unexpected inflation are sensitive to specification. In addition, for contracts with Colas, the estimate of the catch-up effect is sensitive to specification. Only for unindexed contracts is there a consistent catch-up response. Despite the sensitivity of the results, some regularities emerge.

First, in Table 7-4 the response to expected inflation is generally smaller than the estimates in Tables 7-2 and 7-3 (i.e., with no catch-up terms). Further, inspection of Table 7-5 shows estimates of the wage response to a fully anticipated inflation are generally far less than 1. In only one case (*FREE* in column 4) is the response close to 1 (1.23). For all other cases, it ranges from about 0.16 to 0.78. As noted, in contrast to the nonlinear (i.e., uncompensated inflation catch-up) models of Table 7-5, in the linear (i.e., unanticipated inflation) catch-up models of Table 7-4, the NRH requires a future expected inflation term of 1. Inspection of Table 7-4 leads to rejection of this hypothesis in all cases except for PEU_t in column 2. Finally, in the unrestricted catch-up models (Table 7-6), the response to a fully anticipated inflation ranges from 0.34 to 0.87, most of the estimated responses being between 0.4 and 0.6.

Table 7–4. Selected Results for Unanticipated Inflation Catch-up Models (contract is unit of analysis).

	Coefficients			
	Basic Model		Main FREE and MAX Effects and X Omitted	
Explanatory Variables[a]	One PE_t Term for All Contracts (1)	Different PE_t Terms by Cola Status (2)	One PE_t Term for All Contracts (3)	Different PE_t Terms by Cola Status (4)
MAX_t	.0058	.0322[c]	—	—
	(.0056)	(.0126)		
$FREE_t$	.0268[b]	.0415[b]	—	—
	(.0045)	(.0093)		
PE_t	.6854[b]	—	.6260[b]	—
	(.1268)		(.0468)	
PEU_t	—	.7458[b]	—	.4581[b]
		(.1286)		(.0562)
PEM_t	—	.3512[d]	—	.4681[b]
		(.1952)		(.0760)
PEF_t	—	.5352[b]	—	.7703[b]
		(.1612)		(.0524)
$MAX_t(PA_t - PE_t)$	.1169	.0002	.1003[d]	.1158
	(.1286)	(.1379)	(.0579)	(.0943)
$FREE_t(PA_t - PE_t)$	.3614[b]	.2900[b]	.8139[b]	.5059[b]
	(.0974)	(.1080)	(.0388)	(.0629)
$UNCOL_t(PA_{t-1} - PE_{t-1})$	.1408[c]	.1310[c]	.1193[b]	.1770[b]
	(.0554)	(.0555)	(.0374)	(.0390)
$MAX_t(PA_{t-1} - PE_{t-1})$	.0209	−.0205	.0902	.1246
	(.1125)	(.1143)	(.0565)	(.0997)
$FREE_t(PA_{t-1} - PE_{t-1})$	−.1394	−.1732[d]	.3902[b]	.0285
	(.0873)	(.0901)	(.0447)	(.0731)
n	2,682	2,682	2,682	2,682
R^2	.2883	.2903	.2364	.2474

[a] For columns (1) and (2), other explanatory variables are the same as in Table 7–2. For columns (3) and (4), $UMINV$ and the constant term are the only other variables included.

[b] Significant at 0.01 level, two-tailed test.

[c] Significant at 0.05 level, two-tailed test.

[d] Significant at 0.10 level, two-tailed test.

Table 7-5. Selected Results for Uncompensated Inflation Catch-up Models (contract is unit of analysis). [a]

Explanatory Variables	Coefficients			
	(1)	(2)	(3)	(4)
MAX_t	.0387[b]	.0400[b]	—	—
	(.0118)	(.0123)		
$FREE_t$	.0524[b]	.0538[b]	—	—
	(.0084)	(.0088)		
PE_t	.2857[b]	—	.3491[b]	—
	(.0908)		(.0814)	
PEU_t	—	.3406[b]	—	.2444[c]
		(.1302)		(.1297)
PEM_t	—	.2401	—	.4392[c]
		(.1535)		(.2164)
PEF_t	—	.6006[b]	—	1.6330[b]
		(.1147)		(.2077)
$MAX_t(PA_t - aPE_t)$	−.1092	—	.1037[d]	—
	(.1018)		(.0547)	
$FREE_t(PA_t - aPE_t)$	.2409[b]	—	.5699[b]	—
	(.0714)		(.0397)	
$MAX_t(PA_t - a_5 PE_t)$	—	−.0922	—	.1036
		(.1042)		(.0895)
$FREE_t(PA_t - a_6 PE_t)$	—	.2150[c]	—	.6066[b]
		(.0822)		(.0901)
$(PA_{t-1} - aPE_{t-1})UNCOL_t$	.3759[b]	—	.2620[b]	—
	(.0681)		(.0667)	
$(1 - d_{cc})(PA_{t-1} - aPE_{t-1})MAX_t$	−.0735	—	.1996[c]	—
	(.1076)		(.0778)	
$(1 - e_{cc})(PA_{t-1} - aPE_{t-1})FREE_t$	−.4200[b]	—	.2344[c]	—
	(.1149)		(.1154)	
$(PA_{t-1} - a_4 PE_{t-1})UNCOL_t$	—	.3515[b]	—	.3515[b]
		(.0820)		(.0968)
$(1 - \tilde{d}_{cc})(PA_{t-1} - a_5 PE_{t-1})MAX_t$	—	−.0458	—	.1936
		(.1192)		(.1741)
$(1 - \tilde{e}_{cc})(PA_{t-1} - a_6 PE_{t-1})FREE_t$	—	−.2656[c]	—	.0480
		(.1129)		(.1899)

[a] Nonlinear Least Squares used. For description of columns (1) through (4) see Table 7-4. Note that $\tilde{d}_{cc}$ and $\tilde{e}_{cc}$ are the coefficients on $MAX(PA_t - a_5 PE_t)$ and $FREE(PA_t - a_6 PE_t)$, respectively.

[b] Significant at 0.01 level, two-tailed test.

[c] Significant at 0.05 level, two-tailed test.

[d] Significant at 0.10 level, two-tailed test.

Table 7-6.   Selected Results for Unrestricted Catch-up Models.[a]

Explanatory Variables	Coefficients			
	(1)	(2)	(3)	(4)
MAX_t	.0319[b]	.0368[c]	—	—
	(.0102)	(.0126)		
$FREE_t$	.0551[b]	.0398[b]	—	—
	(.0078)	(.0093)		
PE_t	.6095[b]	—	.7149[b]	—
	(.1236)		(.0925)	
PEU_t	—	.5444[b]	—	.3769[b]
		(.1398)		(.1126)
PEM_t	—	.5354[c]	—	.6589[b]
		(.2429)		(.1828)
PEF_t	—	1.1127[b]	—	1.4363[b]
		(.2084)		(.1492)
$MAX(PA_t - PE_t)$	.0302	.0856	.1606[c]	.1938
	(.0988)	(.1529)	(.0757)	(.1204)
$FREE(PA_t - PE_t)$	.3776[b]	.6090[b]	.6370[b]	.8331[b]
	(.0716)	(.1279)	(.0557)	(.0906)
$PA_{t-1} \cdot UNCOL_t$	.2473[b]	.2837[b]	.0004	.2056[c]
	(.0823)	(.0873)	(.0771)	(.0872)
PEU_{t-1}	—	.0468	—	−.1193[d]
		(.0985)		(.0700)
$PA_{t-1} \cdot MAX_t$	−.1362	−.0743	−.0249	.0354
	(.1277)	(.1383)	(.0822)	(.1257)
PEM_{t-1}	—	−.1080	—	−.2685
		(.1889)		(.1813)
$PA_{t-1} \cdot FREE_t$	−.2534[c]	−.3517[b]	.1648[c]	−.2927[b]
	(.1071)	(.1219)	(.0827)	(.1128)
PEF_{t-1}	—	−.2587[d]	—	−.5576[b]
		(.1471)		(.1306)
PE_{t-1}	−.0204	—	−.2390[b]	—
	(.0837)		(.0604)	
n	2,682	2,682	2,682	2,682
R^2	.2944	.2972	.2421	.2546

[a] See note to Table 7–4 for a description of other variables included in each equation for each column.

[b] Significant at 0.01 level, two-tailed test.

[c] Significant at 0.05 level, two-tailed test.

[d] Significant at 0.10 level, two-tailed test.

Second, the "degree of indexation" in contracts with Colas is smaller in the restricted catch-up models (Tables 7–4 and 7–5) than in the no catch-up models reported earlier (Tables 7–2 and 7–3). On the other hand, the main effects of *MAX* and *FREE* are considerably larger in all of the catch-up models than in the no catch-up models. In the unrestricted catch-up models, the degree of indexation is comparable to that in Tables 7–2 and 7–3 for uncapped Colas but smaller for capped agreements.

Given the differences between the no catch-up and catch-up models and between the restricted and unrestricted catch-up models, what conclusions can be made about the effects of Colas on wage inflation? Light can be shed on this question by an examination of the equations as well as some theoretical consideration of the catch-up notion. First, appropriate F-tests can be used to reject certain empirical specifications in favor of others. In particular, the catch-up specifications are favored by such tests over ones with no catch-up terms. In addition, within each model, specifications with different expected price terms (PEU_t, etc.), with *MAX* and *FREE* main effects, and with the other variables (X) included are supported by the F-tests. More importantly, within the "preferred" specification (i.e., including all variables and with different price expectations terms), the linear and nonlinear catch-up models are both decisively rejected against the unrestricted catch-up model. On the basis of these F-tests, column 2 of Table 7–6 would appear to be the best specification.[5] In this version of the model, capped Colas return 8.56 percent (insignificant) and uncapped Colas return 60.9 percent (significant) of current unanticipated inflation. The estimated responses to a perfectly anticipated inflation are as follows:

$$\text{no Cola} = .87; \quad MAX = .36; \quad FREE = .50,$$
$$(.16) \qquad\qquad (.22) \qquad\qquad (.19)$$

indicating a long-run Phillips tradeoff for *MAX* and *FREE*. Of course, problems of serial correlation might complicate the estimation of the effects of past inflation on current wage bargains.

Second, on theoretical grounds, the restricted catch-up models might be problematic because they assume no structural change in the various responses to inflation from one contract to the next. When the models were reestimated with the sample restricted to those contracts that did not change Cola status, the results were similar to those presented here. However, even if Cola type stays the same, the parameters of the Cola might change from one contract to the next.

The unrestricted catch-up models merely assume that past inflation (anticipated and unanticipated) influences current negotiations in a way that cannot be captured by the restricted Equations 7-6 and 7-7.

In summary, whether catch-up or no catch-up models are used, the NRH is accepted for unindexed contracts and rejected for agreements with capped Colas. For agreements with uncapped Colas, acceptance of the NRH depends on specification. When no catch-up terms are allowed, the NRH is accepted; under the most appropriate catch-up specification, it is rejected. The different types of contracts have significantly different responses to anticipated inflation. There are generally significant main *MAX* and *FREE* effects that vary with the level of expected inflation. The main effect of *FREE* is larger and more significant than that of *MAX*. Finally, the wage response to unanticipated inflation for *FREE* is 50 to 60 percent and highly significant; that for *MAX* is 8 to 14 percent and marginally significant or insignificant.

To our knowledge, only two other econometric studies have examined the effects of Colas on wage inflation in the context of catch-up models. Vroman (1981) analyzed a sample of 2,274 contract negotiations over the 1957–79 period. Lacking data on wage levels, he imputed wage levels to each contract using BLS industry wage data, as did Mitchell (1980). As noted earlier, Vroman (1981) used a linear catch-up specification similar to that in Table 7–4. However, he was not able to control for demographic, industry, or bargaining unit characteristics other than industry profits and strikes. In addition, he forced each type of contract (unindexed, *MAX*, and *FREE*) to have the same response to expected inflation and did not include main *MAX* and *FREE* terms. Recall that in our data, these were invalid restrictions. In any case, his results were sensitive to specification. The effect of a perfectly anticipated inflation on wages ranged from 0.46 to 1.17; the "degree of indexation" for capped Colas ranged from 0.14 to 0.29 and for uncapped Colas ranged from 0.51 to 0.66; catch-up terms ranged from −0.07 to 0.12 (no Cola), 0.10 to 0.32 (*MAX*), and −0.01 to 0.12 (*FREE*). Thus, these results are qualitatively similar to ours. However, he did find a positive, significant effect for *UMINV*, indicating that the 1957–79 period was different from the 1966–82 period in this regard.

Kaufman and Woglom (1984) analyzed a small sample of eighty-three negotiations between 1972 and 1981. They attempted to construct and analyze the desired wage increase in each contract. To do this, they computed the actual Cola elasticity and applied this to the expected inflation rate as of the beginning of the contract. In Chapter 6 it was shown that a more appropriate concept is to apply the expected inflation rate to the Cola formula. The Kaufman and Woglom (1984) construct is best viewed as a hybrid between the actual and expected elasticities calculated in Chapter 6. In addition, they treat capped Colas as unindexed contracts, which again was shown in Chapter 6 to be an inappropriate assumption. In any case, using their measure of desired wage increase, the authors estimated augmented Phillips Curves with nonlinear (uncompensated inflation) catch-up terms. Instead of using actual unemployment, they used expected unemployment and its expected rate of change taken from survey data. Their sample of forty-four agreements with Colas supported the NRH, but the sample of thirty-nine unindexed agreements did not support it. Labor market pressure had the expected effects for contracts with Colas but had negative, insignificant effects for contracts without Colas. Finally, Colas exhibited a strong catch-up response, and unindexed agreements did not. No other control variables were included.

Kaufman and Woglom's (1984) result for expected unemployment and its expected rate of change was opposite to ours for actual unemployment or help wanted for a roughly similar time period. Our model was reestimated using a constructed forecast of the rate of change of HELP as well as actual HELP. The forecasts were based on regressions using past HELP data and applied for the life of each contract. Using this procedure, similar results were obtained to those reported in Table 7-2. Clearly, further research is needed on this question; the application of direct expectations regarding unemployment should be made on large samples of collective bargaining agreements.

SUMMARY

The effects of Colas on wage inflation were investigated in this chapter. Using an augmented Phillips Curve approach, capped Colas were estimated to provide an 8 to 14 percent response to unanticipated inflation for janitors and laborers; the response in contracts with uncapped Colas was 50 to 60 percent. These figures are smaller than the direct elasticities calculated in Chapter 6. It is possible that the price a union must pay in order to get a Cola is positively correlated with the amount of unanticipated inflation. Although this finding does not seem consistent with rational expectations, it does suggest that the net effect of Colas on inflation has been slightly smaller than that implied by the elasticities. In addition, unindexed agreements have a response to fully anticipated inflation that is not significantly different from 1. However, the response in capped Colas is less than 1, and the response in uncapped Colas varies depending on the specification used. If the catch-up specification is correct, then neither type of Cola gives complete protection during a perfectly anticipated inflation. This result could be a further illustration of the price workers must pay in order to obtain or keep a Cola. An even more modest estimate of the inflationary impact of Colas would be implied than previously believed.

NOTES

1. See Sachs (1980) and Christofides, Swidinsky, and Wilton (1980).
2. The results of Table 7-2, column 1 are similar to those in our earlier work (Hendricks and Kahn 1983), which used a smaller sample and the specification in column 1.
3. The data were taken from various issues of the *Conference Board Statistical Bulletin.*
4. "Long term" was defined as eighteen months or longer duration.
5. F-tests based on the nonlinear models are based on the asymptotic Chi-square statistics that result from iterative least squares analysis. See Theil (1971: 396).

REFERENCES

Christofides, Louis; Robert Swidinsky; and David Wilton. 1980. "A Micro-econometric Analysis of the Canadian Wage Determination Process." *Economica* 47, no. 186 (May): 165–78.

Conference Board. *Conference Board Statistical Bulletin,* various issues.

Freeman, Richard. 1976. *The Over-Educated American.* New York: Academic Press.

Gordon, Robert J. 1976. "Recent Developments in the Theory of Inflation and Unemployment." *Journal of Monetary Economics* 2 (April): 185–219.

Hendricks, Wallace E., and Lawrence M. Kahn. 1983. "Cost-of-Living Clauses in Union Contracts: Determinants and Effects." *Industrial and Labor Relations Review* 36, no. 3 (April): 447–60.

Kahn, Lawrence M. 1981. "Wage Indexation and Wage Inflation in the U.S.." Unpublished paper, University of Illinois.

Kaufman, Roger, and Geoffrey Woglom. 1984. "The Effects of Expectations on Union Wages." *American Economic Review* 74, no. 3 (June): 418–32.

Mitchell, Daniel J.B. 1980. *Unions, Wages and Inflation.* Washington, D.C.: The Brookings Institution.

Reid, Frank. 1981. "Control and Decontrol of Wages in the United States." *American Economic Review* 71, no. 1 (March): 108–20.

Sachs, Jeffrey. 1980. "The Changing Cyclical Behavior of Wages and Prices." *American Economic Review* 70, no. 1 (March): 78–90.

Theil, Henri. 1971. *Principles of Econometrics.* New York: Wiley.

Vroman, Wayne. 1981. "Wage Contract Settlements in U.S. Manufacturing." Unpublished paper, The Urban Institute.

———. 1982. "Escalator Clauses and Price-Wage Feedback in the U.S. Economy." Unpublished Paper, The Urban Institute.

✳ *Chapter 8*

The Impact of Colas on Strike Activity

Formulating an acceptable theory of strike activity has been an elusive goal for both economists and industrial relations scholars. There are numerous theories of strike incidence, but they almost without exception come down to an assumption that one side causes the strike. We have little to add to this debate. In addition to the theoretical work in this area, there is a growing literature that attempts to relate strike frequency to economic phenomena such as past wage changes or unemployment levels. The theoretical underpinnings of this empirical work may be questioned, but it does serve the function of providing further information with which to evaluate alternative theories.

The relationship between strikes and Cola clauses is investigated in this chapter. In particular, the central question is whether or not wage indexation is associated with fewer strikes (or alternatively, fewer days lost due to strikes) than would occur in the absence of this indexation. Some observers believe this to be the case. For example, Laidler argued that wage indexation in the United States helped cause the low level of strike activity during the inflationary early 1970s (1974: 540).

There are two basic arguments that suggest Colas might decrease strike activity. Aggregate studies of strike activity (e.g., Ashenfelter and Johnson 1969) have found that strike frequency (and duration) is negatively associated with real wage change in the previous period. Gramm (1983) has found a similar result for disaggregated strike data when real wage change over the previous contract was used as an explanatory variable in strike equations. Goldstein (1975) argues that if indexation leads to larger increases in real wages, it should also lead to lower strike activity. However, there is no a priori reason for believing that wage indexation will necessarily lead to larger increases in real wages. This would be true in periods where actual inflation is underestimated by the parties. However, when actual inflation is less than expected inflation, unindexed contracts might be expected to lead to higher changes in real wages. Our results from the previous chapter suggest that, on average, wage changes were higher in contracts with Colas than without Colas during the 1970s. However, this advantage declines and eventually is reversed the more the parties overestimate the inflation rate. In an average period, when actual inflation is approximately equal to expected inflation, the positive main effects of Colas on wage change estimated in the previous chapter might suggest that contracts with Colas would have fewer strikes. However, this prediction might not hold true if these main effects are due to bargaining power. In any case, the real wage argument is certainly open to question.

A second possible reason for Colas to be associated with lower strike propensity concerns long-term contracts. Friedman (1974) and Goldstein (1975) have argued that long-term contracts reduce bargaining costs (including strike costs) because they need to be negotiated less frequently. If contracts are negotiated less frequently, there are fewer chances for strikes and therefore overall strike activity is reduced. This argument implicitly assumes that contracts of unequal lengths have equal probabilities of being associated with strikes at the next negotiation. It is plausible that long-term contracts might be associated with a higher propensity to strike at their conclusion. This might occur, for example, if the stock of grievances accumulates over time. The higher probability of a strike at the conclusion of a long-term contract could offset the lowering of strike opportunities associated with these contracts. Thus, the total effect (opportunity times probability) might be ambiguous.

Interestingly, Swidinsky and Vanderkamp (1982) turn the Friedman–Goldstein argument on its head. They argue that long-term contracts are harder to negotiate due to uncertainties over the longer horizon. They therefore predict that long-term contracts will be associated with a higher probability of a strike. They also point out that Colas might tend to reduce these uncertainties and make negotiation of long-term contracts easier. However, Colas might have unique attributes (e.g., the decision to cap Cola payments) that make them more difficult to negotiate than, for example, wage levels. Thus, the relationship between strikes and subsequently negotiated Colas may be unclear.

The impact of Colas on the overall level of strike activity is thus a complicated interaction of their impact on strike opportunities and strike probabilities. Some authors have stressed one side; other authors have emphasized the other. In the remainder of this chapter, we attempt to disentangle these effects.

STRIKES AND CONTRACT DURATION

If Colas have reduced strike activity by increasing contract length, there should have been a decrease in strike activity between 1950 and 1980 since average contract duration increased over this period. Jacoby and Mitchell (1982) investigated this question using aggregate strike data on strikes per 1,000 union members, strikes as a percentage of union members, and strike days per union member. They divided their data into three periods: 1953–59, 1960–69, and 1970–80. They found no evidence to indicate a decline in "downtime" due to strikes. If anything, strikes actually increased at the same time that contracts become longer.

This result suggests that either the probability of a strike or days lost per strike increase with contract length to offset reduced opportunities. It would be difficult to test such an idea using aggregate data since, in such a sample, there is no way to match individual contract length and strike information. However, Cynthia Gramm has matched our data for manufacturing contracts covering greater than 1,000 workers with Bureau of Labor Statistics (BLS) individual contract data on negotiations and strikes.[1] The resulting data set covers approximately 1,600 negotiations between 1971 and 1981. This allows investigation of the probability question using individual contract negotiations.

Strike data by length of previous contract are tabulated in Table 8–1 for our data set. Three-year contracts are more likely to end with a strike over the new contract than are one- or two-year contracts. Further, the predicted number of strike days for a given negotiation also increases with length of the previous contract. These data illustrate why no long-term decline in total strike activity is evident even though average contract length has increased. The increased probability of

Table 8-1.   Strikes and Length of Previous Contract, 1971–81.[a]

Length of Previous Contract[b]	Strike Probability	Average Days Lost/Negotiation	Sample Size
1 year	.118	3.88	17
2 years	.107	5.46	319
3 years	.150	7.04	1,298

[a] Contracts covering greater than 1,000 workers.

[b] 9–18 months = 1 year
19–29 months = 2 years
30+ months = 3 years

Source: Authors' data base.

Table 8-2.   Strikes and Length of Negotiated Contract, 1971–81.[a]

Length of Negotiated Contract[b]	Strike Probability	Average Days Lost/Negotiation	Sample Size
1 year	.032	.387	31
2 years	.118	5.22	304
3 years	.159	7.12	1,296

[a] Contracts covering greater than 1,000 workers.

[b] 9–18 months = 1 year
19–29 months = 2 years
30+ months = 3 years

Source: Authors' data base.

striking tends to offset the decreased opportunity as contract length increases. This is clearly true for differences between two- and three-year contracts, although less true moving from one- to three-year contracts. However, our sample size of one-year contracts is very small.

Data on strikes and length of the contract that is actually negotiated are presented in Table 8–2. These data present a similar picture to that found by Swidinsky and Vanderkamp (1982) using Canadian data. A short-term contract is much more likely to be negotiated without a strike. There is clearly a cause and effect problem with these data, but they do reinforce the results in Table 8–1. Long-term contracts seem to lead to negotiation problems which largely offset the decline in opportunities to strike.

These results, of course, do not necessarily imply that management would tend to not favor long-term over short-term agreements. There might be fixed costs to a strike that would indicate that one strike after a three-year agreement would be preferable to two strikes in three separate one-year agreements even if the total strike days were equal. For example, there might be costs associated with closing down or starting up operations, assuming that a strike causes production to cease. Thus, two separate strikes each lasting two weeks would be more costly to the firm than one four-week strike if fixed costs are important.

If the major impact of Colas on strike activity is through increasing contract length, this impact appears to be minor. In the next section we will look at this impact directly.

STRIKES AND COLAS

The only previous work of which we are aware that uses individual contract data to analyze U.S. strike activity consists of papers by Gramm (1983) and Mauro (1982). Of these two, only Mauro examines the effects of Colas. He uses a sample of fourteen bargaining relationships over thirty years for a total of 149 contract expirations. Twenty-three percent of these negotiations resulted in strikes (Mauro 1982: 527). Colas in previous contracts were insignificantly (sometimes negatively, sometimes positively) associated with strike probabilities. He concludes that the typically negative (if insignificant) effect of a Cola implies that indexation causes a reduction in strikes by taking away uncertainty about wages (Mauro 1982: 534). Using individual Canadian contract data, Swidinsky and Vanderkamp (1982) found positive (significant) effects of resulting contract duration and positive (generally insignificant) effects of resulting Cola coverage on the propensity to strike. Finally, Kaufman (1981) uses aggregate data to test the hypothesis that Colas reduce the importance of inflation as an influence on strikes. Although they ascribe no independent influence to Colas, his data do support the hypothesis that indexation generally reduces the effect of inflation on strikes. This effect is significant in about half of the models Kaufman reports.

Neither Kaufman nor Mauro examined the effects of Colas through strike opportunities.

Tables 8–3 through 8–5 give the direct associations between strike probabilities and type of wage indexation for our sample. Some clear patterns emerge. First, wage reopeners are associated with considerably less strike activity whether the characteristics of the previously negotiated or currently negotiated contract are used. Second, previous contracts without Colas and previous contracts with free Colas are associated with about the same levels of strike activity. Previous contracts with Colas that are capped, however, have considerably higher levels of strike activity. Third, negotiation of Colas is associated with large increases in strike activity. This is especially evident in Table 8–5, which matches previous and post negotiation contract characteristics. If the previous contract did not contain a Cola and the final negotiated contract does contain a Cola, the probability of a strike is nearly three times as large as when the negotiated contract does not contain a Cola.

Another interesting finding in this table is the apparent asymmetry between the negotiation of a Cola when a Cola did not exist in the previous contract and the concession of dropping a Cola that previously existed. Apparently, management demands to terminate a Cola are less likely to lead to strikes than union demands to begin indexation. Although our "concession" sample of contracts is small (33 contacts) and the cause-effect relationship between negotiated provisions and strikes is open to question, these results might provide further insight into the bargaining process. They suggest that management's position on wage indexation may be less flexible than the union position.

These results conflict with those obtained by Mauro and suggest that, like contract length, Colas increase the probability that a given negotiation will yield a strike and also increase the expected days lost per negotiation. However, the full impact of Colas on strike activity is the combination of their impact on probability of a strike for a given negotiation and on their impact on strike opportunities through their effect on contract length, controlling for other influences on strikes.

This combination can be investigated in the following way: Define "strike propensity" for a single period as

$$SP = \frac{P}{L}, \tag{8-1}$$

Table 8-3.   Strikes and Colas in Previous Contract, 1971-81.[a]

Type of Previous Contract	Probability of a Strike	Average Days Lost/Negotiation	Sample Size
No Cola	.140	6.25	738
Cola	.149	7.32	788
Free Cola	.138	6.38	516
Max Cola	.190	9.57	232
Wage reopener	.078	4.43	77

[a] Contracts covering greater than 1,000 workers.

Source: Authors' data base.

Table 8-4.   Strikes and Colas in Negotiated Contract.[a]

Type of Negotiated Contract	Probability of a Strike	Average Days Lost/Negotiation	Sample Size
No Cola	.108	4.91	628
Cola	.189	8.39	912
Free Cola	.182	7.69	670
Max Cola	.212	10.74	212
Reopener	.038	1.06	80

[a] Contracts covering greater than 1,000 workers.

Source: Authors' data base.

Table 8-5.   Strike Probability by Previous and Negotiated Cola Result.[a]

Previous Contract	Negotiated Contract	Strike Probability	Sample Size
No Cola	No Cola	.111	487
Cola	Cola	.156	720
No Cola	Cola	.313	131
Cola	No Cola	.091	33
Reopener	(either contract)	.043	94

[a] Contracts covering greater than 1,000 workers.

Source: Authors' data base.

where SP is strike propensity, P is the probability of a strike at a given negotiation, and L is the length of the contract. Colas should reduce strike propensity by increasing contract length, but they might increase strike propensity by increasing the probability of a strike for any given contract length. Likewise, define "strike activity," SA, for a single period as

$$SA = \frac{SD}{L}, \tag{8-2}$$

where SD is the number of strike days for a given negotiation.

The derivatives of strike propensity and strike activity with respect to the existence of a Cola will yield direct measures of the total impact of Colas on strikes. To estimate these derivatives, equations are needed relating strike probability, strike days, and contract length to the existence of Colas. Assume the following:

$$P_t = f_1(L_{t-1}, C_{t-1}, X) \tag{8-3}$$

$$SD_t = f_2(L_{t-1}, C_{t-1}, X) \tag{8-4}$$

$$L_t = g(C_t, Y), \tag{8-5}$$

where C represents the existence of a Cola, X is a vector of exogenous variables that influence the probability of a strike (or strike length), and Y is a vector of exogenous variables that influence contract length.

Equation 8-5 can be estimated using ordinary least squares, Equation 8-3 using probit, and Equation 8-4 using Tobit analysis. The derivatives of strike probability and strike duration with respect to Cola existence and contract length are computed at the means of the dependent variables. Assuming a long-run relationship, the total derivatives of strike propensity, SP, and strike activity, SA, can then be written as

$$\frac{dSP}{dC} = \frac{[(\partial L/\partial C \cdot \partial f_1/\partial L) + \partial f_1/\partial C] \cdot g(C, Y) - f_1(L, C, X) \cdot \partial g/\partial C}{g(C, Y)^2} \tag{8-6}$$

$$\frac{dSA}{dC} = \frac{[(\partial L/\partial C \cdot \partial f_2/\partial L) + \partial f_2/\partial C] \cdot g(C, Y) - f_2(L, C, X) \cdot \partial g/\partial C}{g(C, Y)^2}. \tag{8-7}$$

The total influence of Colas on these two measures of strikes depends on the sum of the opportunity-decreasing term $(-f_i(L, C, X) \cdot \partial g/\partial C)$,

$i = 1, 2$, and the term for the strike probability or strike activity per negotiation (the left-hand term of the numerator).

The vector X of exogenous variables in the strike probability and strike duration equations contains the identical variables used by Gramm (1983), except a Cola dummy was substituted for her wage measures.[2] In addition, we test Kaufman's (1981) hypothesis about Colas and inflation (see above). The vector Y of exogenous variables in the contract duration equation contains the same variables we used in Chapter 6 in our analysis of Cola incidence. The strike variables include factors related to the union's willingness to strike and management's resistance to the strike. For example, availability of AFCD (Aid to Families with Dependent Children) payments might make unions more and management less aggressive and thus have an ambiguous effect on strikes (Gramm 1983). Further discussion of the vector of control variables X is given in Appendix 8A. In Equation 8-5, current duration is written as a function of current Cola status. This equation is similar to a "market tradeoff" equation for wages and job safety. Current Cola status "causes" contract length in the sense that management (labor) will have to pay (receive) a price (i.e., the Cola) to get longer contracts. The Cola coefficient in Equation 8–5 summarizes this price. The equation should not be viewed as measuring either management's or labor's indifference curves but rather the ultimate tradeoff both parties can expect. Thus, ordinary least squares is used for 8–5 just as it can be used in a regression of wages on job safety to obtain the tradeoff there (Rosen 1974; Smith 1979).

Several versions of these models are estimated. First, the models are estimated both including and excluding the vectors X and Y. Due to missing data on some variables, the estimates without the variables in X and Y are based on a sample of 1,603 contracts; the estimates with all explanatory variables are based on smaller samples. Second, unexpected inflation over the previous contract is allowed to influence strikes and the Cola effect on strikes. Finally, the effect of capped Colas is allowed to differ from that of uncapped Colas.[3]

The coefficients for the inflation, Cola, and duration variables from Equations 8–3, 8–4, and 8–5 are presented in Table 8–6. As expected, Colas are associated with longer contracts, and the uncapped Cola effect is slightly larger than the capped Cola effect. Turning to the results for strike propensity and strike activity, having a capped Cola has a positive and significant or nearly significant coefficient in each case. This conclusion holds whether unanticipated inflation is excluded from the model or included and the effect of capped Colas is evaluated at the mean difference between actual and expected inflation $(PA - PE)$. Thus, the regression results for capped Colas confirm the information in the descriptive tables. On the other hand, having an uncapped Cola has negative insignificant effects on strike propensity and strike incidence (when evaluated at mean unexpected inflation or excluding $(PA - PE)$ from the model). Of further interest in Table 8-6 are the significant negative interaction effects between unexpected inflation and uncapped Colas. This finding is similar to Kaufman's (1981) results based on aggregate data. These results imply that having an uncapped Cola can reduce strike propensity and strike activity during periods of high unexpected inflation. This result supports Laidler's (1974) claim that Colas reduced strike activity during the OPEC price surge of 1973-74.

In the inflation specifications, the main uncapped and capped Cola terms refer to Cola effects when inflation is completely anticipated. In each case, the main capped Cola effect declines and becomes insignificant. This finding implies that one reason for the high incidence of strikes and high level of strike activity for contracts with capped Colas is that inflation was on average underpredicted in the 1970s. The main uncapped Cola effect is always positive, though insignificant. Again, the unanticipated inflation of the 1970s caused reduced strikes among contracts with uncapped Colas compared with other contracts. Further, the $(PA - PE)$ term is usually positive and is significant whenever all of the control variables ("small sample") are included. Finally, contract duration exerts a positive though insignificant effect on strikes. The sign of this relationship is consistent with Table 8-1.

The calculated derivatives of strike propensity and strike activity with respect to *MAX* and *FREE* are presented in percentage form in Table 8-7. The findings for capped Cola contracts contrast with those for uncapped Cola contracts. In particular, either at mean values of $(PA - PE)$ or in the specifications with inflation excluded, *MAX* raises strike incidence by 26 to 37 percent and strike activity by 34 to 43 percent. On the other hand, *FREE* lowers propensity to strike by 14 to 27 percent and strike activity by 10 to 30 percent. Thus, even though contracts with capped Colas offer fewer opportunities to strike than unindexed agreements, this effect is more than outweighed by the increased strikes per negotiation associated with capped Colas

Table 8-6.   Selected Results for the Impact of Colas on Contract Duration and Colas and Contract Duration on Strike Propensity and Strike Activity (asymptotic standard errors in parentheses).

	Ordinary Least Squares Results for Contract Duration (in months)	
	Large Sample[a] Coefficients	Small Sample[b] Coefficients
MAX	4.26[e]	3.42[e]
	(.22)	(.23)
FREE	4.61[e]	3.80[e]
	(.17)	(.19)

	Probit Results for Strike Propensity			
	Large Sample		Small Sample	
MAX_{t-1}	.1779	.0400	.2353[d]	.2176
	(.1135)	(.1874)	(.1335)	(.2137)
$FREE_{t-1}$	−.0633	.1594	−.1232	.1856
	(.0916)	(.1720)	(.1268)	(.1925)
$DURATION_{t-1}$	.0142[d]	.0143[d]	.0094	.0076
	(.0080)	(.0081)	(.0097)	(.0097)
$(PA-PE)_{t-1}$	—	.2463	—	12.3100[c]
		(2.7348)		(5.2690)
$MAX(PA-PE)_{t-1}$	—	5.6353	—	1.9403
		(5.7760)		(6.5387)
$FREE(PA-PE)_{t-1}$	—	−8.8122[c]	—	−11.7685[c]
		(4.4313)		(5.7801)

	Tobit Results for Strike Activity[f] Standardized Coefficients			
	Large Sample		Small Sample	
MAX_{t-1}	.1777	.0338	.2070	.1514
	(.1101)	(.1825)	(.1287)	(.2065)
$FREE_{t-1}$	−.0419	.1764	−.1171	.1931
	(.0891)	(.1425)	(.1231)	(.1851)
$DURATION_{t-1}$	.0124	.0126	.0104	.0086
	(.0078)	(.0079)	(.0093)	(.0094)

Table 8-6.   (Continued)

	Large Sample		Small Sample	
		Tobit Results for Strike Activity *Standardized Coefficients* (continued)		
$(PA-PE)_{t-1}$	—	−.1177 (2.6771)	—	12.471[c] (5.0846)
$MAX(PA-PE)_{t-1}$	—	5.7742 (5.6094)	—	3.4961 (6.2832)
$FREE(PA-PE)_{t-1}$	—	−8.7917[c] (4.3195)	—	−11.919[c] (5.5821)
Standard error of estimate	98.851	98.245	98.458	97.472

[a] Large sample refers to estimates based on model with no control variables.

[b] Small sample refers to estimates based on model including control variables as noted in text.

[c] Significant at 0.05 level, two-tailed test.

[d] Significant at 0.10 level, two-tailed test.

[e] Significant at 0.01 level, two-tailed test.

[f] For the Tobit results, the standardized coefficients are the regression coefficients divided by the standard error of the estimates.

and longer duration contracts. Contracts with uncapped Colas are associated with reduced incidence and length of strikes. This reduction is achieved through reduced strike opportunities and, sometimes, reduced strikes per negotiation. Thus, on average in the 1970s, having a capped Cola contributed to strikes and having an uncapped Cola inhibited strikes.

The final set of results in Table 8-7 refers to the effects of *MAX* and *FREE* on strikes under the assumption that inflation is completely anticipated. This assumption is implemented by using only the main *MAX* and *FREE* terms in the inflation specifications of Table 8-6. In effect, the derivatives are calculated assuming that actual inflation equals expected inflation. The results of this exercise show positive effects of *MAX* and *FREE* on strikes with the *MAX* effects smaller than when computed at the mean $(PA-PE)$ or without inflation in the model. Thus, having an uncapped Cola inhibits strikes only when there is a sufficient degree of unanticipated inflation. If

Table 8-7. Influence of Colas on Strike Propensity and Strike Activity.

	Strike Propensity[a]		Strike Activity[b]	
	Unexpected Inflation Included	Unexpected Inflation Excluded	Unexpected Inflation Included	Unexpected Inflation Excluded
Large Sample[c]				
MAX	26.2%	26.2%	36.8%	34.8%
FREE	−14.3%	−14.3%	−13.8%	−10.6%
Small Sample[d]				
MAX	36.6%	31.7%	43.1%	37.4%
FREE	−26.8%	−24.4%	−29.6%	−26.8%

	Strike Propensity at $PA = PE$	Strike Activity at $PA = PE$
Large Sample		
MAX	3.3%	5.2%
FREE	22.0%	34.3%
Small Sample		
MAX	28.9%	24.9%
FREE	23.0%	32.5%

Note: Elements of the table are the derivatives in Equations 8-5 and 8-6 (evaluated at mean levels of the dependent variables and unexpected inflation, except when *PA* is forced to equal *PE*, and divided by the mean for *SP/L* or *SA/L*).

[a] Strike Propensity = Expected probability of a strike per time period.

[b] Strike Activity = Expected strike days per time period.

[c] Large Sample = Estimates based on model with no control variables other than Cola existence and contract length (1,603 observations).

[d] Small Sample = Includes control variables as noted in text (1,370 observations).

expectations on average are unbiased, then our point estimates indicate that Colas of both types are associated with higher strike incidence and activity than unindexed agreements. This result should be qualified by noting the insignificant probit and Tobit main effects for *FREE*, *MAX*, and *DURATION* in the inflation specifications. The positive effects of Colas on contract duration (and thus reduced strike opportunities) are highly significant. However, our best point estimates indicate that compared to unindexed agreements, capped Colas are associated with more strike activity and uncapped Colas are associated with less strike activity when inflation is underestimated; both types of Cola are associated with greater strike activity when inflation is fully anticipated, however.

CONCLUSIONS

In this chapter we have attempted to systematically evaluate the influence of Colas and contract duration on strike activity. Colas were hypothesized to have a direct effect on strikes and an indirect effect via their influence on contract duration. On average in the 1970s, having a capped Cola led to greater strike incidence and activity than in unindexed agreements, and having an uncapped Cola led to reduced strikes. However, this reduction only occurs when there is sufficient unanticipated inflation. When inflation is completely anticipated, Colas in previous contracts are associated with more strike activity. This result is compounded by the finding that first-time negotiation or reintroduction of Colas is typically associated with a much higher strike frequency. Thus, under rational expectations, reduction of work time lost due to strikes is not an effect of Colas. However, if there are considerable fixed costs associated with strikes, then the association between Colas and long-term contracts might enable firms to save on these costs.

APPENDIX 8A
CONTROL VARIABLES IN THE STRIKE
PROPENSITY AND STRIKE ACTIVITY
EQUATIONS

The following variables were all defined in Chapter 6: *SIZE, CHILD, MAR, MALE,* and *MULTI.* The following additional variables were included as controls:

DEBT total outstanding consumer installment credit (in millions of dollars) in the month preceding the negotiation;

PROFIT the ratio of after-tax profits to stockholder equity for the unit's industry during the quarter preceding the negotiation;

SHIP	the intrayear coefficient of variation in shipments in the unit's industry for the year preceding the negotiation;
INV	the intrayear coefficient of variation in finished goods inventories in the unit's industry for the year preceding the negotiation;
LC/TC	the ratio of labor costs to value added for the unit's industry;
%ΔORDER	the percentage change in new orders received by the unit's industry over the quarter ending the month preceding the negotiation;
MODCON	dummy variable for eight-firm concentration ratio greater than 40 and less than or equal to 70;
HICON	dummy variable for eight-firm concentration ratio greater than 70;
RORDER	the percentage of the previous year's new orders in the unit's industry that were received during the quarter ending in the month preceding the negotiation;
INTEREST	the average daily effective prime interest rate (in percentages) charged by banks on short-term business loans during the month preceding the negotiation;
UE	the unemployment rate in the state or region in which the unit is located for the month preceding the negotiation;
UNION	the percentage of the total labor force that is unionized in the state or region in which the unit is located;
RIGHT	a dummy variable indicating that the unit is located in a state with a right-to-work statute;
REGION	a dummy variable indicating that the unit spans more than one state;
AFDC	a dummy variable indicating that the state in which the unit is located permits strikers to draw AFDC-UI benefits;
%P&M	the percentage of workers in the unit's industry who are employed in nonsupervisory production and service occupations.

Dummy variables for the years 1972–80 were also included.

As noted, these control variables were used in Gramm's (1983) study of strikes. The variables are intended to proxy union and management willingness to strike or take a strike. According to Gramm, for example, *PROFIT, INTEREST, SHIP, INV, RORDER,*

%∆ORDER, HICON, SIZE, MODCON, and *MULTI* are proxies for a firm's ability to weather a shutdown caused by a strike. Variables such as *UE, RIGHT, %P&M,* and *LC/TC* affect the firm's ability to continue production during a strike. Variables such as *UE, CHILD, MAR, MALE, INTEREST, AFDC,* and *UNION* affect workers' ability to strike. Because the variables that raise union aggressiveness lower management resistance, the reduced form effects cannot be predicted a priori. For example, low unemployment probably raises union demands and firm offers. For further description of this line of reasoning, see Gramm (1983).

NOTES

1. For details on the procedure and more information on the data set, see Gramm (1983).
2. A list of the control variables in the strike propensity and strike activity equations is given in Appendix 8A.
3. Following our procedure of the previous chapter, *PE* is the twelve-month Livingston forecast.

REFERENCES

Ashenfelter, Orley, and George E. Johnson. 1969. "Bargaining Theory, Trade Unions and Industrial Strike Activity." *American Economic Review* 59, no. 1 (March): 35–49.

Braun, Anne R. 1976. "Indexation of Wages and Salaries in Developed Economies." *IMF Staff Papers* 23, no. 1 (March): 226–71.

Friedman, Milton. 1974. "Monetary Correction." In *Essays on Inflation and Indexation,* edited by H. Giersch, pp. 25–62. Washington, D.C.: American Enterprise Institute.

Goldstein, Morris. 1975. "Wage Indexation, Inflation, and the Labor Market." *IMF Staff Papers* 22, no. 3 (November): 680–713.

Gramm, Cynthia. 1983. *A Micro-level Study of Strikes During Contract Negotiations: Determinants and Effects on Wage Changes.* Unpublished doctoral dissertation, University of Illinois.

Jacoby, Sanford M., and Daniel J.B. Mitchell. 1982. "Does Implicit Contracting Explain Explicit Contracting?" *Proceedings of the Thirty-Fifth Annual Meeting of the Industrial Relations Research Association* (B. Dennis, editor). Madison, WS: IRRA, 319–28.

Laidler, David. 1974. "The 1974 Report of the President's Council of Economic Advisors: The Control of Inflation and the Future of the International Monetary System." *American Economic Review* 64, no. 4 (September): 535–43.

Mauro, Martin J. 1982. "Strikes as a Result of Imperfect Information." *Industrial and Labor Relations Review* 35, no. 4 (July): 522–38.

Rosen, Sherwin. 1974. "Hedonic Prices and Implicit Markets." *Journal of Political Economy* 82, no. 1 (January–February): 34–55.

Smith, Robert S. 1979. "Compensating Wage Differentials and Public Policy: A Review." *Industrial and Labor Relations Review* 32, no. 3 (April): 339–52.

Swidinsky, Robert, and John Vanderkamp. 1982. "A Micro-econometric Analysis of Strike Activity in Canada." *Journal of Labor Research* 3, no. 4 (Fall): 455–91.

Chapter 9

Conclusions

In this book we have undertaken a detailed study of the determinants and effects of wage indexation in U.S. collective bargaining. The historical development of Colas has been examined, economic theories and evidence on indexation have been surveyed, and many of these theories were tested on our data base. In this concluding chapter the main findings are summarized and policy and research implications that follow from our results are suggested.

SUMMARY OF MAJOR RESULTS

Evolution and Current Characteristics of Colas

Wage indexation in the United States is almost exclusively a union phenomenon. Historically, Colas have become increasingly widespread during periods of unexpected inflation — principally wars and oil embargoes. However, during the late 1970s, Colas became entrenched in the union sector, in which 55 to 60 percent of workers had some form of wage indexation. The unions that have Colas tend to be relatively strong. Indexation is most prevalent in heavy manufacturing industries such as steel, machinery, and autos and is associated with unions like the United Auto Workers (UAW), United Steelworkers (USW), Machinists, and Teamsters. Colas are positively correlated with high wage rates and long-term contracts. Beginning

239

with the General Motors–UAW agreement of 1948, Colas often have been viewed as the price management must pay to obtain a multiyear, no-strike contract. Strong unions are in the best position to extract such an offer from management.

In the inflationary 1970s and early 1980s, Colas were blamed for helping cause excessive wage rates in many of our basic industries. Companies in troubled sectors such as autos, steel, rubber, and trucking have demanded and won concessions from their unions in an attempt to remain competitive. Union givebacks have often included wage cuts and temporary restrictions on Cola payments. However, in most cases, the union insisted on and won an eventual return to unrestricted cost-of-living protection.

There is considerable variety among the types of indexation in contracts with Colas. For example, the formula relating inflation to wage increases varies, as do the timing of reviews, the presence of minimum or maximum adjustments, the definition of price indices, and the inclusion of Cola payments in the base wage. Formulas have in general become more generous, and the incidence of caps has fallen. Thus, the average actual yield of Colas as a percentage of inflation has risen over time. In addition, the vast majority of Colas return equal cents-per-hour wage increases within the bargaining unit. Thus, Colas serve to narrow wage differentials within such units.

A final recurring theme in the evolution of Colas is government treatment of wage indexation during periods of incomes policy. Government has paid particular attention to Colas during inflationary periods, recognizing that indexation can add to an existing wage-price spiral. However, during the 1970s wage-price controls (1971–74) and guidelines (1978–81), program rules favored workers with Colas. This outcome resulted from unrealistically low inflation assumptions used to cost out the Colas.

Economic Effects of Colas: Theory

Macroeconomists have long been concerned with the effects of indexation on the stability of GNP, employment, and prices. These economists have compared the behavior of a hypothetical economy where wages are set according to expected inflation with behavior of an indexed economy. In effect, the comparison is between regimes of fixed nominal and fixed real wages. The hypothesized impact of indexation depends on the sources of shocks to the economy and on the mechanisms that determines employment when the actual real wage does not equal its market-clearing level.

When economic shocks are monetary — for example, unexpected increases or decreases in the money supply — basic production and demand relationships are unchanged. Therefore, so are market-clearing relative prices including real wages. Under this regime, indexation stabilizes output and employment by keeping real wages at their normal levels. In contrast, real shocks result in unanticipated changes in productivity. If, for example, workers become more productive, then the market-clearing real wage will rise (assuming an upward-sloping supply curve of labor). Indexation in such a case keeps the real wage lower than otherwise. If employment is demand-determined, then greater employment swings result under indexation. However, under supply-determined employment, indexation would lead to smaller fluctuations in employment and output. Since it is reasonable to assume that in the United States, firms determine employment levels, under real shocks indexation is likely to accentuate booms and recessions. In addition to these effects on output and employment, wage indexation has been hypothesized to accentuate price swings by rapidly transmitting an initial surge in prices to wages. The dynamic stability of the economy may become threatened if price-to-wage and wage-to-price responses are quick and of a large magnitude.

Microeconomic effects of Colas include impacts on wage differentials and strike activity. Colas have been hypothesized to raise interindustry wage differentials but lower skill differentials within bargaining units. The interindustry effect results from two sources: (1) workers with Colas have higher base wages than those without Colas and (2) workers with Colas in the 1970s tended to receive higher wage increases than those without Colas due to unanticipated inflation. This effect should not occur when inflation is completely anticipated. The reduced skill differential results from the equal cents-per-hour raises stipulated by most Colas. Regarding strikes, some claim that Colas can reduce workers' opportunities to strike by facilitating long-term agreements. In addition, Colas might reduce uncertainty about real wages and thus reduce the probability that a given negotiation results in a strike. On the other hand, Colas might be difficult to negotiate or change, and grievances might accumulate over the life of a long-term contract. Thus, the effect of a Cola on the probability that a given negotiation results in a strike (and on strike duration) may be ambiguous. Previous empirical research found that Colas have insignificant effects on this strike probability but that having a Cola significantly reduced the impact of inflation on strikes.

The Demand for Indexation: Theory

The microeconomic theory of the demand for Colas views indexation as a way of sharing the risks of uncertain inflation. For workers and firms, these risks involve fluctuating real wages and profits. In addition, for firms, using the Consumer Price Index (CPI) to adjust wages may be a cheap method of obtaining relevant market information. If both labor and management are risk averse, then they are both willing to pay something to have smaller fluctuations in real incomes. Conflicts over the extent to which wages should be tied to the CPI can arise if firm revenues and nonlabor costs are affected by inflation differently from workers' nonlabor income. Realistically, however, nonlabor income is likely to be small compared to wages, implying that workers would probably want complete indexation. In addition, willingness to set wages for short intervals (an alternative to Colas) might differ between the bargaining parties.

Since labor and management have different perspectives on the issue, the degree of indexation (elasticity of wages with respect to prices) that results from negotiations will be a compromise. Theories surveyed suggested that this degree would be closer to 1 the greater union bargaining power is, the more closely the firm's value added follows the CPI, the greater inflation uncertainty there is, and the more risk averse workers are relative to firms. A further implication of such theories is that if workers are more risk averse than firms, as is likely, then workers may pay a premium to get indexation. Finally, these theories imply a strong association between contract length and indexation, since the benefits of a Cola are greater the longer a contract is in force. High costs of negotiation, where the strike threat is considered such a cost, facilitate both Colas and long-term contracts.

Empirical Findings: The Demand for Colas

These theories were tested using a unique data base constructed by examining about 4,000 individual collective bargaining relationships over the 1967–82 period. The demand for indexation was studied in three stages: (1) estimation of the determinants of the probability that a contract had a Cola, (2) analysis among indexed contracts of the proportion of the total wage increase attributable to the Cola, and (3) investigation of the magnitude and determinants of elasticities of wages with respect to prices using the actual Cola formulas and alternative assumptions about inflation. In the second and third stages, particular attention was paid to distinguishing the intentions of the parties from the actual wage outcomes yielded by Colas.

In each analysis, variables associated with union bargaining power (extent of unionism in the industry, bargaining unit size, concentration ratio) significantly positively affected the measure of indexation, as expected. In addition, inflation uncertainty usually had a positive, significant impact on indexation. Regarding the magnitude of Cola elasticities, major differences were found between Colas with and those without caps. The average elasticity with respect to actual inflation in our sample of Colas (for the average union worker) was about 0.6; for uncapped Colas it was 0.74, and for capped Colas it was 0.31. When the response to unanticipated inflation is computed, figures of 0.82 (no cap) and 0.29 (cap) are obtained, with an overall average of 0.66. Thus, there is partial indexation even among uncapped Colas. Further, the response is smaller in capped Colas than those without a maximum; however, the former still yield some return to unanticipated inflation. It therefore makes sense to view capped Colas as a form of wage indexation (albeit limited), even though previous studies have not done so. Finally, elasticities for the average worker are estimated to be 24 percent lower (in relative terms) than for janitors and laborers—a low-paid group. Hence, during inflationary periods, Colas can cause a substantial narrowing of wage differentials within bargaining units.

Empirical Findings: Effects of Colas on Wage Inflation

Measurement of Cola elasticities is of importance in understanding the demand for wage indexation; from a policy perspective, we are also interested in knowing the ultimate effects of Colas on wage inflation. The raw elasticities and total wage changes might differ if scheduled wage increases vary by Cola status. In addition, the possibility that the parties use current negotiations to correct past mistakes in predicting inflation may be taken into account. Our results show that uncapped Colas have significantly higher wage changes than other contracts, *ceteris paribus,* even when inflation is completely anticipated. Further, the wage elasticity for average workers (scheduled plus Cola, if any) with respect to unexpected inflation is about 0.06 to 0.11 for capped Colas, 0.4 to 0.5 for uncapped Colas, and, obviously, 0 for unindexed agreements. The figures for Colas are slightly smaller than the raw elasticities computed in Chapter 6, indicating an even more modest inflation-transmitting effect of Colas.

Empirical Findings: Effects of Colas on Strike Activity

The effects of Colas on strike activity were estimated by using a matched sample of individual contract negotiations, which included data on the occurrence and duration of a strike. The full effects of Colas include both their influence on strike activity per negotiation and on the number of strike opportunities per time period (i.e., contract length). During the 1971–80 period, having a capped Cola led to greater strike incidence and activity than occurred in unindexed agreements; having an uncapped Cola led to reduced strikes. The findings for uncapped Colas are not surprising in light of the substantial amount of unanticipated inflation occurring during this period. However, our estimates imply that during a completely anticipated inflation, Colas of both types are associated with greater strike activity and incidence than in unindexed agreements.

POLICY AND RESEARCH IMPLICATIONS

The major policy concern the government has had about Colas is their possible inflationary impact during periods of rising prices. The low overall incidence of Colas in the economy (at most 10 to 20 percent of workers covered) and the modest return these Colas give when there is unanticipated inflation imply a minor role for Colas in transmitting inflation. This conclusion holds even allowing for substantial spillover effects to workers without Colas. In addition, our strike evidence shows, at least during periods of unexpected inflation, that the prevalent type of Cola—uncapped, about 80 percent of Colas —inhibits strike activity. Therefore, if government were to put limitations, through an incomes policy, on Colas, we estimate that there would be a small reduction in the transmission of inflation. Further, if some unanticipated inflation accompanied such a program, more strike activity would be expected.

In addition to the relatively small consequences for inflation of limiting Colas, other adjustments in collective bargaining agreements would take place if the government restricted Colas. The theory of indexation implies higher wage levels if the government restricts Colas, since workers are willing to pay a price to get indexation. In addition, shorter contracts and more time and resources devoted to negotiations would be expected. Both effects imply a net loss to labor and management due to reduced incentives to economize on negotiation costs and reduced freedom to design mutually advantageous contracts. These adjustments are similar to the effects of any government intervention in the wage–nonwage tradeoff. For example, mandating higher levels of job safety probably leads to lower wage rates (Ehrenberg and Smith 1982).

Colas may not have transmitted much overall inflation, but they have contributed to distortions in relative wages. During the inflationary 1970s and early 1980s, the union–nonunion wage differential rose, in part due to Colas (Moore and Raisian 1981). An immediate consequence of such a distortion would be the shrinking of relative employment in the traditionally unionized sectors. Some of the relative wage distortion has been reversed by the concessions unions have made; in manufacturing, for example, union compensation per hour rose more slowly than nonunion compensation during 1983 for the first time in several years (*Monthly Labor Review,* April 1984). However, most of the legacy of the 1970s and early 1980s remains. Colas might cause further relative wage distortion by narrowing wage differentials within companies. This change can induce firms to hire more skilled workers (as their relative price has fallen) and can lead to morale problems. At least one company (Boeing) has attempted to deal with this issue by negotiating percentage rather than cents-per-hour Cola payments (Harris 1983).

The impact of indexation on relative wages is a particular example of the possible redistributive effects of partial indexation of the economy in an inflationary environment. These effects may well be felt in other areas where there is indexation: Social Security payments, mortgages, and the proposed indexation of income taxes. Indexation will cause unanticipated inflation to redistribute income toward retirees, mortgage holders (banks and savings institutions), and tax-payers (as well as union workers). If the redistribution accompanying the next round of unexpected inflation is substantial, we might observe more groups trying to obtain indexation and more attempts to curb its use. One indication of the direction events could lead is that even though inflation has subsided since 1981, the incidence of Colas has not. After previous inflations, the percentage of workers covered by Colas declined (see Table 2–7). The large unanticipated inflations of the 1970s apparently left an impression on union workers that is not easily forgotten. This suggests a spread of indexation during the next bout of unanticipated inflation. In addition, there might be an increase in creative compromises in Cola negotiations as firms attempt to protect themselves against uncontrollable labor costs. For example, the two-tiered wage system (in which new workers get substantially lower wages than incumbents) might spread. If this occurs, Colas will likely move toward equal percentage rather than cents-per-hour increases.

Our study of wage indexation indicates that in the research agenda on Colas there is much room for theoretical and empirical improvement in our understanding of the subject. On the theoretical side, issues of efficient and noncooperative bargaining are not yet settled. The "pure" efficient bargaining model implies no role for bargaining power in the determination of the incidence or strength of wage indexation. However, we have found abundant evidence linking worker bargaining power to indexation. If bargaining power truly does influence Colas — as is the case in the partial efficient bargaining models of Ehrenberg, Danziger, and San (1983) and Card (1982) — then what prevents the attainment of efficient bargaining? An additional theoretical issue concerns the government's role as an actor in the system. What affects the government's demand for indexation?

On the empirical side, the basic issue of measuring indexation remains. We have attempted to distinguish the Cola yield when inflation is anticipated and the Cola response to unanticipated inflation, but there are other dimensions to this relationship. For example, the array of starting dates, triggers, corridors, and caps associated with Colas indicates that labor and management often are designing a highly nonlinear response to inflation. It may be very difficult to capture this response in one number, "the" elasticity of indexation.

A second measurement problem concerns the nonunion sector. Although a small percentage of nonunion firms indicate that they give cost-of-living raises, the nature of these increases remains unknown. How automatic is this response? What implicit inflation protection exists in the nonunion sector? Can nonunion workers expect to be fully caught up to inflation each year? If so, then nonunion wage setting would resemble a Cola with one-year reviews. We doubt whether the connection between inflation and wages is so direct and immediate in the nonunion sector. If it were, neither the sharp declines in real wages following the inflation of 1973–75 and 1979–81 nor the rising union–nonunion wage differential would likely have been observed. Measuring the nonunion response probably requires the same kind of micro-level data that we have collected for union contracts.

The proper representation of price expectations constitutes a third measurement issue. We (and others) have used survey data to guess what labor and management perceived, but there is no reason for their expectations to always equal those from survey data. The result is an errors-in-variables problem of unknown proportion. The economic environment of a firm or employer association bargaining over Colas must also be specified more accurately. For reasons of data availability, industry averages are invariably used, again producing an errors-in-variables problem. Finally, the price workers must pay in order to obtain a Cola deserves further study. Is this price simply a reduced wage level or does it take a more complicated form?

Even if these measurement problems could be solved, there are some questions that available data do not allow us to answer. For example, the United States has had limited indexation and inflation rates of 3 to 13 percent over the last five years. Brazil and Israel have extensive indexation with inflation rates occasionally over 100 percent (ILO 1982). What inflation rate and volatility would it take to induce institution of widespread indexation in the United States?

Finally, many of the effects we estimated for Colas in the United States were based on the 1970s, a period in which inflation was largely underpredicted. From December 1980 to December 1983, however, survey data indicate that people have consistently overpredicted inflation. If such overprediction continues, will we observe the effects of Colas in reverse? We believe that it will take a long period of stable inflation rates before union workers begin to give up their Colas.

REFERENCES

Card, David. 1982. "Indexation in Long Term Labor Agreements: A Theoretical and Empirical Analysis." Unpublished paper, University of Chicago.

Ehrenberg, Ronald, and Robert Smith. 1982. *Modern Labor Economics.* Glenview, Ill.: Scott–Foresman.

Ehrenberg, Ronald; Leif Danziger; and Gee San. 1983. "Cost-of-Living Adjustment Clauses in Union Contracts: A Summary of Results." *Journal of Labor Economics* 1, no. 3 (July): 215–45.

Harris, Roy H., Jr. 1983. "Boeing Accord Attacks Narrowing Pay Gap Between Skilled and Less-Skilled Workers." *Wall Street Journal,* (October 11).

International Labor Office (ILO). 1982. *Year Book of Labor Statistics 1982.* Geneva: ILO.

Moore, William J., and John Raisian. 1981. "A Time Series Analysis of the Growth and Determinants of Union/Nonunion Relative Wage Effects, 1967–77." BLS Working Paper No. 115.

U.S. Bureau of Labor Statistics. 1984. *Monthly Labor Review* 107, no. 4 (April): 93.

Index

About the Authors

Wallace E. Hendricks is Professor of Economics and Labor and Industrial Relations at the University of Illinois at Urbana–Champaign. He received his B.A. and Ph.D. degrees in Economics from the University of California, Berkeley, and has been a consultant for many public and private institutions including the U.S. Department of Energy, the Illinois Commerce Commission, Commonwealth Edison, and Continental Airlines. He has coauthored several state and federal monographs reports on collective bargaining and utility services, and his articles have appeared in *Journal of Human Resources*, *Industrial Relations*, *Journal of Labor Research*, and *Bell Journal of Economics*, among others.

Lawrence M. Kahn is Professor of Economics and Labor and Industrial Relations at the University of Illinois at Urbana–Champaign. He received his Ph.D. in Economics from the University of California, Berkeley, and is currently a member of the Board of Editors of *Industrial Relations*. He has published articles in *Journal of Human Resources*, *Labor History*, and *International Economic Review*, among others, as well as coauthoring several federal monographs on labor and union issues.